The Story of S

James Baldwin

Alpha Editions

This edition published in 2024

ISBN : 9789362929891

Design and Setting By
Alpha Editions
www.alphaedis.com
Email - info@alphaedis.com

As per information held with us this book is in Public Domain.
This book is a reproduction of an important historical work. Alpha Editions uses the best technology to reproduce historical work in the same manner it was first published to preserve its original nature. Any marks or number seen are left intentionally to preserve its true form.

Contents

The Fore Word...- 1 -

Adventure I. Mimer, the Master. ....- 5 -

Adventure II. Greyfell...- 15 -

Adventure III. The Curse of Gold.............................- 24 -

Adventure IV. Fafnir, the Dragon.............................- 35 -

Adventure V. In AEgir's Kingdom.............................- 42 -

Adventure VI. Brunhild. ....- 53 -

Adventure VII. In Nibelungen Land..........................- 58 -

Adventure VIII. Siegfried's Welcome Home..- 65 -

Adventure IX. The Journey to Burgundy-Land. ....- 69 -

Adventure X. Kriemhild's Dream............................- 73 -

Adventure XI. How the Spring-time Came. ....- 75 -

Adventure XII. The War with the North-kings...- 81 -

Adventure XIII. The Story of Balder. ....- 89 -

Adventure XIV. How Gunther Outwitted Brunhild. ....- 97 -

Adventure XV. In Nibelungen Land Again. ....- 106 -

Adventure XVI. How Brunhild Was Welcomed Home. ....- 118 -

Adventure XVII. How Siegfried Lived in Nibelungen Land. ....- 129 -

Adventure XVIII. How the Mischief Began to Brew. ....- 141 -

Adventure XIX. How They Hunted in the Odenwald. ....- 153 -

Adventure XX. How the Hoard Was Brought to Burgundy. ....- 161 -

The After Word. ....- 165 -

The Story of Siegfried Endnotes. ....- 166 -

The Fore Word.

When the world was in its childhood, men looked upon the works of Nature with a strange kind of awe. They fancied that every thing upon the earth, in the air, or in the water, had a life like their own, and that every sight which they saw, and every sound which they heard, was caused by some intelligent being. All men were poets, so far as their ideas and their modes of expression were concerned, although it is not likely that any of them wrote poetry. This was true in regard to the Saxon in his chilly northern home, as well as to the Greek in the sunny southland. But, while the balmy air and clear sky of the south tended to refine men's thoughts and language, the rugged scenery and bleak storms of the north made them uncouth, bold, and energetic. Yet both the cultured Greek and the rude Saxon looked upon Nature with much the same eyes, and there was a strange resemblance in their manner of thinking and speaking. They saw, that, in all the phenomena which took place around them, there was a certain system or regularity, as if these were controlled by some law or by some superior being; and they sought, in their simple poetical way, to account for these appearances. They had not yet learned to measure the distances of the stars, nor to calculate the motions of the earth. The changing of the seasons was a mystery which they scarcely sought to penetrate. But they spoke of these occurrences in a variety of ways, and invented many charming, stories with reference to them, not so much with a view towards accounting for the mystery, as towards giving expression to their childlike but picturesque ideas.

Thus, in the south, when reference was made to the coming of winter and to the dreariness and discomforts of that season of the year, men did not know nor care to explain it all, as our teachers now do at school; but they sometimes told how Hades had stolen Persephone (the summer) from her mother Demetre (the earth), and had carried her, in a chariot drawn by four coal black steeds, to the gloomy land of shadows; and how, in sorrow for her absence, the Earth clothed herself in mourning, and no leaves grew upon the trees, nor flowers in the gardens, and the very birds ceased singing, because Persephone was no more. But they added, that in a few months the fair maiden would return for a time to her sorrowing mother, and that then the flowers would bloom, and the trees would bear fruit, and the harvest-fields would again be full of golden grain.

In the north a different story was told, but the meaning was the same. Sometimes men told how Odin (the All-Father) had become angry with Brunhild (the maid of spring), and had wounded her with the thorn of sleep, and how all the castle in which she slept was wrapped in deathlike slumber until Sigurd or Siegfried (the sunbeam) rode through flaming fire, and awakened her with a kiss. Sometimes men told how Loki (heat) had betrayed Balder (the sunlight), and had induced blind old Hoder (the winter months) to slay him, and how all things, living and inanimate, joined in weeping for the bright god, until Hela (death) should permit him to revisit the earth for a time.

So, too, when the sun arose, and drove away the darkness and the hidden terrors of the night, our ancestors thought of the story of a noble young hero slaying a hideous dragon, or taking possession of the golden treasures of Mist Land. And when the springtime came, and the earth renewed its youth, and the fields and woods were decked in beauty, and there was music everywhere, they loved to tell of Idun (the spring) and her youth-giving apples, and of her wise husband Bragi (Nature's musician). When storm-clouds loomed up from the horizon and darkened the sky, and thunder rolled overhead, and lightning flashed on every hand, they talked about the mighty Thor riding over the clouds in his goat-drawn chariot, and battling with the giants of the air. When the mountain-meadows were green with long grass, and the corn was yellow for the sickles of the reapers, they spoke of Sif, the golden-haired wife of Thor, the queen of the pastures and the fields. When the seasons were mild, and the harvests were plentiful, and peace and gladness prevailed, they blessed Frey, the giver of good gifts to men.

To them the blue sky-dome which everywhere hung over them like an arched roof was but the protecting mantle which the All-Father had suspended above the earth. The rainbow was the shimmering bridge which stretches from earth to heaven. The sun and the moon were the children of a giant, whom two wolves chased forever around the earth. The stars were sparks from the fire-land of the south, set in the heavens by the gods. Night was a giantess, dark and swarthy, who rode in a car drawn by a steed the foam from whose bits sometimes covered the earth with dew. And Day was the son of Night; and the steed which he rode lighted all the sky and the earth with the beams which glistened from his mane.

It was thus that men in the earlier ages of the world looked upon and spoke of the workings of Nature; and it was in this manner that many myths, or poetical fables, were formed. By and by, as the world grew older, and mankind became less poetical and more practical, the first or mythical meaning of these stories was forgotten, and they were regarded no longer as mere poetical fancies, but as historical facts. Perhaps some real hero had indeed performed daring deeds, and had made the world around him happier and better. It was easy to liken him to Sigurd, or to some other mythical slayer of giants; and soon the deeds of both were ascribed to but one. And thus many myth-stories probably contain some historical facts blended with the mass of poetical fancies which mainly compose them; but, in such cases, it is generally impossible to distinguish what is fact from what is mere fancy.

All nations have had their myth-stories; but, to my mind, the purest and grandest are those which we have received from our northern ancestors. They are particularly interesting to us; because they are what our fathers once believed, and because they are ours by right of inheritance. And, when we are able to make them still more our own by removing the blemishes which rude and barbarous ages have added to some of them, we shall discover in them many things that are beautiful and true, and well calculated to make us wiser and better.

It is not known when or by whom these myth-stories were first put into writing, nor when they assumed the shape in which we now have them. But it is said, that, about the year 1100, an Icelandic scholar called Saemund the Wise collected a number of songs and poems into a book which is now known as the "Elder Edda;" and that, about a century later, Snorre Sturleson, another Icelander, wrote a prose-work of a similar character, which is called the "Younger Edda." And it is to these two books that we owe the preservation of almost all that is now known of the myths and the strange religion of our Saxon and Norman forefathers. But, besides these, there are a number of semi-mythological stories of great interest and beauty,—stories partly mythical, and partly founded upon remote and forgotten historical facts. One of the oldest and finest of these is the story of Sigurd, the son of Sigmund. There are many versions of this story, differing from each other according to the time in which they were written and the character of the people among whom they were received. We find the first mention of Sigurd and his strange daring deeds in the song of Fafnir, in the "Elder Edda." Then, in the "Younger Edda," the story is repeated in the myth of the Niflungs and the Gjukungs. It is told again in the "Volsunga Saga" of Iceland. It is repeated and re-repeated in various forms and different languages, and finally appears in the "Nibelungen Lied," a grand old German poem, which may well be compared with the Iliad of the Greeks. In this last version, Sigurd is called Siegfried; and the story is colored and modified by the introduction of many notions peculiar to the middle ages, and unknown to our Pagan fathers of the north. In our own time this myth has been woven into a variety of forms. William Morris has embodied it in his noble poem of "Sigurd the Volsung;" Richard Wagner, the famous German composer, has constructed from it his inimitable drama, the "Nibelungen Ring;" W. Jordan, another German writer, has given it to the world in his "Sigfrid's Saga;" and Emanuel Geibel has derived from it the materials for his "Tragedy of Brunhild."

And now I, too, come with the STORY OF SIEGFRIED, still another version of the time-honored legend. The story as I shall tell it you is not in all respects a literal rendering of the ancient myth; but I have taken the liberty to change and recast such portions of it as I have deemed advisable. Sometimes I have drawn materials from one version of the story, sometimes from another, and sometimes largely from my own imagination alone. Nor shall I be accused of impropriety in thus reshaping a narrative, which, although hallowed by an antiquity of a thousand years and more, has already appeared in so many different forms, and been clothed in so many different garbs; for, however much I may have allowed my fancy or my judgment to retouch and remodel the immaterial portions of the legend, the essential parts of this immortal myth remain the same. And, if I succeed in leading you to a clearer understanding and a wiser appreciation of the thoughts and feelings of our old northern ancestors, I shall have accomplished the object for which I have written this Story of Siegfried.

Adventure I. Mimer, the Master.

At Santen, in the Lowlands, there once lived a young prince named Siegfried. His father, Siegmund, was king of the rich country through which the lazy Rhine winds its way just before reaching the great North Sea; and he was known, both far and near, for his good deeds and his prudent thrift. And Siegfried's mother, the gentle Sigelind, was loved by all for her goodness of heart and her kindly charity to the poor. Neither king nor queen left aught undone that might make the young prince happy, or fit him for life's usefulness. Wise men were brought from far-off lands to be his teachers; and every day something was added to his store of knowledge or his stock of happiness. And very skilful did he become in warlike games and in manly feats of strength. No other youth could throw the spear with so great force, or shoot the arrow with surer aim. No other youth could run more swiftly, or ride with more becoming ease. His gentle mother took delight in adding to the beauty of his matchless form, by clothing him in costly garments decked with the rarest jewels. The old, the young, the rich, the poor, the high, the low, all praised the fearless Siegfried, and all vied in friendly strife to win his favor. One would have thought that the life of the young prince could never be aught but a holiday, and that the birds would sing, and the flowers would bloom, and the sun would shine forever for his sake.

But the business of man's life is not mere pastime; and none knew this truth better than the wise old king, Siegmund.

"All work is noble," said he to Siegfried; "and he who yearns to win fame must not shun toil. Even princes should know how to earn a livelihood by the labor of their hands."

And so, while Siegfried was still a young lad, his father sent him to live with a smith called Mimer, whose smithy was among the hills not far from the great forest. For in those early times the work of the smith was looked upon as the most worthy of all trades,—a trade which the gods themselves were not ashamed to follow. And this smith Mimer was a wonderful master,—the wisest and most cunning that the world had ever seen. Men said that he was akin to the dwarf-folk who had ruled the earth in the early days, and who were learned in every lore, and skilled in every craft; and they said that he was so exceeding old that no one could remember the day when he came to dwell in the land of Siegmund's fathers. And some said, too, that he was the keeper of a wonderful well, or flowing spring, the waters of which imparted wisdom and far-seeing knowledge to all who drank of them.

To Mimer's school, then, where he would be taught to work skilfully and to think wisely, Siegfried was sent, to be in all respects like the other pupils there. A coarse blue blouse, and heavy leggings, and a leathern apron, took the place of the costly clothing which he had worn in his father's dwelling. His feet were incased in awkward wooden shoes, and his head was covered with a wolf-skin cap. The dainty bed, with its downy pillows, wherein every night his mother had been wont, with gentle care, to see him safely covered, was given up for a rude heap of straw in a corner of the smithy. And the rich food to which he had been used gave place to the coarsest and humblest fare. But the lad did not complain. The days which he passed in the smithy were mirthful and happy; and the sound of his hammer rang cheerfully, and the sparks from his forge flew briskly, from morning till night.

And a wonderful smith he became. No one could do more work than he, and none wrought with greater skill. The heaviest chains and the strongest bolts, for prison or for treasure-house, were but as toys in his stout hands, so easily and quickly did he beat them into shape. And he was alike cunning in work of the most delicate and brittle kind. Ornaments of gold and silver, studded with the rarest jewels, were fashioned into beautiful forms by his deft fingers. And among all of Mimer's apprentices none learned the master's lore so readily, nor gained the master's favor more.[EN#1]

One morning the master, Mimer, came to the smithy with a troubled look upon his face. It was clear that something had gone amiss; and what it was the apprentices soon learned from the smith himself. Never, until lately, had any one questioned Mimer's right to be called the foremost smith in all the world; but now a rival had come forward. An unknown upstart—one Amilias, in Burgundy-land—had made a suit of armor, which, he boasted, no stroke of sword could dint, and no blow of spear could scratch; and he had sent a challenge to all other smiths, both in the Rhine country and elsewhere, to equal that piece of workmanship, or else acknowledge themselves his underlings and vassals. For many days had Mimer himself toiled, alone and vainly, trying to forge a sword whose edge the boasted armor of Amilias could not foil; and now, in despair, he came to ask the help of his pupils and apprentices.

"Who among you is skilful enough to forge such a sword?" he asked.

One after another, the pupils shook their heads. And Veliant, the foreman of the apprentices, said, "I have heard much about that wonderful armor, and its extreme hardness, and I doubt if any skill can make a sword with edge so sharp and true as to cut into it. The best that can be done is to try to make another war-coat whose temper shall equal that of Amilias's armor."

Then the lad Siegfried quickly said, "I will make such a sword as you want,—a blade that no war-coat can foil. Give me but leave to try!"

The other pupils laughed in scorn, but Mimer checked them. "You hear how this boy can talk: we will see what he can do. He is the king's son, and we know that he has uncommon talent. He shall make the sword; but if, upon trial, it fail, I will make him rue the day."

Then Siegfried went to his task. And for seven days and seven nights the sparks never stopped flying from his forge; and the ringing of his anvil, and the hissing of the hot metal as he tempered it, were heard continuously. On the eighth day the sword was fashioned, and Siegfried brought it to Mimer.

The smith felt the razor-edge of the bright weapon, and said, "This seems, indeed, a fair fire-edge. Let us make a trial of its keenness."

Then a thread of wool as light as thistle-down was thrown upon water, and, as it floated there, Mimer struck it with the sword. The glittering blade cleft the slender thread in twain, and the pieces floated undisturbed upon the surface of the liquid.

"Well done!" cried the delighted smith. "Never have I seen a keener edge. If its temper is as true as its sharpness would lead us to believe, it will indeed serve me well."

But Siegfried took the sword again, and broke it into many pieces; and for three days he welded it in a white-hot fire, and tempered it with milk and oatmeal. Then, in sight of Mimer and the sneering apprentices, he cast a light ball of fine-spun wool upon the flowing water of the brook; and it was caught in the swift eddies of the stream, and whirled about until it met the bared blade of the sword, which was held in Mimer's hands. And it was parted as easily and clean as the rippling water, and not the smallest thread was moved out of its place.

Then back to the smithy Siegfried went again; and his forge glowed with a brighter fire, and his hammer rang upon the anvil with a cheerier sound, than ever before. But he suffered none to come near, and no one ever knew what witchery he used. But some of his fellow-pupils afterwards told how, in the dusky twilight, they had seen a one-eyed man, long-bearded, and clad in a cloud-gray kirtle, and wearing a sky-blue hood, talking with Siegfried at the smithy door. And they said that the stranger's face was at once pleasant and fearful to look upon, and that his one eye shone in the gloaming like the evening star, and that, when he had placed in Siegfried's hands bright shards, like pieces of a broken sword, he faded suddenly from their sight, and was seen no more.

For seven weeks the lad wrought day and night at his forge; and then, pale and haggard, but with a pleased smile upon his face, he stood before Mimer, with the gleaming sword in his hands. "It is finished," he said. "Behold the glittering terror!—the blade Balmung. Let us try its edge, and prove its temper once again, that so we may know whether you can place your trust in it."

And Mimer looked long at the ruddy hilts of the weapon, and at the mystic runes that were scored upon its sides, and at the keen edge, which gleamed like a ray of sunlight in the gathering gloom of the evening. But no word came from his lips, and his eyes were dim and dazed; and he seemed as one lost in thoughts of days long past and gone.

Siegfried raised the blade high over his head; and the gleaming edge flashed hither and thither, like the lightning's play when Thor rides over the storm-clouds. Then suddenly it fell upon the master's anvil, and the great block of iron was cleft in two; but the bright blade was no whit dulled by the stroke, and the line of light which marked the edge was brighter than before.

Then to the flowing brook they went; and a great pack of wool, the fleeces of ten sheep, was brought, and thrown upon the swirling water. As the stream bore the bundle downwards, Mimer held the sword in its way. And the whole was divided as easily and as clean as the woollen ball or the slender woollen thread had been cleft before.

"Now, indeed," cried Mimer, "I no longer fear to meet that upstart, Amilias. If his war-coat can withstand the stroke of such a sword as Balmung, then I shall not be ashamed to be his underling. But, if this good blade is what it seems to be, it will not fail me; and I, Mimer the Old, shall still be called the wisest and greatest of smiths."

And he sent word at once to Amilias, in Burgundy-land, to meet him on a day, and settle forever the question as to which of the two should be the master, and which the underling. And heralds proclaimed it in every town and dwelling. When the time which had been set drew near, Mimer, bearing the sword Balmung, and followed by all his pupils and apprentices, wended his way towards the place of meeting. Through the forest they went, and then along the banks of the sluggish river, for many a league, to the height of land which marked the line between King Siegmund's country and the country of the Burgundians. It was in this place, midway between the shops of Mimer and Amilias, that the great trial of metal and of skill was to be made. And here were already gathered great numbers of people from the

Lowlands and from Burgundy, anxiously waiting for the coming of the champions. On the one side were the wise old Siegmund and his gentle queen, and their train of knights and courtiers and fair ladies. On the other side were the three Burgundian kings, Gunther, Gernot, and Giselher, and a mighty retinue of warriors, led by grim old Hagen, the uncle of the kings, and the wariest chief in all Rhineland.

When every thing was in readiness for the contest, Amilias, clad in his boasted war-coat, went up to the top of the hill, and sat upon a great rock, and waited for Mimer's coming. As he sat there, he looked, to the people below, like some great castle-tower; for he was almost a giant in size, and his coat of mail, so skilfully wrought, was so huge that twenty men of common mould might have found shelter, or hidden themselves, within it. As the smith Mimer, so dwarfish in stature, toiled up the steep hillside, Amilias smiled to see him; for he felt no fear of the slender, gleaming blade that was to try the metal of his war-coat. And already a shout of expectant triumph went up from the throats of the Burgundian hosts, so sure were they of their champion's success.

But Mimer's friends waited in breathless silence, hoping, and yet fearing. Only King Siegmund whispered to his queen, and said, "Knowledge is stronger than brute force. The smallest dwarf who has drunk from the well of the Knowing One may safely meet the stoutest giant in battle."

When Mimer reached the top of the hill, Amilias folded his huge arms, and smiled again; for he felt that this contest was mere play for him, and that Mimer was already as good as beaten, and his thrall. The smith paused a moment to take breath, and as he stood by the side of his foe he looked to those below like a mere black speck close beside a steel-gray castle-tower.

"Are you ready?" asked the smith.

"Ready," answered Amilias. "Strike!"

Mimer raised the beaming blade in the air, and for a moment the lightning seemed to play around his head. The muscles on his short, brawny arms, stood out like great ropes; and then Balmung, descending, cleft the air from right to left. The waiting lookers-on in the plain below thought to hear the noise of clashing steel; but they listened in vain, for no sound came to their ears, save a sharp hiss like that which red-hot iron gives when plunged into a tank of cold water. The huge Amilias sat unmoved, with his arms still folded upon his breast; but the smile had faded from his face.

"How do you feel now?" asked Mimer in a half-mocking tone.

"Rather strangely, as if cold iron had touched me," faintly answered the upstart.

"Shake thyself!" cried Mimer.

Amilias did so, and, lo! he fell in two halves; for the sword had cut sheer through the vaunted war-coat, and cleft in twain the great body incased within. Down tumbled the giant head and the still folded arms, and they rolled with thundering noise to the foot of the hill, and fell with a fearful splash into the deep waters of the river; and there, fathoms down, they may even now be seen, when the water is clear, lying like great gray rocks among the sand and gravel below. The rest of the body, with the armor which incased it, still sat upright in its place; and to this day travellers sailing down the river are shown on moonlit evenings the luckless armor of Amilias on the high hill-top. In the dim, uncertain light, one easily fancies it to be the ivy covered ruins of some old castle of feudal times.

The master, Mimer, sheathed his sword, and walked slowly down the hillside to the plain, where his friends welcomed him with glad cheers and shouts of joy. But the Burgundians, baffled, and feeling vexed, turned silently homeward, nor cast a single look back to the scene of their disappointment and their ill-fated champion's defeat.

And Siegfried went again with the master and his fellows to the smoky smithy, to his roaring bellows and ringing anvil, and to his coarse fare, and rude, hard bed, and to a life of labor. And while all men praised Mimer and his knowing skill, and the fiery edge of the sunbeam blade, no one knew that it was the boy Siegfried who had wrought that piece of workmanship.

But after a while it was whispered around that not Mimer, but one of his pupils, had forged the sword. And, when the master was asked what truth there was in this story, his eyes twinkled, and the corners of his mouth twitched strangely, and he made no answer. But Veliant, the foreman of the smithy, and the greatest of boasters said, "It was I who forged the fire-edge of the blade Balmung." And, although none denied the truth of what he said, but few who knew what sort of a man he was believed his story. And this is the reason, my children, that, in the ancient songs and stories which tell of this wondrous sword, it is said by most that Mimer, and by a few that Veliant, forged its blade. But I prefer to believe that it was made by Siegfried, the hero who afterwards wielded it in so many adventures. [EN#3] Be this as it may, however, blind hate and jealousy were from this time uppermost in the coarse and selfish mind of Veliant; and he sought how he might drive the lad away from the smithy in disgrace. "This boy has done what no one else could do," said he. "He may yet do greater deeds, and set himself up as the master smith of the world, and then we shall all have to humble ourselves before him as his underlings and thralls."

And he nursed this thought, and brooded over the hatred which he felt towards the blameless boy; but he did not dare to harm him, for fear of their master, Mimer. And Siegfried busied himself at his forge, where the sparks flew as briskly and as merrily as ever before, and his bellows roared from early morning till late at evening. Nor did the foreman's unkindness trouble him for a moment, for he knew that the master's heart was warm towards him.

Oftentimes, when the day's work was done, Siegfried sat with Mimer by the glowing light of the furnace-fire, and listened to the sweet tales which the master told of the deeds of the early days, when the world was young, and the dwarf-folk and the giants had a name and a place upon earth. And one night, as they thus sat, the master talked of Odin the All-Father, and of the gods who dwell with him in Asgard, and of the puny men-folk whom they protect and befriend, until his words grew full of bitterness, and his soul of a fierce longing for something he dared not name. And the lad's heart was stirred with a strange uneasiness, and he said,—

"Tell me, I pray, dear master, something about my own kin, my father's fathers,—those mighty kings, who, I have heard said, were the bravest and best of men."

Then the smith seemed pleased again. And his eyes grew brighter, and lost their far-away look; and a smile played among the wrinkles of his swarthy face, as he told a tale of old King Volsung and of the deeds of the Volsung kings:—

"Long years ago, before the evil days had dawned, King Volsung ruled over all the land which lies between the sea and the country of the Goths. The days were golden; and the good Frey dropped peace and plenty everywhere, and men went in and out and feared no wrong. King Volsung had a dwelling in the midst of fertile fields and fruitful gardens. Fairer than any dream was that dwelling. The roof was thatched with gold, and red turrets and towers rose above. The great feast-hall was long and high, and its walls were hung with sun-bright shields; and the door-nails were of silver. In the middle of the hall stood the pride of the Volsungs,—a tree whose blossoms filled the air with fragrance, and whose green branches, thrusting themselves through the ceiling, covered the roof with fair foliage. It was Odin's tree, and King Volsung had planted it there with his own hands.

"On a day in winter King Volsung held a great feast in his hall in honor of Siggeir, the King of the Goths, who was his guest. And the fires blazed bright in the broad chimneys, and music and mirth went round. But in the midst of the merry-making the guests were startled by a sudden peal of thunder, which seemed to come from the cloudless sky, and which made the shields upon the walls rattle and ring. In wonder they looked around. A strange man stood in the doorway, and laughed, but said not a word. And they noticed that he wore no shoes upon his feet, but that a cloud-gray cloak was thrown over his shoulders, and a blue hood was drawn down over his head. His face was half-hidden by a heavy beard; and he had but one eye, which twinkled and glowed like a burning coal. And all the guests sat moveless in their seats, so awed were they in the presence of him who stood at the door; for they knew that he was none other than Odin the All-Father, the king of gods and men. He spoke not a word, but straight into the hall he strode, and he paused not until he stood beneath the blossoming branches of the tree. Then, forth from beneath his cloud-gray cloak, he drew a gleaming sword, and struck the blade deep into the wood,—so deep that nothing but the hilt was left in sight. And, turning to the awe-struck guests, he said, 'A blade of mighty worth have I hidden in this tree. Never have the earth-folk wrought better steel, nor has any man ever wielded a more trusty sword. Whoever there is among you brave enough and strong enough to draw it forth from the wood, he shall have it as a gift from Odin.' Then slowly to the door he strode again, and no one saw him any more.

"And after he had gone, the Volsungs and their guests sat a long time silent, fearing to stir, lest the vision should prove a dream. But at last the old king arose, and cried, 'Come, guests and kinsmen, and set your hands to the ruddy hilt! Odin's gift stays, waiting for its fated owner. Let us see which one of you is the favored of the All-Father.' First Siggeir, the King of the Goths, and his earls, the Volsungs' guests, tried their hands. But the blade stuck fast; and the stoutest man among them failed to move it. Then King Volsung, laughing, seized the hilt, and drew with all his strength; but the sword held still in the wood of Odin's tree. And one by one the nine sons of Volsung tugged and strained in vain; and each was greeted with shouts and laughter, as, ashamed and beaten, he wended to his seat again. Then, at last, Sigmund, the youngest son, stood up, and laid his hand upon the ruddy hilt, scarce thinking to try what all had failed to do. When, lo! the blade came out of the tree as if therein it had all along lain loose. And Sigmund raised it high over his head, and shook it, and the bright flame that leaped from its edge lit up the hall like the lightning's gleaming; and the Volsungs and their guests rent the air with cheers and shouts of gladness. For no one among all the men of the mid-world was more worthy of Odin's gift than young Sigmund the brave."

But the rest of Mimer's story would be too long to tell you now; for he and his young apprentice sat for hours by the dying coals, and talked of Siegfried's kinfolk,—the Volsung kings of old. And he told how Siggeir, the Goth king, was wedded to Signy the fair, the only daughter of Volsung, and the pride of the old king's heart; and how he carried her with him to his home in the land of the Goths; and how he coveted Sigmund's sword, and plotted to gain it by guile; and how, through presence of friendship, he invited the Volsung kings to visit him in Gothland, as the guests of himself and Signy; and how he betrayed and slew them, save Sigmund alone, who escaped, and for long years lived an outlaw in the land of his treacherous foe. And then he told how Sigmund afterwards came back to his own country of the Volsungs; and how his people welcomed him, and he became a mighty king, such as the world had never known before; and how, when he had grown old, and full of years and honors, he went out with his earls and fighting-men to battle against the hosts of King Lyngi the Mighty; and how, in the midst of the fight, when his sword had hewn down numbers of the foe, and the end of the strife and victory seemed near, an old man, one eyed and bearded, and wearing a cloud-gray cloak, stood up before him in the din, and his sword was broken in pieces, and he fell dead on the heap of the slain.[EN#4] And, when Mimer had finished his tale, his dark face seemed to grow darker, and his twinkling eyes grew brighter, as he cried out in a tone of despair and hopeless yearning,—

"Oh, past are those days of old and the worthy deeds of the brave! And these are the days of the home-stayers,—of the wise, but feeble-hearted. Yet the Norns have spoken; and it must be that another hero shall arise of the Volsung blood, and he shall restore the name and the fame of his kin of the early days. And he shall be my bane; and in him shall the race of heroes have an end."[EN#7]

Siegfried's heart was strangely stirred within him as he hearkened to this story of ancient times and to the fateful words of the master, and for a long time he sat in silent thought; and neither he nor Mimer moved, or spoke again, until the darkness of the night had begun to fade, and the gray light of morning to steal into the smithy. Then, as if moved by a sudden impulse, he turned to the master, and said,—

"You speak of the Norns, dear master, and of their foretelling; but your words are vague, and their meaning very broad. When shall that hero come? and who shall he be? and what deeds shall be his doing?"

"Alas!" answered Mimer, "I know not, save that he shall be of the Volsung race, and that my fate is linked with his."

"And why do you not know?" returned Siegfried. "Are you not that old Mimer, in whom it is said the garnered wisdom of the world is stored? Is there not truth in the old story that even Odin pawned one of his eyes for a single draught from your fountain of knowledge? And is the possessor of so much wisdom unable to look into the future with clearness and certainty?"

"Alas!" answered Mimer again, and his words came hard and slow, "I am not that Mimer, of whom old stories tell, who gave wisdom to the All-Father in exchange for an eye. He is one of the giants, and he still watches his fountain in far-off Jotunheim.[EN#2] I claim kinship with the dwarfs, and am sometimes known as an elf, sometimes as a wood-sprite. Men have called me Mimer because of my wisdom and skill, and the learning which I impart to my pupils. Could I but drink from the fountain of the real Mimer, then the wisdom of the world would in truth be mine, and the secrets of the future would be no longer hidden. But I must wait, as I have long waited, for the day and the deed and the doom that the Norns have foretold."

And the old strange look of longing came again into his eyes, and the wrinkles on his swarthy face seemed to deepen with agony, as he arose, and left the smithy. And Siegfried sat alone before the smouldering fire, and pondered upon what he had heard.

Adventure II. Greyfell.

Many were the pleasant days that Siegfried spent in Mimer's smoky smithy; and if he ever thought of his father's stately dwelling, or of the life of ease which he might have enjoyed within its halls, he never by word or deed showed signs of discontent. For Mimer taught him all the secrets of his craft and all the lore of the wise men. To beat hot iron, to shape the fire-edged sword, to smithy war-coats, to fashion the slender bracelet of gold and jewels,—all this he had already learned. But there were many other things to know, and these the wise master showed him. He told him how to carve the mystic runes which speak to the knowing ones with silent, unseen tongues; he told him of the men of other lands, and taught him their strange speech; he showed him how to touch the harp-strings, and bring forth bewitching music: and the heart of Siegfried waxed very wise, while his body grew wondrous strong. And the master loved his pupil dearly.

But the twelve apprentices grew more jealous day by day, and when Mimer was away they taunted Siegfried with cruel jests, and sought by harsh threats to drive him from the smithy; but the lad only smiled, and made the old shop ring again with the music from his anvil. On a day when Mimer had gone on a journey, Veliant, the foreman, so far forgot himself as to strike the boy. For a moment Siegfried gazed at him with withering scorn; then he swung his hammer high in air, and brought it swiftly down, not upon the head of Veliant, who was trembling with expectant fear, but upon the foreman's anvil. The great block of iron was shivered by the blow, and flew into a thousand pieces. Then, turning again towards the thoroughly frightened foreman, Siegfried said, while angry lightning-flashes darted from his eyes,—

"What if I were to strike you thus?"

Veliant sank upon the ground, and begged for mercy.

"You are safe," said Siegfried, walking away. "I would scorn to harm a being like you!"

The apprentices were struck dumb with amazement and fear; and when Siegfried had returned to his anvil they one by one dropped their hammers, and stole away from the smithy. In a secret place not far from the shop, they met together, to plot some means by which they might rid themselves of him whom they both hated and feared.

The next morning Veliant came to Siegfried's forge, with a sham smile upon his face. The boy knew that cowardice and base deceit lurked, ill concealed, beneath that smile; yet, as he was wont to do, he welcomed the foreman kindly.

"Siegfried," said Veliant, "let us be friends again. I am sorry that I was so foolish and so rash yesterday, and I promise that I will never again be so rude and unmanly as to become angry at you. Let us be friends, good Siegfried! Give me your hand, I pray you, and with it your forgiveness."

Siegfried grasped the rough palm of the young smith with such a gripe, that the smile vanished from Veliant's face, and his muscles writhed with pain.

"I give you my hand, certainly," said the boy, "and I will give you my forgiveness when I know that you are worthy of it."

As soon as Veliant's aching hand allowed him speech, he said,—

"Siegfried, you know that we have but little charcoal left for our forges, and our master will soon return from his journey. It will never do for him to find us idle, and the fires cold. Some one must go to-day to the forest-pits, and bring home a fresh supply of charcoal. How would you like the errand? It is but a pleasant day's journey to the pits; and a ride into the greenwood this fine summer day would certainly be more agreeable than staying in the smoky shop."

"I should like the drive very much," answered Siegfried; "but I have never been to the coal-pits, and I might lose my way in the forest."

"No danger of that," said Veliant. "Follow the road that goes straight into the heart of the forest, and you cannot miss your way. It will lead you to the house of Regin, the master, the greatest charcoal-man in all Rhineland. He will be right glad to see you for Mimer's sake, and you may lodge with him for the night. In the morning he will fill your cart with the choicest charcoal, and you can drive home at your leisure; and, when our master comes again, he will find our forges flaming, and our bellows roaring, and our anvils ringing, as of yore."

Siegfried, after some further parley, agreed to undertake the errand, although he felt that Veliant, in urging him to do so, wished to work him some harm. He harnessed the donkey to the smith's best cart, and drove merrily away along the road which led towards the forest.[EN#5] The day was bright and clear; and as Siegfried rode through the flowery meadows, or betwixt the fields of corn, a thousand sights and sounds met him, and made him glad. Now and then he would stop to watch the reapers in the fields, or to listen to the song of some heaven-soaring lark lost to sight in the blue sea overhead. Once he met a company of gayly dressed youths and maidens, carrying sheaves of golden grain,—for it was now the harvest-time,—and singing in praise of Frey, the giver of peace and plenty.

"Whither away, young prince?" they merrily asked.

"To Regin, the coal-burner, in the deep greenwood," he answered.

"Then may the good Frey have thee in keeping!" they cried. "It is a long and lonesome journey." And each one blessed him as they passed.

It was nearly noon when he drove into the forest, and left the blooming meadows and the warm sunshine behind him. And now he urged the donkey forwards with speed; for he knew that he had lost much precious time, and that many miles still lay between him and Regin's charcoal-pits. And there was nothing here amid the thick shadows of the wood to make him wish to linger; for the ground was damp, and the air was chilly, and every thing was silent as the grave. And not a living creature did Siegfried see, save now and then a gray wolf slinking across the road, or a doleful owl sitting low down in some tree-top, and blinking at him in the dull but garish light. Evening at last drew on, and the shadows in the wood grew deeper; and still no sign of charcoal-burner, nor of other human being, was seen. Night came, and thick darkness settled around; and all the demons of the forest came forth, and clamored and chattered, and shrieked and howled. But Siegfried was not afraid. The bats and vampires came out of their hiding-places, and flapped their clammy wings in his face; and he thought that he saw ogres and many fearful creatures peeping out from behind every tree and shrub. But, when he looked upwards through the overhanging tree-tops, he saw the star-decked roof of heaven, the blue mantle which the All-Father has hung as a shelter over the world; and he went bravely onwards, never doubting but that Odin has many good things in store for those who are willing to trust him.

And by and by the great round moon arose in the east, and the fearful sounds that had made the forest hideous began to die away; and Siegfried saw, far down the path, a red light feebly gleaming. And he was glad, for he knew that it must come from the charcoal-burners' pits. Soon he came out upon a broad, cleared space; and the charcoal-burners' fires blazed bright before him; and some workmen, swarthy and soot-begrimed, came forwards to meet him.

"Who are you?" they asked; "and why do you come through the forest at this late hour?"

"I am Siegfried," answered the boy; "and I come from Mimer's smithy. I seek Regin, the king of charcoal-burners; for I must have coal for my master's smithy."

"Come with me," said one of the men: "I will lead you to Regin."

Siegfried alighted from his cart, and followed the man to a low-roofed hut not far from the burning pits. As they drew near, they heard the sound of a harp, and strange, wild music within; and Siegfried's heart was stirred with wonder as he listened. The man knocked softly at the door, and the music ceased.

"Who comes to break into Regin's rest at such a time as this?" said a rough voice within.

"A youth who calls himself Siegfried," answered the man. "He says that he comes from Mimer's smithy, and he would see you, my master."

"Let him come in," said the voice.

Siegfried passed through the low door, and into the room beyond; and so strange was the sight that met him that he stood for a while in awe, for never in so lowly a dwelling had treasures so rich been seen. Jewels sparkled from the ceiling; rare tapestry covered the walls; and on the floor were heaps of ruddy gold and silver, still unfashioned. And in the midst of all this wealth stood Regin, the king of the forest, the greatest of charcoal-men. And a strange old man he was, wrinkled and gray and beardless; but out of his eyes sharp glances gleamed of a light that was not human, and his heavy brow and broad forehead betokened wisdom and shrewd cunning. And he welcomed Siegfried kindly for Mimer's sake, and set before him a rich repast of venison, and wild honey, and fresh white bread, and luscious grapes. And, when the meal was finished, the boy would have told his errand, but Regin stopped him.

"Say nothing of your business to-night," said he; "for the hour is already late, and you are weary. Better lie down, and rest until the morrow; and then we will talk of the matter which has brought you hither."

And Siegfried was shown to a couch of the fragrant leaves of the myrtle and hemlock, overspread with soft white linen, such as is made in the far-off Emerald Isle; and he was lulled to sleep by sweet strains of music from Regin's harp,—music which told of the days when the gods were young on the earth. And as he slept he dreamed. He dreamed that he stood upon the crag of a high mountain, and that the eagles flew screaming around him, and the everlasting snows lay at his feet, and the world in all its beauty was stretched out like a map below him; and he longed to go forth to partake of its abundance, and to make for himself a name among men. Then came the Norns, who spin the thread, and weave the woof, of every man's life; and they held in their hands the web of his own destiny. And Urd, the Past, sat on the tops of the eastern mountains, where the sun begins to rise at dawn; while Verdanda, the Present, stood in the western sea, where sky and water meet. And they stretched the web between them, and its ends were hidden in the far-away mists. Then with all their might the two Norns span the purple and golden threads, and wove the fatal woof. But as it began to grow in beauty and in strength, and to shadow the earth with its gladness and its glory, Skuld, the pitiless Norn of the Future, seized it with rude fingers, and tore it into shreds, and cast it down at the feet of Hela, the white queen of the dead.[EN#6] And the eagles shrieked, and the mountain shook, and the crag toppled, and Siegfried awoke.

The next morning, at earliest break of day, the youth sought Regin, and made known his errand.

"I have come for charcoal for my master Mimer's forges. My cart stands ready outside; and I pray you to have it filled at once, for the way is long, and I must be back betimes."

Then a strange smile stole over Regin's wrinkled face, and he said,—

"Does Siegfried the prince come on such a lowly errand? Does he come to me through the forest, driving a donkey, and riding in a sooty coal-cart? I have known the day when his kin were the mightiest kings of earth, and they fared through every land the noblest men of men-folk."

The taunting word, the jeering tones, made Siegfried's anger rise. The blood boiled in his veins; but he checked his tongue, and mildly answered,—

"It is true that I am a prince, and my father is the wisest of kings; and it is for this reason that I come thus to you. Mimer is my master, and my father early taught me that even princes must obey their masters' behests."

Then Regin laughed, and asked, "How long art thou to be Mimer's thrall? Does no work wait for thee but at his smoky forge?"

"When Mimer gives me leave, and Odin calls me," answered the lad, "then I, too, will go faring over the world, like my kin of the earlier days, to carve me a name and great glory, and a place with the noble of earth."

Regin said not a word; but he took his harp, and smote the strings, and a sad, wild music filled the room. And he sang of the gods and the dwarf-folk, and of the deeds that had been in the time long past and gone. And a strange mist swam before Siegfried's eyes; and so bewitching were the strains that fell upon his ears, and filled his soul, that he forgot about his errand, and his master Mimer, and his father Siegmund, and his lowland home, and thought only of the heart-gladdening sounds. By and by the music ended, the spell was lifted, and Siegfried turned his eyes towards the musician. A wonderful change had taken place. The little old man still stood before him with the harp in his hand; but his wrinkled face was hidden by a heavy beard, and his thin gray locks were covered with a long black wig, and he seemed taller and stouter than before. As Siegfried started with surprise, his host held out his hand, and said,—

"You need not be alarmed, my boy. It is time for you to know that Regin and Mimer are the same person, or rather that Mimer is Regin disguised.[EN#8] The day has come for you to go your way into the world, and Mimer gives you leave."

Siegfried was so amazed he could not say a word. He took the master's hand, and gazed long into his deep, bright eyes. Then the two sat down together, and Mimer, or Regin as we shall now call him, told the prince many tales of the days that had been, and of his bold, wise forefathers. And the lad's heart swelled within him; and he longed to be like them,—to dare and do and suffer, and gloriously win at last. And he turned to Regin and said,—

"Tell me, wisest of masters, what I shall do to win fame, and to make myself worthy to rule the fair land which my fathers held."

"Go forth in your own strength, and with Odin's help," answered Regin,—"go forth to right the wrong, to help the weak, to punish evil, and come not back to your father's kingdom until the world shall know your noble deeds."

"But whither shall I go?" asked Siegfried.

"I will tell you," answered Regin. "Put on these garments, which better befit a prince than those soot-begrimed clothes you have worn so long. Gird about you this sword, the good Balmung, and go northward. When you come to the waste lands which border upon the sea, you will find the ancient Gripir, the last of the kin of the giants. Ask of him a war-steed, and Odin will tell you the rest."

So, when the sun had risen high above the trees, Siegfried bade Regin good-by, and went forth like a man, to take whatsoever fortune should betide. He went through the great forest, and across the bleak moorland beyond, and over the huge black mountains that stretched themselves across his way, and came to a pleasant country all dotted with white farmhouses, and yellow with waving, corn. But he tarried not here, though many kind words were spoken to him, and all besought him to stay. Right onwards he went, until he reached the waste land which borders the sounding sea. And there high mountains stood, with snow-crowned crags beetling over the waves; and a great river, all foaming with the summer floods, went rolling through the valley. And in the deep dales between the mountains were rich meadows, green with grass, and speckled with thousands of flowers of every hue, where herds of cattle and deer, and noble elks, and untamed horses, fed in undisturbed peace. And Siegfried, when he saw, knew that these were the pastures of Gripir the ancient.

High up among the gray mountain-peaks stood Gripir's dwelling,—a mighty house, made of huge bowlders brought by giant hands from the far north-land. And the wild eagle, built their nests around it, and the mountain vultures screamed about its doors. But Siegfried was not afraid. He climbed the steep pathway which the feet of men had never touched before, and, without pausing, walked straightway into the high-built hall. The room was so dark that at first he could see nothing save the white walls, and the glass-green pillars which upheld the roof. But the light grew stronger soon; and Siegfried saw, beneath a heavy canopy of stone, the ancient Gripir, seated in a chair made from the sea-horse's teeth.[EN#9] And the son of the giants held in his hand an ivory staff; and a purple mantle was thrown over his shoulders, and his white beard fell in sweeping waves almost to the sea-green floor. Very wise he seemed, and he gazed at Siegfried with a kindly smile.

"Hail, Siegfried!" he cried. "Hail, prince with the gleaming eye! I know thee, and I know the woof that the Norns have woven for thee. Welcome to my lonely mountain home! Come and sit by my side in the high-seat where man has never sat, and I will tell thee of things that have been, and of things that are yet to be."

Then Siegfried fearlessly went and sat by the side of the ancient wise one. And long hours they talked together,—strong youth and hoariest age; and each was glad that in the other he had found some source of hope and comfort. And they talked of the great midworld, and of the starry dome above it, and of the seas which gird it, and of the men who live upon it. All night long they talked, and in the morning Siegfried arose to go.

"Thou hast not told me of thy errand," said Gripir; "but I know what it is. Come first with me, and see this great mid-world for thyself."

Then Gripir, leaning on his staff, led the way out of the great hall, and up to the top of the highest mountain-crag. And the wild eagles circled in the clear, cold air above them; and far below them the white waves dashed against the mountain's feet; and the frosty winds swept around them unchecked, bringing to their ears the lone lamenting of the north giants, moaning for the days that had been and for the glories that were past. Then Siegfried looked to the north, and he saw the dark mountain-wall of Norway trending away in solemn grandeur towards the frozen sea, but broken here and there by sheltering fjords, and pleasant, sunny dales. He looked to the east, and saw a great forest stretching away and away until it faded to sight in the blue distance. He looked to the south, and saw a pleasant land, with farms and vineyards, and towns and strong-built castles;

and through it wound the River Rhine, like a great white serpent, reaching from the snow-capped Alps to the northern sea. And he saw his father's little kingdom of the Netherlands lying like a green speck on the shore of the ocean. Then he looked to the west, and nothing met his sight but a wilderness of rolling, restless waters, save, in the far distance, a green island half hidden by sullen mists and clouds. And Siegfried sighed, and said,—

"The world is so wide, and the life of man so short!"

"The world is all before thee," answered Gripir. "Take what the Norns have allotted thee. Choose from my pastures a battle-steed, and ride forth to win for thyself a name and fame among the sons of men."

Then Siegfried ran down the steep side of the mountain to the grassy dell where the horses were feeding. But the beasts were all so fair and strong, that he knew not which to choose. While he paused, uncertain what to do, a strange man stood before him. Tall and handsome was the man, with one bright eye, and a face beaming like the dawn in summer; and upon his head he wore a sky-blue hood bespangled with golden stars, and over his shoulder was thrown a cloak of ashen gray.

"Would you choose a horse, Sir Siegfried?" asked the stranger.

"Indeed I would," answered he. "But it is hard to make a choice among so many."

"There is one in the meadow," said the man, "far better than all the rest. They say that he came from Odin's pastures on the green hill-slopes of Asgard, and that none but the noblest shall ride him."

"Which is he?" asked Siegfried.

"Drive the herd into the river," was the answer, "and then see if you can pick him out."

And Siegfried and the stranger drove the horses down the sloping bank, and into the rolling stream; but the flood was too strong for them. Some soon turned back to the shore; while others, struggling madly, were swept away, and carried out to the sea. Only one swam safely over. He shook the dripping water from his mane, tossed his head in the air, and then plunged again into the stream. Right bravely he stemmed the torrent the second time. He clambered up the shelving bank, and stood by Siegfried's side.

"What need to tell you that this is the horse?" said the stranger. "Take him: he is yours. He is Greyfell, the shining hope that Odin sends to his chosen heroes."

And then Siegfried noticed that the horse's mane glimmered and flashed like a thousand rays from the sun, and that his coat was as white and clear as the fresh-fallen snow on the mountains. He turner to speak to the stranger, but he was nowhere to be seen and Siegfried bethought him how he had talked with Odin unawares. Then he mounted the noble Greyfell and rode with a light heart across the flowery meadows.

"Whither ridest thou?" cried Gripir the ancient, from his doorway among the crags.

"I ride into the wide world," said Siegfried; "but I know not whither. I would right the wrong, and help the weak, and make myself a name on the earth, as did my kinsmen of yore. Tell me, I pray you, where I shall go; for you are wise, and you know the things which have been, and those which shall befall."

"Ride back to Regin, the master of masters," answered Gripir. "He will tell thee of a wrong to be righted."

And the ancient son of the giants withdrew into his lonely abode; and Siegfried, on the shining Greyfell, rode swiftly away towards the south.

Adventure III. The Curse of Gold.

Forth then rode Siegfried, upon the beaming Greyfell, out into the broad mid-world. And the sun shone bright above him, and the air was soft and pure, and the earth seemed very lovely, and life a gladsome thing. And his heart was big within him as he thought of the days to come, of the deeds of love and daring, of the righting of many wrongs, of the people's praise, and the glory of a life well lived. And he wended his way back again toward the south and the fair lands of the Rhine. He left the barren moorlands behind him, and the pleasant farms and villages of the fruitful countryside, and after many days came once more to Regin's woodland dwelling. For he said to himself, "My old master is very wise; and he knows of the deeds that were done when yet the world was young, and my kin were the mightiest of men. I will go to him, and learn what grievous evil it is that he has so often vaguely hinted at."

Regin, when he saw the lad and the beaming Greyfell standing like a vision of light at his door, welcomed them most gladly, and led Siegfried into the inner room, where they sat down together amid the gold, and the gem-stones, and the fine-wrought treasures there.

"Truly," said the master, "the days of my long waiting are drawing to a close, and at last the deed shall be done."

And the old look of longing came again into his eyes, and his pinched face seemed darker and more wrinkled than before, and his thin lips trembled with emotion as he spoke.

"What is that deed of which you speak?" asked Siegfried.

"It is the righting of a grievous wrong," answered Regin, "and the winning of treasures untold. Lo, many years have I waited for the coming of this day; and now my heart tells me that the hero so long hoped for is here, and the wisdom and the wealth of the world shall be mine."

"But what is the wrong to be righted?" asked Siegfried. "And what is this treasure that you speak of as your own?"

"Alas!" answered Regin, "the treasure is indeed mine; and yet wrongfully has it been withheld from me. But listen a while to a tale of the early days, and thou shalt know what the treasure is, and what is the wrong to be righted."

He took his harp and swept the strings, and played a soft, low melody which told of the dim past, and of blighted hopes, and of a nameless, never-satisfied yearning for that which might have been. And then he told Siegfried this story:

Regin's Story.

When the earth was still very young, and men were feeble and few, and the Dwarfs were many and strong, the Asa-folk were wont oft-times to leave their halls in heaven-towering Asgard in order to visit the new-formed mid-world, and to see what the short-lived sons of men were doing. Sometimes they came in their own godlike splendor and might; sometimes they came disguised as feeble men-folk, with all man's weaknesses and all his passions. Sometimes Odin, as a beggar, wandered from one country to another, craving charity; sometimes, as a warrior clad in coat of mail, he rode forth to battle for the cause of right; or as a minstrel he sang from door to door, and played sweet music in the halls of the great; or as a huntsman he dashed through brakes and fens, and into dark forests, and climbed steep mountains in search of game; or as a sailor he embarked upon the sea, and sought new scenes in unknown lands. And many times did men-folk entertain him unawares.

Once on a time he came to the mid-world in company with Hoenir and Loki; and the three wandered through many lands and in many climes, each giving gifts wherever they went. Odin gave knowledge and strength, and taught men how to read the mystic runes; Hoenir gave gladness and good cheer, and lightened many hearts with the glow of his comforting presence; but Loki had nought to give but cunning deceit and base thoughts, and he left behind him bitter strife and many aching breasts. At last, growing tired of the fellowship of men, the three Asas sought the solitude of the forest, and as huntsmen wandered long among the hills and over the wooded heights of Hunaland. Late one afternoon they came to a mountain-stream at a place where it poured over a ledge of rocks, and fell in clouds of spray into a rocky gorge below. As they stood, and with pleased eyes gazed upon the waterfall, they saw near the bank an otter lazily making ready to eat a salmon which he had caught. And Loki, ever bent on doing mischief, hurled a stone at the harmless beast, and killed it. And he boasted loudly that he had done a worthy deed. And he took both the otter, and the fish which it had caught, and carried them with him as trophies of the day's success.

Just at nightfall the three huntsmen came to a lone farmhouse in the valley, and asked for food, and for shelter during the night.

"Shelter you shall have," said the farmer, whose name was Hreidmar, "for the rising clouds foretell a storm. But food I have none to give you. Surely huntsmen of skill should not want for food; since the forest teems with game, and the streams are full of fish."

Then Loki threw upon the ground the otter and the fish, and said, "We have sought in both forest and stream, and we have taken from them at one blow both flesh and fish. Give us but the shelter you promise, and we will not trouble you for food."

The farmer gazed with horror upon the lifeless body of the otter, and cried out, "This creature which you mistook for an otter, and which you have robbed and killed, is my son Oddar, who for mere pastime had taken the form of the furry beast. You are but thieves and murderers!"

Then he called loudly for help: and his two sons Fafnir and Regin, sturdy and valiant kin of the dwarf-folk, rushed in, and seized upon the huntsmen, and bound them hand and foot; for the three Asas, having taken upon themselves the forms of men, had no more than human strength, and were unable to withstand them.

Then Odin and his fellows bemoaned their ill fate. And Loki said, "Wherefore did we foolishly take upon ourselves the likenesses of puny men? Had I my own power once more, I would never part with it in exchange for man's weaknesses."

And Hoenir sighed, and said, "Now, indeed, will darkness win: and the frosty breath of the Reimthursen giants will blast the fair handiwork of the sunlight and the heat; for the givers of life and light and warmth are helpless prisoners in the hands of these cunning and unforgiving jailers."

"Surely," said Odin, "not even the highest are free from obedience to heaven's behests and the laws of right. I, whom men call the Preserver of Life, have demeaned myself by being found in evil company; and, although I have done no other wrong, I suffer rightly for the doings of this mischief-maker with whom I have stooped to have fellowship. For all are known, not so much by what they are as by what they seem to be, and they bear the bad name which their comrades bear. Now I am fallen from my high estate. Eternal right is higher than I. And in the last Twilight of the gods I must needs meet the dread Fenris-wolf, and in the end the world will be made new again, and the shining Balder will rule in sunlight majesty forever."

Then the Asas asked Hreidmar, their jailer, what ransom they should pay for their freedom; and he, not knowing who they were, said, "I must first know what ransom you are able to give."

"We will give any thing you may ask," hastily answered Loki.

Hreidmar then called his sons, and bade them strip the skin from the otter's body. When this was done, they brought the furry hide and spread it upon the ground; and Hreidmar said, "Bring shining gold and precious stones enough to cover every part of this otter-skin. When you have paid so much ransom, you shall have your freedom."

"That we will do," answered Odin. "But one of us must have leave to go and fetch it: the other two will stay fast bound until the morning dawns. If, by that time, the gold is not here, you may do with us as you please."

Hreidmar and the two young men agreed to Odin's offer; and, lots being cast, it fell to Loki to go and fetch the treasure. When he had been loosed from the cords which bound him, Loki donned his magic shoes, which had carried him over land and sea from the farthest bounds of the mid-world, and hastened away upon his errand. And he sped with the swiftness of light, over the hills and the wooded slopes, and the deep dark valleys, and the fields and forests and sleeping hamlets, until he came to the place where dwelt the swarthy elves and the cunning dwarf Andvari. There the River Rhine, no larger than a meadow-brook, breaks forth from beneath a mountain of ice, which the Frost giants and blind old Hoder, the Winter-king, had built long years before; for they had vainly hoped that they might imprison the river at its fountain-head. But the baby-brook had eaten its way beneath the frozen mass, and had sprung out from its prison, and gone on, leaping and smiling, and kissing the sunlight, in its ever-widening course towards Burgundy and the sea.

Loki came to this place, because he knew that here was the home of the elves who had laid up the greatest hoard of treasures ever known in the mid-world. He scanned with careful eyes the mountain-side, and the deep, rocky caverns, and the dark gorge through which the little river rushed; but in the dim moonlight not a living being could he see, save a lazy salmon swimming in the quieter eddies of the stream. Any one but Loki would have lost all hope of finding treasure there, at least before the dawn of day; but his wits were quick, and his eyes were very sharp.

"One salmon has brought us into this trouble, and another shall help us out of it!" he cried.

Then, swift as thought, he sprang again into the air; and the magic shoes carried him with greater speed than before down the Rhine valley, and through Burgundy-land, and the low meadows, until he came to the shores of the great North Sea. He sought the halls of old AEgir, the Ocean-king; but he wist not which way to go,—whether across the North Sea towards Isenland, or whether along the narrow channel between Britain-land and the main. While he paused, uncertain where to turn, he saw the pale-haired daughters of old AEgir, the white-veiled Waves, playing in the moonlight near the shore. Of them he asked the way to AEgir's hall.

"Seven days' journey westward," said they, "beyond the green Isle of Erin, is our father's hall. Seven days' journey northward, on the bleak Norwegian shore, is our father's hall."

And they stopped not once in their play, but rippled and danced on the shelving beach, or dashed with force against the shore.

"Where is your mother Ran, the Queen of the Ocean?" asked Loki.

And they answered,—

> *"In the deep sea-caves*
> *By the sounding shore,*
> *In the dashing waves*
> *When the wild storms roar,*
> *In her cold green bowers*
> *In the northern fiords,*
> *She lurks and she glowers,*
> *She grasps and she hoards,*
> *And she spreads her strong net for her prey."*

Loki waited to hear no more; but he sprang into the air, and the magic shoes carried him onwards over the water in search of the Ocean-queen. He had not gone far when his sharp eyes espied her, lurking near a rocky shore against which the breakers dashed with frightful fury. Half hidden in the deep dark water, she lay waiting and watching; and she spread her cunning net upon the waves, and reached out with her long greedy fingers to seize whatever booty might come near her.

When the wary queen saw Loki, she hastily drew in her net, and tried to hide herself in the shadows of an overhanging rock. But Loki called her by name, and said,—

"Sister Ran, fear not! I am your friend Loki, whom once you served as a guest in AEgir's gold-lit halls."

Then the Ocean-queen came out into the bright moonlight, and welcomed Loki to her domain, and asked, "Why does Loki thus wander so far from Asgard, and over the trackless waters?"

And Loki answered, "I have heard of the net which you spread upon the waves, and from which no creature once caught in its meshes can ever escape. I have found a salmon where the Rhine-spring gushes from beneath the mountains, and a very cunning salmon he is for no common skill can catch him. Come, I pray, with your wondrous net, and cast it into the stream where he lies. Do but take the wary fish for me, and you shall have more gold than you have taken in a year from the wrecks of stranded vessels."

"I dare not go," cried Ran. "A bound is set, beyond which I may not venture. If all the gold of earth were offered me, I could not go."

"Then lend me your net," entreated Loki. "Lend me your net, and I will bring it back to-morrow filled with gold."

"Much I would like your gold," answered Ran; "but I cannot lend my net. Should I do so, I might lose the richest prize that has ever come into my husband's kingdom. For three days, now, a gold-rigged ship, bearing a princely crew with rich armor and abundant wealth, has been sailing carelessly over these seas. To-morrow I shall send my daughters and the bewitching mermaids to decoy the vessel among the rocks. And into my net the ship, and the brave warriors, and all their armor and gold, shall fall. A rich prize it will be. No: I cannot part with my net, even for a single hour."

But Loki knew the power of flattering words.

"Beautiful queen," said he, "there is no one on earth, nor even in Asgard, who can equal you in wisdom and foresight. Yet I promise you, that, if you will but lend me your net until the morning dawns, the ship and the crew of which you speak shall be yours, and all their golden treasures shall deck your azure halls in the deep sea."

Then Ran carefully folded the net, and gave it to Loki.

"Remember your promise," was all that she said.

"An Asa never forgets," he answered.

And he turned his face again towards Rhineland; and the magic shoes bore him aloft, and carried him in a moment back to the ice-mountain and the gorge and the infant river, which he had so lately left. The salmon still rested in his place, and had not moved during Loki's short absence.

Loki unfolded the net, and cast it into the stream. The cunning fish tried hard to avoid being caught in its meshes; but, dart which way he would, he met the skilfully woven cords, and these drew themselves around him, and held him fast. Then Loki pulled the net up out of the water, and grasped the helpless fish in his right hand. But, lo! as he held the struggling creature high in the air, it was no longer a fish, but the cunning dwarf Andvari.

"Thou King of the Elves," cried Loki, "thy cunning has not saved thee. Tell me, on thy life, where thy hidden treasures lie!"

The wise dwarf knew who it was that thus held him as in a vise; and he answered frankly, for it was his only hope of escape, "Turn over the stone upon which you stand. Beneath it you will find the treasure you seek."

Then Loki put his shoulder to the rock, and pushed with all his might. But it seemed as firm as the mountain, and would not be moved.

"Help us, thou cunning dwarf," he cried,—"help us, and thou shalt have thy life!"

The dwarf put his shoulder to the rock, and it turned over as if by magic, and underneath was disclosed a wondrous chamber, whose walls shone brighter than the sun, and on whose floor lay treasures of gold and glittering gem-stones such as no man had ever seen. And Loki, in great haste, seized upon the hoard, and placed it in the magic net which he had borrowed from the Ocean-queen. Then he came out of the chamber; and Andvari again put his shoulder to the rock which lay at the entrance, and it swung back noiselessly to its place.

"What is that upon thy finger?" suddenly cried Loki. "Wouldst keep back a part of the treasure? Give me the ring thou hast!"

But the dwarf shook his head, and made answer, "I have given thee all the riches that the elves of the mountain have gathered since the world began. This ring I cannot give thee, for without its help we shall never be able to gather more treasures together."

And Loki grew angry at these words of the dwarf; and he seized the ring, and tore it by force from Andvari's fingers. It was a wondrous little piece of mechanism shaped like a serpent, coiled, with its tail in its mouth; and its scaly sides glittered with many a tiny diamond, and its ruby eyes shone with an evil light. When the dwarf knew that Loki really meant to rob him of the ring, he cursed it and all who should ever possess it, saying,—

"May the ill-gotten treasure that you have seized tonight be your bane, and the bane of all to whom it may come, whether by fair means or by foul! And the ring which you have torn from my hand, may it entail upon the one who wears it sorrow and untold ills, the loss of friends, and a violent death! The Norns have spoken, and thus it must be."

Loki was pleased with these words, and with the dark curses which the dwarf pronounced upon the gold; for he loved wrong-doing, for wrong-doing's sake, and he knew that no curses could ever make his own life more cheerless than it always had been. So he thanked Andvari for his curses and his treasures; and, throwing the magic net upon his shoulder, he sprang again into the air, and was carried swiftly back to Hunaland; and, just before the dawn appeared in the east, he alighted at the door of the farmhouse where Odin and Hoenir still lay bound with thongs, and guarded by Fafnir and Regin.

Then the farmer, Hreidmar, brought the otter's skin, and spread it upon the ground; and, lo! it grew, and spread out on all sides, until it covered an acre of ground. And he cried out, "Fulfil now your promise! Cover every hair of this hide with gold or with precious stones. If you fail to do this, then your lives, by your own agreement, are forfeited, and we shall do with you as we list."

Odin took the magic net from Loki's shoulder; and opening it, he poured the treasures of the mountain elves upon the otter-skin. And Loki and Hoenir spread the yellow pieces carefully and evenly over every part of the furry hide. But, after every piece had been laid in its place; Hreidmar saw near the otter's mouth a single hair uncovered; and he declared, that unless this hair, too, were covered, the bargain would be unfulfilled, and the treasures and lives of his prisoners would be forfeited. And the Asas looked at each other in dismay; for not another piece of gold, and not another precious stone, could they find in the net, although they searched with the greatest care. At last Odin took from his bosom the ring which Loki had stolen from the dwarf; for he had been so highly pleased with its form and workmanship, that he had hidden it, hoping that it would not be needed to complete the payment of the ransom. And they laid the ring upon the uncovered hair. And now no portion of the otter's skin could be seen. And Fafnir and Regin, the ransom being paid, loosed the shackles of Odin and Hoenir, and bade the three huntsmen go on their way.

Odin and Hoenir at once shook off their human disguises, and, taking their own forms again, hastened with all speed back to Asgard. But Loki tarried a little while, and said to Hreidmar and his sons,—

"By your greediness and falsehood you have won for yourselves the Curse of the Earth, which lies before you. It shall be your bane. It shall be the bane of every one who holds it. It shall kindle strife between father and son, between brother and brother. It shall make you mean, selfish, beastly. It shall transform you into monsters. The noblest king among men-folk shall feel its curse. Such is gold, and such it shall ever be to its worshippers. And the ring which you have gotten shall impart to its possessor its own nature. Grasping, snaky, cold, unfeeling, shall he live; and death through treachery shall be his doom."

Then he turned away, delighted that he had thus left the curse of Andvari with Hreidmar and his sons, and hastened northward toward the sea; for he wished to redeem the promise that he had made to the Ocean-queen, to bring back her magic net, and to decoy the richly laden ship into her clutches.

No sooner were the strange huntsmen well out of sight than Fafnir and Regin began to ask their father to divide the glittering hoard with them.

"By our strength and through our advice," said they, "this great store has come into your hands. Let us place it in three equal heaps, and then let each take his share and go his way."

At this the farmer waxed very angry; and he loudly declared that he would keep all the treasure for himself, and that his sons should not have any portion of it whatever. So Fafnir and Regin, nursing their disappointment, went to the fields to watch their sheep; but their father sat down to guard his new-gotten treasure. And he took in his hand the glittering serpent-ring, and gazed into its cold ruby eyes: and, as he gazed, all his thoughts were fixed upon his gold; and there was no room in his heart for love toward his fellows, nor for deeds of kindness, nor for the worship of the All-Father. And behold, as he continued to look at the snaky ring, a dreadful change came over him. The warm red blood, which until that time had leaped through his veins, and given him life and strength and human feelings, became purple and cold and sluggish; and selfishness, like serpent-poison, took hold of his heart. Then, as he kept on gazing at the hoard which lay before him, he began to lose his human shape; his body lengthened into many scaly folds, and he coiled himself around his loved treasures,—the very likeness of the ring upon which he had looked so long.

When the day drew near its close, Fafnir came back from the fields with his herd of sheep, and thought to find his father guarding the treasure, as he had left him in the morning; but instead he saw a glittering snake, fast asleep, encircling the hoard like a huge scaly ring of gold. His first thought was that the monster had devoured his father; and, hastily drawing his sword, with one blow he severed the serpent's head from its body. And, while yet the creature writhed in the death-agony, he gathered up the hoard, and fled with it beyond the hills of Hunaland, until on the seventh day he came to a barren heath far from the homes of men. There he placed the treasures in one glittering heap; and he clothed himself in a wondrous mail-coat of gold that was found among them, and he put on the Helmet of Dread, which had once been the terror of the mid-world, and the like of which no man had ever seen; and then he gazed with greedy eyes upon the fateful ring, until he, too, was changed into a cold and slimy reptile,—a monster dragon. And he coiled himself about the hoard; and, with his restless eyes forever open, he gloated day after day upon his loved gold, and watched with ceaseless care that no one should come near to despoil him of it. This was ages and ages ago; and still he wallows among his treasures on the Glittering Heath, and guards as of yore the garnered wealth of Andvari.[EN#10]

When I, Regin, the younger brother, came back in the late evening to my father's dwelling, I saw that the treasure had been carried away; and, when I beheld the dead serpent lying in its place, I knew that a part of Andvari's curse had been fulfilled. And a strange fear came over me; and I left every thing behind me, and fled from that dwelling, never more to return. Then I came to the land of the Volsungs, where your father's fathers dwelt, the noblest king-folk that the world has ever seen. But a longing for the gold and the treasure, a hungry yearning, that would never be satisfied, filled my soul. Then for a time I sought to forget this craving. I spent my days in the getting of knowledge and in teaching men-folk the ancient lore of my kin, the Dwarfs. I taught them how to plant and to sow, and to reap the yellow grain. I showed them where the precious metals of the earth lie hidden, and how to smelt iron from its ores,—how to shape the ploughshare and the spade, the spear and the battle-axe. I taught them how to tame the wild horses of the meadows, and how to train the yoke-beasts to the plough; how to build lordly dwellings and mighty strongholds, and how to sail in ships across old AEgir's watery kingdom. But they gave me no thanks for what I had done; and as the years went by they forgot who had been their teacher, and they said that it was Frey who had given them this knowledge and skill. And I taught the young maidens how to spin and weave, and to handle the needle deftly,—to make rich garments, and to work in tapestry and embroidery. But they, too, forgot me, and said that it was Freyja who had taught them. Then I showed men how to read the mystic runes aright, and how to make the sweet beverage of poetry, that charms all hearts, and enlightens the world. But they say now that they had these gifts from Odin. I taught them how to fashion the tales of old into rich melodious songs, and with music and sweet-mouthed eloquence to move the minds of their fellow-men. But they say that Bragi taught them this; and they remember me only as Regin, the elfin schoolmaster, or at best as Mimer, the master of smiths. At length my heart grew bitter because of the neglect and ingratitude of men; and the old longing for Andvari's hoard came back to me, and I forgot much of my cunning and lore. But I lived on and on, and generations of short-lived men arose and passed, and still the hoard was not mine; for I was weak, and no man was strong enough to help me.

Then I sought wisdom of the Norns, the weird women who weave the woof of every creature's fate.[EN#6] and [EN#7]

"How long," asked I, "must I hope and wait in weary expectation of that day when the wealth of the world and the garnered wisdom of the ages shall be mine?"

And the witches answered, "When a prince of the Volsung race shall come who shall excel thee in the smithying craft, and to whom the All-Father shall give the Shining Hope as a helper, then the days of thy weary watching, shall cease."

"How long," asked I, "shall I live to enjoy this wealth and this wisdom, and to walk as a god among men? Shall I be long-lived as the Asa-folk, and dwell on the earth until the last Twilight comes?"

"It is written," answered Skuld, "that a beardless youth shall see thy death. But go thou now, and bide thy time."

Here Regin ended his story, and both he and Siegfried sat for a long time silent and thoughtful.

"I know what you wish," said Siegfried at last. "You think that I am the prince of whom the weird sisters spoke; and you would have me slay the dragon Fafnir, and win for you the hoard of Andvari."

"It is even so," answered Regin.

"But the hoard is accursed," said the lad.

"Let the curse be upon me," was the answer. "Is not the wisdom of the ages mine? And think you that I cannot escape the curse? Is there aught that can prevail against him who has all knowledge and the wealth of the world at his call?"

"Nothing but the word of the Norns and the will of the All-Father," answered Siegfried.

"But will you help me?" asked Regin, almost wild with earnestness. "Will you help me to win that which is rightfully mine, and to rid the world of a horrible evil?"

"Why is the hoard of Andvari more thine than Fafnir's?"

"He is a monster, and he keeps the treasure but to gloat upon its glittering richness. I will use it to make myself a name upon the earth. I will not hoard it away. But I am weak, and he is strong and terrible. Will you help me?"

"To-morrow," said Siegfried, "be ready to go with me to the Glittering Heath. The treasure shall be thine, and also the curse."

"And also the curse," echoed Regin.

Adventure IV. Fafnir, the Dragon.

Regin took up his harp, and his fingers smote the strings; and the music which came forth sounded like the wail of the winter's wind through the dead treetops of the forest. And the song which he sang was full of grief and wild hopeless yearning for the things which were not to be. When he had ceased, Siegfried said,—

"That was indeed a sorrowful song for one to sing who sees his hopes so nearly realized. Why are you so sad? Is it because you fear the curse which you have taken upon yourself? or is it because you know not what you will do with so vast a treasure, and its possession begins already to trouble you?"

"Oh, many are the things I will do with that treasure!" answered Regin; and his eyes flashed wildly, and his face grew red and pale. "I will turn winter into summer; I will make the desert-places glad; I will bring back the golden age; I will make myself a god: for mine shall be the wisdom and the gathered wealth of the world. And yet I fear"—

"What do you fear?"

"The ring, the ring—it is accursed! The Norns, too, have spoken, and my doom is known. I cannot escape it."

"The Norns have woven the woof of every man's life," answered Siegfried. "To-morrow we fare to the Glittering Heath, and the end shall be as the Norns have spoken."

And so, early the next morning, Siegfried mounted Greyfell, and rode out towards the desert-land that lay beyond the forest and the barren mountain-range; and Regin, his eyes flashing with desire, and his feet never tiring, trudged by his side. For seven days they wended their way through the thick greenwood, sleeping at night on the bare ground beneath the trees, while the wolves and other wild beasts of the forest filled the air with their hideous howlings. But no evil creature dared come near them, for fear of the shining beams of light which fell from Greyfell's gleaming mane. On the eighth day they came to the open country and to the hills, where the land was covered with black bowlders and broken by yawning chasms. And no living thing was seen there, not even an insect, nor a blade of grass; and the silence of the grave was over all. And the earth was dry and parched, and the sun hung above them like a painted shield in a blue-black sky, and there was neither shade nor water anywhere. But Siegfried rode onwards in the way which Regin pointed out, and faltered not, although he grew faint with thirst and with the overpowering heat. Towards the evening of the next day they came to a dark mountain-wall which stretched far out on either hand, and rose high above them, so steep that it seemed to close up the way, and to forbid them going farther.

"This is the wall!" cried Regin. "Beyond this mountain is the Glittering Heath, and the goal of all my hopes."

And the little old man ran forwards, and scaled the rough side of the mountain, and reached its summit, while Siegfried and Greyfell were yet toiling among the rocks at its foot. Slowly and painfully they climbed the steep ascent, sometimes following a narrow path which wound along the edge of a precipice, sometimes leaping, from rock to rock, or over some deep gorge, and sometimes picking their way among the crags and cliffs. The sun at last went down, and one by one the stars came out; and the moon was rising, round and red, when Siegfried stood by Regin's side, and gazed from the mountain-top down upon the Glittering Heath which lay beyond. And a strange, weird scene it was that met his sight. At the foot of the mountain was a river, white and cold and still; and beyond it was a smooth and barren plain, lying silent and lonely in the pale moonlight. But in the distance was seen a circle of flickering flames, ever changing,—now growing brighter, now fading away, and now shining with a dull, cold light, like the glimmer of the glow-worm or the fox-fire. And as Siegfried gazed upon the scene, he saw the dim outline of some hideous monster moving hither and thither, and seeming all the more terrible in the uncertain light.

"It is he!" whispered Regin, and his lips were ashy pale, and his knees trembled beneath him. "It is Fafnir, and he wears the Helmet of Terror! Shall we not go back to the smithy by the great forest, and to the life of ease and safety that may be ours there? Or will you rather dare to go forwards, and meet the Terror in its abode?"

"None but cowards give up an undertaking once begun," answered Siegfried. "Go back to Rhineland yourself, if you are afraid; but you must go alone. You have brought me thus far to meet the dragon of the heath, to win the hoard of the swarthy elves, and to rid the world of a terrible evil. Before the setting of another sun, the deed which you have urged me to do will be done."

Then he dashed down the eastern slope of the mountain, leaving Greyfell and the trembling Regin behind him. Soon he stood on the banks of the white river, which lay between the mountain and the heath; but the stream was deep and sluggish, and the channel was very wide. He paused a moment, wondering how he should cross; and the air seemed heavy with deadly vapors, and the water was thick and cold. While he thus stood in thought, a boat came silently out of the mists, and drew near; and the boatman stood up and called to him, and said,—

"What man are you who dares come into this land of loneliness and fear?"

"I am Siegfried," answered the lad; "and I have come to slay Fafnir, the Terror."

"Sit in my boat," said the boatman, "and I will carry you across the river."

And Siegfried sat by the boatman's side; and without the use of an oar, and without a breath of air to drive it forwards, the little vessel turned, and moved silently towards the farther shore.

"In what way will you fight the dragon?" asked the boatman.

"With my trusty sword Balmung I shall slay him," answered Siegfried.

"But he wears the Helmet of Terror, and he breathes deathly poisons, and his eyes dart forth lightning, and no man can withstand his strength," said the boatman.

"I will find some way by which to overcome him."

"Then be wise, and listen to me," said the boatman. "As you go up from the river you will find a road, worn deep and smooth, starting from the water's edge, and winding over the moor. It is the trail of Fafnir, adown which he comes at dawn of every day to slake his thirst at the river. Do you dig a pit in this roadway,—a pit narrow and deep,—and hide yourself within it. In the morning, when Fafnir passes over it, let him feel the edge of Balmung."

As the man ceased speaking, the boat touched the shore, and Siegfried leaped out. He looked back to thank his unknown friend, but neither boat nor boatman was to be seen. Only a thin white mist rose slowly from the cold surface of the stream, and floated upwards and away towards the mountain-tops. Then the lad remembered that the strange boatman had worn a blue hood bespangled with golden stars, and that a gray kirtle was thrown over his shoulders, and that his one eye glistened and sparkled with a light that was more than human. And he knew that he had again talked with Odin. Then, with a braver heart than before, he went forwards, along the river-bank, until he came to Fafnir's trail,—a deep, wide furrow in the earth, beginning at the river's bank, and winding far away over the heath, until it was lost to sight in the darkness. The bottom of the trail was soft and slimy, and its sides had been worn smooth by Fafnir's frequent travel through it.

In this road, at a point not far from the river, Siegfried, with his trusty sword Balmung, scooped out a deep and narrow pit, as Odin had directed. And when the gray dawn began to appear in the east he hid himself within this trench, and waited for the coming of the monster. He had not long to wait; for no sooner had the sky begun to redden in the light of the coming sun than the dragon was heard bestirring himself. Siegfried peeped warily from his hiding-place, and saw him coming far down the road, hurrying with all speed, that he might quench his thirst at the sluggish river, and hasten back to his gold; and the sound which he made was like the trampling of many feet and the jingling of many chains. With bloodshot eyes, and gaping mouth, and flaming nostrils, the hideous creature came rushing onwards. His sharp, curved claws dug deep into the soft earth; and his bat-like wings, half trailing on the ground, half flapping in the air, made a sound like that which is heard when Thor rides in his goat-drawn chariot over the dark thunder-clouds. It was a terrible moment for Siegfried, but still he was not afraid. He crouched low down in his hiding-place, and the bare blade of the trusty Balmung glittered in the morning light. On came the hastening feet and the flapping wings: the red gleam from the monster's flaming nostrils lighted up the trench where Siegfried lay. He heard a roaring and a rushing like the sound of a whirlwind in the forest; then a black, inky mass rolled above him, and all was dark. Now was Siegfried's opportunity. The bright edge of Balmung gleamed in the darkness one moment, and then it smote the heart of Fafnir as he passed. Some men say that Odin sat in the pit with Siegfried, and strengthened his arm and directed his sword, or else he could not thus have slain the Terror. But, be this as it may, the victory was soon won. The monster stopped short, while but half of his long body had glided over the pit; for sudden death had overtaken him. His horrid head fell lifeless upon the ground; his cold wings flapped once, and then lay, quivering and helpless, spread out on either side; and streams of thick black blood flowed from his heart, through the wound beneath, and filled the trench in which Siegfried was hidden, and ran like a mountain-torrent down the road towards the river. Siegfried was covered from head to foot with the slimy liquid, and, had he not quickly leaped from his hiding-place, he would have been drowned in the swift-rushing, stream.[EN#11]

The bright sun rose in the east, and gilded the mountain-tops, and fell upon the still waters of the river, and lighted up the treeless plains around. The south wind played gently against Siegfried's cheeks and in his long hair, as he stood gazing on his fallen foe. And the sound of singing birds, and rippling waters, and gay insects,—such as had not broken the silence of the Glittering Heath for ages,—came to his ears. The Terror was dead, and Nature had awakened from her sleep of dread. And as the lad leaned upon his sword, and thought of the deed he had done, behold! the shining

Greyfell, with the beaming, hopeful mane, having crossed the now bright river, stood by his side. And Regin, his face grown wondrous cold, came trudging over the meadows; and his heart was full of guile. Then the mountain vultures came wheeling downwards to look upon the dead dragon; and with them were two ravens, black as midnight. And when Siegfried saw these ravens he knew them to be Odin's birds,—Hugin, thought, and Munin, memory. And they alighted on the ground near by; and the lad listened to hear what they would say. Then Hugin flapped his wings, and said,—

"The deed is done. Why tarries the hero?"

And Munin said,—

"The world is wide. Fame waits for the hero."

And Hugin answered,—

"What if he win the Hoard of the Elves? That is not honor. Let him seek fame by nobler deeds."

Then Munin flew past his ear, and whispered,—

"Beware of Regin, the master! His heart is poisoned. He would be thy bane."

And the two birds flew away to carry the news to Odin in the happy halls of Gladsheim.

When Regin drew near to look upon the dragon, Siegfried kindly accosted him: but he seemed not to hear; and a snaky glitter lurked in his eyes, and his mouth was set and dry, and he seemed as one walking in a dream.

"It is mine now," he murmured: "it is all mine, now,—the Hoard of the swarthy elf-folk, the garnered wisdom of ages. The strength of the world is mine. I will keep, I will save, I will heap up; and none shall have part or parcel of the treasure which is mine alone."

Then his eyes fell upon Siegfried; and his cheeks grew dark with wrath, and he cried out,—

"Why are you here in my way? I am the lord of the Glittering Heath: I am the master of the Hoard. I am the master, and you are my thrall."

Siegfried wondered at the change which had taken place in his old master; but he only smiled at his strange words, and made no answer.

"You have slain my brother!" Regin cried; and his face grew fearfully black, and his mouth foamed with rage.

"It was my deed and yours," calmly answered Siegfried. "I have rid the world of a Terror: I have righted a grievous wrong."

"You have slain my brother," said Regin; "and a murderer's ransom you shall pay!"

"Take the Hoard for your ransom, and let us each wend his way," said the lad.

"The Hoard is mine by rights," answered Regin still more wrathfully. "I am the master, and you are my thrall. Why stand you in my way?"

Then, blinded with madness, he rushed at Siegfried as if to strike him down; but his foot slipped in a puddle of gore, and he pitched headlong against the sharp edge of Balmung. So sudden was this movement, and so unlooked for, that the sword was twitched out of Siegfried's hand, and fell with a dull splash into the blood-filled pit before him; while Regin, slain by his own rashness, sank dead upon the ground. Full of horror, Siegfried turned away, and mounted Greyfell.[EN#12]

"This is a place of blood," said he, "and the way to glory leads not through it. Let the Hoard still lie on the Glittering Heath: I will go my way from hence; and the world shall know me for better deeds than this."

And he turned his back on the fearful scene, and rode away; and so swiftly did Greyfell carry him over the desert land and the mountain waste, that, when night came, they stood on the shore of the great North Sea, and the white waves broke at their feet. And the lad sat for a long time silent upon the warm white sand of the beach, and Greyfell waited at his side. And he watched the stars as they came out one by one, and the moon, as it rose round and pale, and moved like a queen across the sky. And the night wore away, and the stars grew pale, and the moon sank to rest in the wilderness of waters. And at day-dawn Siegfried looked towards the west, and midway between sky and sea he thought he saw dark mountain-tops hanging above a land of mists that seemed to float upon the edge of the sea.

While he looked, a white ship, with sails all set, came speeding over the waters towards him. It came nearer and nearer, and the sailors rested upon their oars as it glided into the quiet harbor. A minstrel, with long white beard floating in the wind, sat at the prow; and the sweet music from his harp was wafted like incense to the shore. The vessel touched the sands: its white sails were reefed as if by magic, and the crew leaped out upon the beach.

"Hail, Siegfried the Golden!" cried the harper. "Whither do you fare this summer day?"

"I have come from a land of horror and dread," answered the lad; "and I would fain fare to a brighter."

"Then go with me to awaken the earth from its slumber, and to robe the fields in their garbs of beauty," said the harper. And he touched the strings of his harp, and strains of the softest music arose in the still morning air. And Siegfried stood entranced, for never before had he heard such music.

"Tell me who you are!" he cried, when the sounds died away. "Tell me who you are, and I will go to the ends of the earth with you."

"I am Bragi," answered the harper, smiling. And Siegfried noticed then that the ship was laden with flowers of every hue, and that thousands of singing birds circled around and above it, filling the air with the sound of their glad twitterings.

Now, Bragi was the sweetest musician in all the world. It was said by some that his home was with the song-birds, and that he had learned his skill from them. But this was only part of the truth: for wherever there was loveliness or beauty, or things noble and pure, there was Bragi; and his wondrous power in music and song was but the outward sign of a blameless soul. When he touched the strings of his golden harp, all Nature was charmed with the sweet harmony: the savage beasts of the wood crept near to listen; the birds paused in their flight; the waves of the sea were becalmed, and the winds were hushed; the leaping waterfall was still, and the rushing torrent tarried in its bed; the elves forgot their hidden treasures, and joined in silent dance around him; and the strom-karls and the musicians of the wood vainly tried to imitate him. And he was as fair of speech as he was skilful in song. His words were so persuasive that he had been known to call the fishes from the sea, to move great lifeless rocks, and, what is harder, the hearts of kings. He understood the voice of the birds, and the whispering of the breeze, the murmur of the waves, and the roar of the waterfalls. He knew the length and breadth of the earth, and the secrets of the sea, and the language of the stars. And every day he talked with Odin the All-Father, and with the wise and good in the sunlit halls of Gladsheim. And once every year he went to the North-lands, and woke the earth from its long winter's sleep, and scattered music and smiles and beauty everywhere.[EN#13]

Right gladly did Siegfried agree to sail with Bragi over the sea; for he wot that the bright Asa-god would be a very different guide from the cunning, evil-eyed Regin. So he went on board with Bragi, and the gleaming Greyfell followed them, and the sailors sat at their oars. And Bragi stood in the prow, and touched the strings of his harp. And, as the music arose, the white sails leaped up the masts, and a warm south breeze began to blow; and the little vessel, wafted by sweet sounds and the incense of spring, sped gladly away over the sea.

Adventure V. In AEgir's Kingdom.

The vessel in which Siegfried sailed was soon far out at sea; for the balmy south wind, and the songs of the birds, and the music from Bragi's harp, all urged it cheerily on. And Siegfried sat at the helm, and guided it in its course. By and by they lost all sight of land, and the sailors wist not where they were; but they knew that Bragi, the Wise, would bring them safely into some haven whenever it should so please him, and they felt no fear. And the fishes leaped up out of the water as the white ship sped by on woven wings; and the monsters of the deep paused, and listened to the sweet music which floated down from above. After a time the vessel began to meet great ice-mountains in the sea,—mountains which the Reifriesen, and old Hoder, the King of the winter months, had sent drifting down from the frozen land of the north. But these melted at the sound of Bragi's music and at the sight of Siegfried's radiant armor. And the cold breath of the Frost-giants, which had driven them in their course, turned, and became the ally of the south wind.

At length they came in sight of a dark shore, which stretched on either hand, north and south, as far as the eye could reach; and as they drew nearer they saw a line of huge mountains, rising, as it were, out of the water, and stretching their gray heads far above the clouds. And the overhanging cliffs seemed to look down, half in anger, half in pity, upon the little white winged vessel which had dared thus to sail through these unknown waters. But the surface of the sea was smooth as glass; and the gentle breeze drove the ship slowly forwards through the calm water, and along the rock-bound coast, and within the dark shadows of the mountain-peaks. Long ago the Frost-giants had piled great heaps of snow upon these peaks, and built huge fortresses of ice between, and sought, indeed, to clasp in their cold embrace the whole of the Norwegian land. But the breezes of the South-land that came with Bragi's ship now played among the rocky steeps, and swept over the frozen slopes above, and melted the snow and ice; and thousands of rivulets of half-frozen water ran down the mountain-sides, and tumbled into rocky gorges, or plunged into the sea. And the grass began to grow on the sunny slopes, and the flowers peeped up through the half-melted snow, and the music of spring was heard on every side. Now and then the little vessel passed by deep, dark inlets enclosed between high mountain-walls, and reaching many leagues far into land. But the sailors steered clear of these shadowy fjords; for they said that Ran, the dread Ocean-queen, lived there, and spread her nets in the deep green waters to entangle unwary seafaring men. And the sound of Bragi's harp awakened all sleeping things;

and it was carried from rock to rock, and from mountain-height to valley, and was borne on the breeze far up the fjords, and all over the land.

One day, as they were sailing through these quiet waters, beneath the overhanging cliffs, Bragi tuned his harp, and sang a song of sea. And then he told Siegfried a story of AEgir and his gold-lit hall.

Old AEgir was the Ocean-king. At most times he was rude and rough, and his manners were uncouth and boisterous. But when Balder, the Shining One, smiled kindly upon him from above, or when Bragi played his harp by the seashore, or sailed his ship on the waters, the heart of the bluff old king was touched with a kindly feeling, and he tried hard to curb his ungentle passions, and to cease his blustering ways. He was one of the old race of giants; and men believe that he would have been a very good and quiet giant, had it not been for the evil ways of his wife, the crafty Queen Ran. For, however kind at heart the king might be, his good intentions were almost always thwarted by the queen. Ran could never be trusted; and no one, unless it were Loki, the Mischief-maker, could ever say any thing in her praise. She was always lurking among hidden rocks, or in the deep sea, or along the shores of silent fjords, and reaching out with her long lean fingers, seeking to clutch in her greedy grasp whatever prey might unwarily come near her. And many richly-laden vessels, and many brave seamen and daring warriors, had she dragged down to her blue-hung chamber in old AEgir's hall.

And this is the story that Bragi told of

The Feast in AEgir's Hall.

It happened long ago, when the good folk at Gladsheim were wont to visit the mid-world oftener than now. On a day in early autumn Queen Ran, with her older daughters,—Raging Sea, Breaker, Billow, Surge, and Surf,—went out to search for plunder. But old AEgir staid at home, and with him his younger daughters,—fair Purple-hair, gentle Diver, dancing Ripple, and smiling Sky-clear. And as they played around him, and kissed his old storm-beaten cheeks, the heart of the king was softened into gentleness, and he began to think kindly of the green earth which bordered his kingdom, and of the brave men who lived there; but most of all did he think of the great and good Asa-folk, who dwell in Asgard, and overlook the affairs of the world. Then he called his servants, Funfeng and Elder, and bade them prepare a feast in his gold-lit hall. And he sent fleet messengers to invite the Asa-folk to come and partake of the good cheer. And his four young daughters played upon the beach, and smiled and danced in the beaming sunlight. And the hearts of many seafaring men were gladdened that day, as they spread their sails to the wind; for they saw before them a pleasant voyage, and the happy issue of many an undertaking.

Long before the day had begun to wane, the Asa-folk arrived in a body at AEgir's hall; for they were glad to answer the bidding of the Ocean-king. Odin came, riding Sleipner, his eight-footed steed; Thor rode in his iron chariot drawn by goats; Frey came with Gullinburste, his golden-bristled boar. There, too, was the war-like Tyr, and blind Hoder, and the silent Vidar, and the sage Forsete, and the hearkening Heimdal, and Niord, the Ruler of the Winds, and Bragi, with his harp; and lastly came many elves, the thralls of the Asa-folk, and Loki, the cunning Mischief-maker. In his rude but hearty way old AEgir welcomed them; and they went down into his amber hall, and rested themselves upon the sea-green couches that had been spread for them. And a thousand fair mermaids stood around them, and breathed sweet melodies through sea-shells of rainbow hue, while the gentle white-veiled daughters of the Ocean-king danced to the bewitching music.

Hours passed by, and the sun began to slope towards the west, and the waiting guests grew hungry and ill at ease; and then they began to wonder why the feast was so long in getting ready. At last the host himself became impatient; and he sent out in haste for his servants, Funfeng and Elder. Trembling with fear, they came and stood before him.

"Master," said they, "we know that you are angry because the feast is not yet made ready; but we beg that your anger may not fall upon us. The truth is, that some thief has stolen your brewing-kettle, and we have no ale for your guests."

Then old AEgir's brow grew dark, and his breath came quick and fast; and, had not Niord held the winds tightly clutched in his hand, there would have been a great uproar in the hall. Even as it was, the mermaids fled away in great fright, and the white-veiled Waves stopped dancing, and a strange silence fell upon all the company.

"Some enemy has done this!" crier AEgir, as soon as he could speak. "Some enemy has taken away my brewing-kettle; and, unless we can find it, I fear our feast will be but a dry one."

Then Thor said,—

"If any one knows where this kettle is, let him speak, and I will bring it back; and I promise you you shall not wait long for the feast."

But not one in all this company knew aught about the missing kettle. At last Tyr stood up and said,—

"If we cannot find the same vessel that our host has lost, mayhap we may find another as good. I know a dogwise giant who lives east of the Rivers Elivagar, and who has a strong kettle, fully a mile deep, and large enough to brew ale for all the world."

"That is the very kettle we want!" cried Thor. "Think you that we can get it?"

"If we are cunning enough, we may," answered Tyr. "But old Hymer will never give it up willingly."

"Is it Hymer of whom you speak?" asked Thor. "Then I know him well; and, willingly or not willingly he must let us have his kettle. For what is a feast without the gladsome ale?"

Then Thor and Tyr set out on their journey towards the land of Elivagar; and they travelled many a league northwards, across snowy mountains and barren plains, until they came to the shores of the frozen sea. And there the sun rises and sets but once a year, and even in summer the sea is full of ice. On the lonely beach, stood Hymer's dwelling,—a dark and gloomy abode. Tyr knocked at the door; and it was opened by Hymer's wife, a strangely handsome woman, who bade them come in. Inside the hall they saw Hymer's old mother, sitting in the chimney-corner, and crooning over the smouldering fire. She was a horribly ugly old giantess, with nine hundred heads; but every head was blind and deaf and toothless. Ah, me! what a wretched old age that must have been!

"Is your husband at home?" asked Thor, speaking to the pretty woman who had opened the door.

"He is not," was the answer. "He is catching fish in the warm waters of the sheltered bay; or, mayhap, he is tending his cows in the open sea, just around the headland."

For the great icebergs that float down from the frozen sea are called old Hymer's cows.

"We have come a very long journey," said Tyr. "Will you not give two tired strangers food and lodging until they shall have rested themselves?"

The woman seemed in nowise loath to do this; and she set before the two Asa-folk a plentiful meal of the best that she had in the house. When they had eaten, she told them that it would be far safer for them to hide themselves under the great kettles in the hall; for, she said, her husband would soon be home, and he might not be kind to them. So Thor and Tyr hid themselves, and listened for Hymer's coming. After a time, the great hall-door opened, and they heard the heavy steps of the giant.

"Welcome home!" cried the woman, as Hymer shook the frost from his hair and beard, and stamped the snow from his feet. "I am so glad that you have come! for there are two strangers in the hall, and they have asked for you. One of them I know is Thor, the foe of the giants, and the friend of man. The other is the one-armed god of war, the brave Tyr. What can be their errand at Hymer's hall?"

"Where are they?" roared Hymer, stamping so furiously, that even his deaf old mother seemed to hear, and lifted up her heads.

"They are under the kettles, at the gable-end of the hall," answered the woman.

Hymer cast a wrathful glance towards the place. The post at the end of the hall was shivered in pieces by his very look; the beam that upheld the floor of the loft was broken, and all the kettles tumbled down with a fearful crash. Thor and Tyr crept out from among the rubbish, and stood before old Hymer. The giant was not well pleased at the sight of such guests come thus unbidden to his hall. But he knew that his rude strength would count as nothing if matched with their skill and weapons: hence he deemed it wise to treat the two Asas as his friends, and to meet them with cunning and strategy.

"Welcome to my hall!" he cried. "Fear no hurt from Hymer, for he was never known to harm a guest."

And Thor and Tyr were given the warmest seats at the fireside. And the giant ordered his thralls to kill the fatted oxen, and to make ready a great feast in honor of his guests. And, while the meal was being got ready, he sat by Thor's side, and asked him many questions about what was going on in the great South-land. And Thor answered him pleasantly, meeting guile with guile. When the feast was in readiness, all sat down at the table, which groaned beneath its weight of meat and drink; for Hymer's thralls had killed three fat oxen, and baked them whole for this meal, and they had filled three huge bowls with ale from his great brewing-kettle. Hymer ate and drank very fast, and wished to make his guests fear him, because he could eat so much. But Thor was not to be taken aback in this way; for he at once ate two of the oxen, and quaffed a huge bowl of ale which the giant had set aside for himself. The giant saw that he was outdone, and he arose from the table, saying,—

"Not all my cows would serve to feed two guests so hungry as these. We shall be obliged to live on fish now."

He strode out of the hall without another word, and began getting his boat ready for a sail. But Thor followed him.

"It is a fine day for fishing," said Thor gayly. "How I should like to go out with you!"

"Such little fellows as you would better stay at home," growled Hymer.

"But let me go with you," persisted Thor. "I can certainly row the boat while you fish."

"I have no need of help from such a stunted pygmy," muttered the giant. "You could not be of the least use to me: you would only be in my way. Still, if you are bent on doing so, you may go, and you shall take all the risks. If I go as far as I do sometimes, and stay as long as I often do, you may make up your mind never to see the dry land again; for you will certainly catch your death of cold, and be food for the fishes—if, indeed, they would deign to eat such a scrawny scrap!"

These taunting words made Thor so angry, that he grasped his hammer, and was sorely tempted to crush the giant's skull. But he checked himself, and coolly said,—

"I pray you not to trouble yourself on my account I have set my head on going with you, and go I will. Tell me where I can find something that I can use for bait, and I will be ready in a trice."

"I have no bait for you," roughly answered Hymer "You must look for it yourself."

Half a dozen oxen, the very finest and fattest of Hymer's herd, were grazing on the short grass which grew on the sunnier slopes of the hillside; for not all of the giant's cattle had yet taken to the water. When Thor saw these great beasts, he ran quickly towards them, and seizing the largest one, which Hymer called the Heaven-breaker, he twisted off his head as easily as he would that of a small fowl, and ran back with it to the boat. Hymer looked at him in anger and amazement, but said nothing; and the two pushed the boat off from the shore. The little vessel sped through the water more swiftly than it had ever done before, for Thor plied the oars.

In a moment the long, low beach was out of sight; and Hymer, who had never travelled so fast, began to feel frightened.

"Stop!" he cried. "Here is the place to fish: I have often caught great store of flat-fish here. Let us out with our lines!"

"No, no!" answered Thor; and he kept on plying the oars. "We are not yet far enough from shore. The best fish are still many leagues out."

And the boat skimmed onwards through the waters, and the white spray dashed over the prow; and Hymer, now very much frightened, sat still, and looked at his strange fellow-fisherman, but said not a word. On and on they went; and the shore behind them first grew dim, and then sank out of sight; and the high mountain-tops began to fade away in the sky, and then were seen no more. And when at last the fishermen were so far out at sea that nothing was in sight but the rolling waters on every side, Thor stopped his rowing.

"We have come too far!" cried the giant, trembling in every limb. "The great Midgard snake lies hereabouts. Let us turn back!"

"Not yet," answered Thor quietly. "We will fish here a little while."

Without loss of time he took from his pocket a strong hook, wonderfully made, to which he fastened a long line as strong as ten ships' cables twisted together; then he carefully baited the hook with the gory head of the Heaven-breaker ox, and threw it into the water. As the giant had feared, they were now right over the head of the great Midgard snake. The huge beast looked upward with his sleepy eyes, and saw the tempting bait falling slowly through the water; but he did not see the boat, it was so far above him. Thinking of no harm, he opened his leathern jaws, and greedily gulped the morsel down; but the strong iron hook stuck fast in his throat. Maddened by the pain, he began to lash his tail against the floor of the sea; and he twisted and writhed until the ocean was covered with foam, and the waves ran mountain-high. But Thor pulled hard upon the line above, and strove to lift the reptile's head out of the water; then the snake darted with lightning speed away, pulling the boat after him so swiftly, that, had not Thor held on to the oar-locks, he would have been thrown into the sea. Quickly he tightened his magic girdle of strength around him, and, standing up in the boat, he pulled with all his might. The snake would not be lifted. But the boat split in two; and Thor slid into the water, and stood upon the bottom of the sea. He seized the great snake in his hands, and raised his head clean above the water. What a scene of frightful turmoil was there then! The earth shook; the mountains belched forth fire; the lightnings flashed; the caves howled; and the sky grew black and red. Nobody knows what the end would have been, had not Hymer reached over, and cut the strong cord. The slippery snake glided out of Thor's hands, and hid himself in the deep sea; and every thing became quiet again.

Silently Thor and Hymer sat in the broken boat, and rowed swiftly back towards land. Thor felt really ashamed of himself, because he had gained nothing by his venture. And the giant was not at all happy.

When they reached the frozen shore and Hymer's cheerless castle again, they found Tyr there, anxiously waiting for them. He felt that they were tarrying too long in this dreary place; and he wished to be back among his fellows in old Ægir's hall. Hymer felt very cross and ugly because his boat had been broken; and, when they came into the hall, he said to Thor,—

"You may think that you are very stout,—you who dared attack the Midgard snake, and lifted him out of the sea. Yet there are many little things that you cannot do. For instance, here is the earthen goblet from which I drink my ale. Great men, like myself, can crush such goblets between their thumbs and fingers; but such puny fellows as you will find that they cannot break it by any means."

"Let me try!" cried Thor.

He took the great goblet in his hands, and threw it with all his strength against a stone post in the middle of the hall. The post was shattered into a thousand pieces, but the goblet was unharmed.

"Ha, ha!" laughed the giant. "Try again!"

Thor did so. This time he threw it against a huge granite rock that stood like a mountain near the seashore. The rock crumbled in pieces and fell, but the goblet was whole as ever.

"What a very stout fellow you are!" cried Hymer in glee. "Go home now, and tell the good Asa-folk that you cannot even break a goblet!"

"Let me try once more," said Thor, amazed, but not disheartened.

"Throw it against Hymer's forehead," whispered some one over his shoulder. "It is harder than any rock."

Thor looked, and saw that it was the giant's handsome wife who had given him this kind advice. He took the goblet, and hurled it quickly, straight at old Hymer's head. The giant had no time to dodge. The vessel struck him squarely between the eyes, and was shattered into ten thousand little pieces. But the giant's forehead was unhurt.

"That drink was rather hot!" cried Hymer, trying to joke at his ill luck. "But it doesn't take a very great man to break a goblet. There is one thing, however, that you cannot do. Yonder is my great brewing-kettle, a mile deep. No man has ever lifted it. Now, if you will carry it out of the hall, where it sits, you may have it for your own."

"Agreed!" cried Thor. "It is a fair bargain; and, if I fail, I will go home and never trouble you again."

Then he took hold of the edge of the great kettle, and lifted it with all his might. The floor of Hymer's hall broke under him, and the walls and roof came tumbling down; but he turned the kettle over his head, and walked away with it, the great rings of the vessel clattering at his heels. Tyr went before him, and cleared the way; and Hymer gazed after him in utter amazement. The two Asa-folk had fairly won the brewing-kettle.

In due time they reached old AEgir's hall, where the guests were still waiting for them. Some said that they had been gone three days, but most agreed that it was only three hours. Be that as it may, AEgir's thralls, Funfeng and Elder, brewed great store of ale in the kettle which Thor had brought; and, when the guests were seated at the table, the foaming liquor passed itself around to each, and there was much merriment and glad good cheer. And old AEgir was so happy in the pleasant company of the Asa-folk, that men say that he forgot to blow and bluster for a full six months thereafter.[EN#14]

Such was the story which the wise harper told to Siegfried as they sailed gayly along the Norwegian shore. And with many other pleasant tales did they beguile the hours away. And no one ever thought of danger, for the sky was blue and cloudless. And, besides this, Bragi himself was on board; and he could charm and control the rudest elements.

One day, however, the sea became unaccountably ruffled. There was no wind; but yet the waves rose suddenly, and threatened to overwhelm the little ship. Quickly the sailors sprang to their oars, and tried by rowing to drive the vessel away from the shore and into the quieter waters of the open sea. But all their strength was of no avail: the swift stream carried the little bark onward in its course, as an autumn leaf is borne on the bosom of a mighty river. Then the whole surface of the water seemed lashed into fury. The waves formed hundreds of currents, each stronger than a mountain torrent, and each seeming to follow a course of its own. They clashed wildly against each other; they heaved, and boiled, and hissed, and threw great clouds of spray high into the air; they formed deep whirlpools, which twisted and twirled, and broke into a thousand eddies, and then plunged deep down into rocky caverns beneath, or laid bare the bottom of the sea. The helpless ship was carried round and round, swiftly and more swiftly still; and vain were the efforts of the crew to steer her out of the seething caldron of waters. Then the cheeks of the sailors grew white with fear; and they dropped their oars, and clung to the masts and ropes, and cried out,—

"Alas, we are lost! This is old AEgir's brewing-kettle!"

But Siegfried stood by the helm, and said,—

"If that be true, then we may sup with him in his gold-lit hall."

And all this time Bragi slept in the hold, and no one dared awaken him. Faster and faster the ship was carried round the seething pool. The flying spray was frozen in the air; and it filled the masts with snow, and pattered like heavy hail upon the deck. The light of the sun seemed shut out, and darkness closed around. A dismal chasm yawned deep before them, and in the gray gloom the ship's crew saw many wondrous things. Great sea-monsters swam among the rocks, and seemed not to heed the uproar above them. Lovely mermaids sat in their green-and-purple caves, and combed their tresses of golden hair; and thoughtful mermen groped among the seaweeds, searching hopefully for lost or hidden treasures. Then Siegfried caught a glimpse of the mighty AEgir, sitting in his banquet-room; and, as he quaffed his foaming ale, he called aloud to his daughters to leave their play, and come to their father in his gold-lit hall. And the white-veiled Waves answered to their names, and came at his call. First, Raging Sea entered the wide hall, and sat by the Ocean-king's side; then Billow, then Surge, then Surf, and Breakers; then came the Purple-haired, and the Diver; but AEgir's two youngest daughters, Laughing Ripple and Smiling Sky-clear, came not at their father's beck, but lingered to play among the rocks and in the open sea.

So deeply engaged was Siegfried in watching this scene, that he did not notice Bragi, who now came upon the deck with his harp in his hand. And sweet music arose from among the dashing waves, and was heard far down in the deep sea-caverns, and even in AEgir's hall. And, when Siegfried looked up again, the eddying whirlpools, and the threatening waves, and the flying spray, were no more; but the ship was gliding over the quiet waters of a deep blue sea, and the sun was shining brightly in the clear sky above. Then an east wind filled the sails; and, as Bragi's music rose sweeter and higher, they glided swiftly away from the coast, and soon the snow-capped mountain-peaks grew dim in the distance, and then sank from sight.

Many days they sailed over an unknown sea, and towards an unknown land; and none but Bragi knew what the end of their voyage would be. And yet no one doubted or was afraid, for the secrets of the earth and the sea were known to the sweet singer. After a time, the water became as smooth as glass: not a ripple moved upon its surface, and not the slightest breath of air stirred among the idly-hanging sails. Then the sailors went to their oars; but they seemed overcome with languor and sleepiness, and only when Bragi played upon his harp did they move their oars with their wonted strength and quickness. And at last they came in sight of a long, low coast, and a shelving beach up which the tide was slowly creeping in drowsy silence. And not half a league from the shore was a grand old castle, with a tall tower and many turrets, and broad halls and high battlements; and in the light of the setting sun every thing was as green as emerald or as the fresh grass of early spring. And a pale flickering light gleamed on the castle-walls, and the moat seemed filled with a glowing fire.

The ship glided silently up to the sandy beach, and the sailors moored it to the shore. But Siegfried heard no sound upon the land, nor could he see any moving, living thing. Silence brooded everywhere, and the castle and its inmates seemed to be wrapped in slumber. The sentinels could be seen upon the ramparts, standing like statues of stone, and showing no signs of life; while above the barbacan gate the watchman was at his post, motionless and asleep.

Adventure VI. Brunhild.

Siegfried and the harper sat together in the little ship as it lay moored to the sandy shore; and their eyes were turned towards the sea-green castle and its glowing walls, and they looked in vain for any movement, or any sign of wakeful life. Every thing was still. Not a breath of air was stirring. The leaves of the trees hung motionless, as if they, too, were asleep. The great green banner on the tower's top clung around the flagstaff as if it had never fluttered to the breeze. No song of birds, nor hum of insects, came to their ears. There was neither sound nor motion anywhere.

"Play your harp, good Bragi, and awaken all these sleepers," said Siegfried.

Then the harper touched the magic strings, and strains of music, loud and clear, but sweet as a baby's breath, rose up in the still air, and floated over the quiet bay, and across the green meadows which lay around the castle-walls; and it was borne upward over the battlements, and among the shining turrets and towers, and was carried far out over the hills, and among the silent trees of the plain. And Bragi sung of the beginning of all things, and of whatsoever is beautiful on the land, or in the sea, or in the sky. And Siegfried looked to see every thing awakened, and quickened into life, as had oft been done before by Bragi's music; but nothing stirred. The sun went down, and the gray twilight hung over sea and land, and the red glow in the castle-moat grew redder still; and yet every thing slept. Then Bragi ended his song, and the strings of his harp were mute.

"Music has no charms to waken from sleep like that," he said.

And then he told Siegfried what it all meant; and, to make the story plain, he began by telling of Odin's bright home at Gladsheim and of the many great halls that were there.

One of the halls in Gladsheim is called Valhal. This hall is so large and wide, that all the armies of the earth might move within it. Outside, it is covered with gold and with sun-bright shields. A fierce wolf stands guard before it, and a mountain-eagle hovers over it. It has five hundred and forty doors, each large enough for eight hundred heroes to march through abreast. Inside, every thing is glittering bright. The rafters are made of spears, and the ceiling is covered with shields, and the walls are decked with war-coats. In this hall Odin sets daily a feast for all the heroes that have been slain in battle. These sit at the great table, and eat of the food which Odin's servants have prepared, and drink of the heavenly mead which the Valkyries, Odin's handmaids, bring them.

But the Valkyries have a greater duty. When the battle rages, and swords clash, and shields ring, and the air is filled with shouts and groans and all the din of war, then these maidens hover over the field of blood and death, and carry the slain heroes home to Valhal.[EN#15]

One of Odin's Valkyries was named Brunhild, and she was the most beautiful of all the maidens that chose heroes for his war-host. But she was wilful too, and did not always obey the All-Father's behests. And when Odin knew that she had sometimes snatched the doomed from death, and sometimes helped her chosen friends to victory, he was very angry. And he drove her away from Gladsheim, and sent her, friendless and poor, to live among the children of men, and to be in all ways like them. But, as she wandered weary and alone over the earth, the good old King of Isenland saw her beauty and her distress, and pity and love moved his heart; and, as he had no children of his own, he took her for his daughter, and made her his heir. And not long afterward he died, and the matchless Brunhild became queen of all the fair lands of Isenland and the hall of Isenstein. When Odin heard of this, he was more angry still; and he sent to Isenstein, and caused Brunhild to be stung with the thorn of Sleep. And he said,—

"She shall sleep until one shall come who is brave enough to ride through fire to awaken her."

And all Isenland slept too, because Brunhild, the Maiden of Spring, lay wounded with the Sleepful thorn.

When Siegfried heard this story, he knew that the land which lay before them was Isenland, and that the castle was Isenstein, and that Brunhild was sleeping within that circle of fire.

"My songs have no power to awaken such a sleeper," said Bragi. "A hero strong and brave must ride through the flame to arouse her. It is for this that I have brought you hither; and here I will leave you, while I sail onwards to brighten other lands with my music."

Siegfried's heart leaped up with gladness; for he thought that here, at last, was a worthy deed for him to do. And he bade his friend Bragi good-by, and stepped ashore; and Greyfell followed him. And Bragi sat at the prow of the ship, and played his harp again; and the sailors plied their oars; and the little vessel moved swiftly out of the bay, and was seen no more. And Siegfried stood alone on the silent, sandy beach.

As he thus stood, the full moon rose white and dripping from the sea; and its light fell on the quiet water, and the sloping meadows, and the green turrets of the castle. And the last notes of Bragi's harp came floating to him over the sea.

Then a troop of fairies came down to dance upon the sands. It was the first sign of life that Siegfried had seen. As the little creatures drew near, he hid himself among the tall reeds which grew close to the shore; for he wished to see them at their gambols, and to listen to their songs. At first, as if half afraid of their own tiny shadows, they danced in silence; but, as the moon rose higher, they grew bolder, and began to sing. And their music was so sweet and soft, that Siegfried forgot almost every thing, else for the time: they sang of the pleasant summer days, and of cooling shades, and still fountains, and silent birds, and peaceful slumber. And a strange longing for sleep took hold of Siegfried; and his eyes grew heavy, and the sound of the singing seemed dim and far away. But just as he was losing all knowledge of outward things, and his senses seemed moving in a dream, the fairies stopped dancing, and a little brown elf came up from the sea, and saluted the queen of the tiny folk.

"What news bring you from the great world beyond the water?" asked the queen.

"The prince is on his way hither," answered the elf.

"And what will he do?"

"If he is brave enough, he will awaken the princess, and arouse the drowsy people of Isenstein; for the Norns have said that such a prince shall surely come."

"But he must be the bravest of men ere he can enter the enchanted castle," said the queen; "for the wide moat is filled with flames, and no faint heart will ever dare battle with them."

"But I will dare!" cried Siegfried; and he sprang from his hiding-place, forgetful of the little folk, who suddenly flitted away, and left him alone upon the beach. He glanced across the meadows at the green turrets glistening in the mellow moonlight, and then at the flickering flames around the castle walls, and he resolved that on the morrow he would at all hazards perform the perilous feat.

In the morning, as soon as the gray dawn appeared, he began to make ready for his difficult undertaking. But, when he looked again at the red flames, he began to hesitate. He paused, uncertain whether to wait for a sign and for help from the All-Father, or whether to go straightway to the castle, and, trusting in his good armor alone, try to pass through the burning moat. While he thus stood in doubt, his eyes were dazzled by a sudden flash of light. He looked up. Greyfell came dashing across the sands; and from his long mane a thousand sunbeams gleamed and sparkled in the morning light. Siegfried had never seen the wondrous creature so radiant; and as the steed stood by him in all his strength and beauty he felt new hope and courage, as if Odin himself had spoken to him. He hesitated no longer, but mounted the noble horse; and Greyfell bore him swiftly over the plain, and paused not until he had reached the brink of the burning moat.

Now, indeed, would Siegfried's heart have failed him, had he not been cheered by the sunbeam presence of Greyfell. For filling the wide, deep ditch, were angry, hissing flames, which, like a thousand serpent-tongues, reached out, and felt here and there, for what they might devour; and ever and anon they took new forms, and twisted and writhed like fiery snakes, and then they swirled in burning coils high over the castle-walls. Siegfried stopped not a moment. He spoke the word, and boldly the horse with his rider dashed into the fiery lake; and the vile flames fled in shame and dismay before the pure sunbeam flashes from Greyfell's mane. And, unscorched and unscathed, Siegfried rode through the moat, and through the wide-open gate, and into the castle-yard.

The gate-keeper sat fast asleep in his lodge, while the chains and the heavy key with which, when awake, he was wont to make the great gate fast, lay rusting at his feet; and neither he, nor the sentinels on the ramparts above, stirred or awoke at the sound of Greyfell's clattering hoofs. As Siegfried passed from one part of the castle to another, many strange sights met his eyes. In the stables the horses slumbered in their stalls, and the grooms lay snoring by their sides. The birds sat sound asleep on their nests beneath the eaves. The watch-dogs, with fast-closed eyes, lay stretched at full-length before the open doors. In the garden the fountain no longer played, the half-laden bees had gone to sleep among the blossoms of the apple-trees, and the flowers themselves had forgotten to open their petals to the sun. In the kitchen the cook was dozing over the half-baked meats in front of the smouldering fire; the butler was snoring in the pantry; the dairy-maid was quietly napping among the milk-pans; and even the house-flies had gone to sleep over the crumbs of sugar on the table. In the great banquet-room a thousand knights, overcome with slumber, sat silent at the festal board; and their chief, sitting on the dais, slept, with his half-emptied goblet at his lips.

Siegfried passed hurriedly from room to room and from hall to hall, and cast but one hasty glance at the strange sights which met him at every turn; for he knew that none of the drowsy ones in that spacious castle could be awakened until he had aroused the Princess Brunhild. In the grandest hall of the palace he found her. The peerless maiden, most richly dight, reclined upon a couch beneath a gold-hung canopy; and her attendants, the ladies of the court, sat near and around her. Sleep held fast her eyelids, and her breathing was so gentle, that, but for the blush upon her cheeks, Siegfried would have thought her dead. For long, long years had her head thus lightly rested on that gold-fringed pillow; and in all that time neither her youth had faded, nor her wondrous beauty waned.

Siegfried stood beside her. Gently he touched his lips to that matchless forehead; softly he named her name,—

"Brunhild!"

The charm was broken. Up rose the peerless princess in all her queen-like beauty; up rose the courtly ladies round her. All over the castle, from cellar to belfry-tower, from the stable to the banquet hall, there was a sudden awakening, a noise of hurrying feet and mingled voices, and sounds which had long been strangers to the halls of Isenstein. The watchman on the tower, and the sentinels on the ramparts, yawned, and would not believe they had been asleep; the porter picked up his keys, and hastened to lock the long-forgotten gates; the horses neighed in their stalls; the watchdogs barked at the sudden hubbub; the birds, ashamed at having allowed the sun to find them napping, hastened to seek their food in the meadows; the servants hurried here and there, each intent upon his duty; the warriors in the banquet-hall clattered their knives and plates, and began again their feast; and their chief dropped his goblet, and rubbed his eyes, and wondered that sleep should have overtaken him in the midst of such a meal.[EN#16]

And Siegfried, standing at an upper window, looked out over the castle-walls; and he saw that the flames no longer raged in the moat, but that it was filled with clear sparkling water from the fountain which played in the garden. And the south wind blew gently from the sea, bringing from afar the sweetest strains of music from Bragi's golden harp; and the breezes whispered among the trees, and the flowers opened their petals to the sun, and birds and insects made the air melodious with their glad voices. Then Brunhild, radiant with smiles, stood by the hero's side, and welcomed him kindly to Isenland and to her green-towered castle of Isenstein.

Adventure VII. In Nibelungen Land.

Every one in the castle of Isenstein, from the princess to the kitchen-maid, felt grateful to the young hero for what he had done. The best rooms were fitted up for his use, and a score of serving men and maidens were set apart to do his bidding, and ordered to be mindful of his slightest wish. And all the earl-folk and brave men, and all the fair ladies, and Brunhild, fairest of them all, besought him to make his home there, nor ever think of going back to Rhineland. Siegfried yielded to their persuasions, and for six months he tarried in the enchanted land in one long round of merry-making and gay enjoyment. But his thoughts were ever turned toward his father's home in the Lowlands across the sea, and he longed to behold again his gentle mother Sigelind. Then he grew tired of his life of idleness and ease, and he wished that he might go out again into the busy world of manly action and worthy deeds. And day by day this feeling grew stronger, and filled him with unrest.

One morning, as he sat alone by the seashore, and watched the lazy tide come creeping up the sands, two ravens lighted near him. Glad was he to see them, for he knew them to be Hugin and Munin, the sacred birds of Odin, and he felt sure that they brought him words of cheer from the All-Father. Then Hugin flapped his wings, and said, "In idleness the stings of death lie hidden, but in busy action are the springs of life. For a hundred years fair Brunhild slept, but why should Siegfried sleep? The world awaits him, but it waits too long."

Then Munin flapped his wings also, but he said nothing. And busy memory carried Siegfried back to his boyhood days; and he called to mind the wise words of his father Siegmund, and the fond hopes of his gentle mother, and he thought, too, of the noble deeds of his kinsfolk of the earlier days. And he rose in haste, and cried, "Life of ease, farewell! I go where duty leads. To him who wills to do, the great All-Father will send strength and help."

While he spoke, his eyes were dazzled with a flash of light. He looked; and the beaming Greyfell, his long mane sparkling like a thousand sunbeams, dashed up the beach, and stood beside him. As the noble steed in all his strength and beauty stood before him, the youth felt fresh courage; for, in the presence of the shining hope which the All-Father had given him, all hinderances seemed to vanish, and all difficulties to be already overcome. He looked toward the sea again, and saw in the blue distance a white-sailed ship drawing swiftly near, its golden dragon-stem ploughing through the waves like some great bird of the deep. And as with straining, eager eyes, he watched its coming, he felt that Odin had sent it, and that the time had come wherein he must be up and doing. The hour for thriving action comes to us once: if not seized upon and used, it may never come again.

The ship drew near the shore. The sailors rested on their oars. Siegfried and the steed Greyfell sprang upon the deck; then the sailors silently bent again to their rowing. The flapping sails were filled and tightened by the strong west wind; and the light vessel leaped from wave to wave like a thing of life, until Isenstein, with its tall towers and its green marble halls, sank from sight in the distance and the mist. And Siegfried and his noble steed seemed to be the only living beings on board; for the sailors who plied the oars were so silent and phantom-like, that they appeared to be nought but the ghosts of the summer sea-breezes. As the ship sped swiftly on its way, all the creatures in the sea paused to behold the sight. The mermen rested from their weary search for hidden treasures, and the mermaids forgot to comb their long tresses, as the radiant vessel and its hero-freight glided past. And even old King AEgir left his brewing-kettle in his great hall, and bade his daughters, the white-veiled Waves, cease playing until the vessel should safely reach its haven.

When, at length, the day had passed, and the evening twilight had come, Siegfried saw that the ship was nearing land; but it was a strange land.[EN#17] Like a fleecy cloud it appeared to rest above the waves, midway between the earth and the sky; a dark mist hung upon it, and it seemed a land of dreams and shadows. The ship drew nearer and nearer to the mysterious shore, and as it touched the beach the sailors rested from their rowing. Then Siegfried and the horse Greyfell leaped ashore; but, when they looked back, the fair vessel that had carried them was nowhere to be seen. Whether it had suddenly been clutched by the greedy fingers of the Sea-queen Ran, and dragged down into her deep sea-caverns, or whether, like the wondrous ship Skidbladner, it had been folded up, and made invisible to the eyes of men, Siegfried never knew. The thick mists and the darkness of night closed over and around both hero and horse; and they dared not stir, but stood long hours in the silent gloom, waiting for the coming of the dawn.

At length the morning came, but the light was not strong enough to scatter the fogs and thick vapors that rested upon the land. Then Siegfried mounted Greyfell; and the sunbeams began to flash from the horse's mane and from the hero's glittering mail-coat; and the hazy clouds fled upward and away, until they were caught and held fast by great mist-giants, who stood like sentinels on the mountain-tops. As the shining pair came up from the sea, and passed through the woods and valleys of the Nibelungen

Land, there streamed over all that region such a flood of sunlight as had never before been seen.

In every leafy tree, and behind every blade of grass, elves and fairies were hidden; and under every rock and in every crevice lurked cunning dwarfs. But Siegfried rode straight forward until he came to the steep side of a shadowy mountain. There, at the mouth of a cavern, a strange sight met his eyes. Two young men, dressed in princes' clothing, sat upon the ground: their features were all haggard and gaunt, and pinched with hunger, and their eyes wild with wakefulness and fear; and all around them were heaps of gold and precious stones,—more than a hundred wagons could carry away. And neither of the two princes would leave the shining hoard for food, nor close his eyes in sleep, lest the other might seize and hide some part of the treasure. And thus they had watched and hungered through many long days and sleepless nights, each hoping that the other would die, and that the whole inheritance might be his own.

When they saw Siegfried riding near, they called out to him, and said, "Noble stranger, stop a moment! Come and help us divide this treasure."

"Who are you?" asked Siegfried; "and what treasure is it that lies there?"

"We are the sons of Niblung, who until lately was king of this Mist Land. Our names are Schilbung and the young Niblung," faintly answered the princes.

"And what are you doing here with this gold and these glittering stones?"

"This is the great Nibelungen Hoard, which our father not long ago brought from the South-land. It is not clear just how he obtained it.[EN#18] Some say that he got it unjustly from his brother, whose vassals had digged it from the earth. Others say that he found it lying on the Glittering Heath, where Fafnir the Dragon had guarded it zealously for ages past, until he was slain by a hero who cared nought for his gold. But, be this as it may, our father is now dead, and we have brought the hoard out of the cavern where he had hidden it, in order that we may share it between us equally. But we cannot agree, and we pray you to help us divide it."

Then Siegfried dismounted from the horse Greyfell, and came near the two princes.

"I will gladly do as you ask," said he; "but first I must know more about your father,—who he was, and whether this is really the Hoard of the Glittering Heath."

Then Niblung answered, as well as his feeble voice would allow, "Our father was, from the earliest times, the ruler of this land, and the lord of the fog and the mist. Many strongholds, and many noble halls, had he in this land; and ten thousand brave warriors were ever ready to do his bidding. The trolls, and the swarthy elves of the mountains, and the giants of the cloudy peaks, were his vassals. But he did more than rule over the Nibelungen Land. Twice every year he crossed the sea and rambled through the Rhine valleys, or loitered in the moist Lowlands; and now and then he brought rich trophies back to his island home. The last time, he brought this treasure with him; but, as we have said, it is not clear how he obtained it. We have heard men say that it was the Hoard of Andvari, and that when Fafnir, the dragon who watched it, was slain, the hero who slew him left it to be taken again by the swarthy elves who had gathered it; but because of a curse which Andvari had placed upon it, no one would touch it, until some man would assume its ownership, and take upon himself the risk of incurring the curse. This thing, it is said, our father did. And the dwarf Alberich undertook to keep it for him; and he, with the help of the ten thousand elves who live in these caverns, and the twelve giants whom you see standing on the mountain-peaks around, guarded it faithfully so long as our father lived. But, when he died, we and our thralls fetched it forth from the cavern, and spread it here on the ground. And, lo! for many days we have watched and tried to divide it equally. But we cannot agree."

"What hire will you give me if I divide it for you?" asked Siegfried.

"Name what you will have," answered the princes.

"Give me the sword which lies before you on the glittering heap."

Then Niblung handed him the sword, and said, "Right gladly will we give it. It is a worthless blade that our father brought from the South-land. They say that he found it also on the Glittering Heath, in the trench where Fafnir was slain. And some will have it that it was forged by Regin, Fafnir's own brother. But how that is, I do not know. At any rate, it is of no use to us; for it turns against us whenever we try to use it."

Siegfried took the sword. It was his own Balmung, that had been lost so long.

Forthwith he began the task of dividing the treasure; and the two brothers, so faint from hunger and want of sleep that they could scarcely lift their heads, watched him with anxious, greedy eyes. First he placed a piece of gold by Niblung's side, and then a piece of like value he gave to Schilbung. And this he did again and again, until no more gold was left. Then, in the same manner, he divided the precious gem-stones until none remained. And the brothers were much pleased; and they hugged their glittering treasures, and thanked Siegfried for his kindness, and for the fairness with which he had given to each his own. But one thing was left which had not fallen to the lot of either brother. It was a ring of curious workmanship,—a serpent coiled, with its tail in its mouth, and with ruby eyes glistening and cold.

"What shall I do with this ring?" asked Siegfried.

"Give it to me!" cried Niblung.

"Give it to me!" cried Schilbung.

And both tried to snatch it from Siegfried's hand.

But the effort was too great for them. Their arms fell helpless at their sides, their feet slipped beneath them, their limbs failed: they sank fainting, each upon his pile of treasures.

"O my dear, dear gold!" murmured Niblung, trying to clasp it all in his arms,—"my dear, dear gold! Thou art mine, mine only. No one shall take thee from me. Here thou art, here thou shalt rest. O my dear, dear gold!" And then, calling up the last spark of life left in his famished body, he cried out to Siegfried, "Give me the ring!—the ring, I say!"

He hugged his cherished gold nearer to his bosom; he ran his thin fingers deep down into the shining yellow heap; he pressed his pale lips to the cold and senseless metal; he whispered faintly, "My dear, dear gold!" and then he died.

"O precious, precious gem-stones," faltered Schilbung, "how beautiful you are! And you are mine, all mine. I will keep you safe. Come, come, my bright-eyed beauties! No one but me shall touch you. You are mine, mine, mine!" And he chattered and laughed as only madmen laugh. And he kissed the hard stones, and sought to hide them in his bosom. But his hands trembled and failed, dark mists swam before his eyes; he fancied that he heard the black dwarfs clamoring for his treasure; he sprang up quickly, he shrieked—and then fell lifeless upon his hoard of sparkling gems.

A strange, sad sight it was,—boundless wealth, and miserable death; two piles of yellow gold and sun-bright diamonds, and two thin, starved corpses stretched upon them. Some stories relate that the brothers were slain by Siegfried, because their foolish strife and greediness had angered him.[EN#19] But I like not to think so. It was the gold, and not Siegfried, that slew them.

"O gold, gold!" cried the hero sorrowfully, "truly thou art the mid-world's curse; thou art man's bane. But when the bright spring-time of the new world shall come, and Balder shall reign in his glory, then will the curse be taken from thee, and thy yellow brightness will be the sign of purity and enduring worth; and then thou wilt be a blessing to mankind, and the precious plaything of the gods."

But Siegfried had little time for thought and speech. A strange sound was heard upon the mountain-side. The twelve great giants who had stood as watchmen upon the peaks above were rushing down to avenge their masters, and to drive the intruder out of Nibelungen Land. Siegfried waited not for their onset; but he mounted the noble horse Greyfell, and, with the sword Balmung in his hand, he rode forth to meet his foes, who, with fearful threats and hideous roars, came striding toward him. The sunbeams flashed from Greyfell's mane, and dazzled the dull eyes of the giants, unused as they were to the full light of day. Doubtful, they paused, and then again came forward. But they mistook every tree in their way for an enemy, and every rock they thought a foe; and in their fear they fancied a great host to be before them. Did you ever see the dark and threatening storm-clouds on a summer's day scattered and put to flight by the bright beams of the sun? It was thus that Siegfried's giant foes were routed. One and all, they dropped their heavy clubs, and stood ashamed and trembling, not knowing what to do. And Siegfried made each one swear to serve him faithfully; and then he sent them back to the snow-covered mountain-peaks to stand again as watchmen at their posts.

And now another danger appeared. Alberich the dwarf, the master of the swarthy elves who guarded the Nibelungen Hoard, had come out from his cavern, and seen the two princes lying dead beside their treasures, and he thought that they had been murdered by Siegfried; and, when he beheld the giants driven back to the mountain-tops, he lifted a little silver horn to his lips, and blew a shrill bugle-call. And the little brown elves came trooping forth by thousands: from under every rock, from the nooks and crannies and crevices in the mountain-side, from the deep cavern and the narrow gorge, they came at the call of their chief. Then, at Alberich's word, they formed in line of battle, and stood in order around the hoard and the bodies of their late masters. Their little golden shields and their sharp-pointed spears were thick as the blades of grass in a Rhine meadow. And Siegfried, when he saw them, was pleased and surprised; for never before had such a host of pygmy warriors stood before him.

While he paused and looked, the elves became suddenly silent, and Siegfried noticed that Alberich stood no longer at their head, but had strangely vanished from sight.

"Ah, Alberich!" cried the hero. "Thou art indeed cunning. I have heard of thy tricks. Thou hast donned the Tarnkappe, the cloak of darkness, which hides thee from sight, and makes thee as strong as twelve common men. But come on, thou brave dwarf!"

Scarcely had he spoken, when he felt a shock which almost sent him reeling from his saddle, and made Greyfell plunge about with fright. Quickly, then, did Siegfried dismount, and, with every sense alert, he waited for the second onset of the unseen dwarf. It was plain that Alberich wished to strike him unawares, for many minutes passed in utter silence. Then a brisk breath of wind passed by Siegfried's face, and he felt another blow; but, by a quick downward movement of his hand, he caught the plucky elf-king, and tore off the magic Tarnkappe, and then, with firm grasp, he held him, struggling in vain to get free.

"Ah, Alberich!" he cried, "now I know thou art cunning. But the Tarnkappe I must have for my own. What wilt thou give for thy freedom?"

"Worthy prince," answered Alberich humbly, "you have fairly overcome me in fight, and made me your prisoner. I and all mine, as well as this treasure, rightfully belong to you. We are yours, and you we shall obey."

"Swear it!" said Siegfried. "Swear it, and thou shalt live, and be the keeper of my treasures."

And Alberich made a sign to his elfin host, and every spear was turned point downwards, and every tiny shield was thrown to the ground, and the ten thousand little warriors kneeled, as did also their chief, and acknowledged Siegfried to be their rightful master, and the lord of the Nibelungen Land, and the owner of the Hoard of Andvari.

Then, by Alberich's orders, the elves carried the Hoard back into the cavern, and there kept faithful watch and ward over it. And they buried the starved bodies of the two princes on the top of the mist-veiled mountain; and heralds were sent to all the strongholds in Nibelungen Land, proclaiming that Siegfried, through his wisdom and might, had become the true lord and king of the land. Afterwards the prince, riding on the beaming Greyfell, went from place to place, scattering sunshine and smiles where shadows and frowns had been before. And the Nibelungen folk welcomed him everywhere with glad shouts and music and dancing; and ten thousand warriors, and many noble earl-folk, came to meet him, and plighted their faith to him. And the pure brightness of his hero-soul, and the gleaming sunbeams from Greyfell's mane,—the light of hope and faith,—lifted the curtain of mists and fogs that had so long darkened the land, and let in the glorious glad light of day and the genial warmth of summer.

Adventure VIII. Siegfried's Welcome Home.

In Santen Castle, one day, there was a strange uproar and confusion. Everybody was hurrying aimlessly about, and no one seemed to know just what to do. On every side there were restless whisperings, and hasty gestures, and loud commands. The knights and warriors were busy donning their war-coats, and buckling on their swords and helmets. Wise King Siegmund sat in his council-chamber, and the knowing men of the kingdom stood around him; and the minds of all seemed troubled with doubt, if not with fear.

What could have caused so great an uproar in the once quiet old castle? What could have brought perplexity to the mind of the wisest king in all Rhineland? It was this: a herald had just come from the seashore, bringing word that a strange fleet of a hundred white-sailed vessels had cast anchor off the coast, and that an army of ten thousand fighting men had landed, and were making ready to march against Santen. Nobody had ever heard of so large a fleet before; and no one could guess who the strangers might be, nor whence they had come, nor why they should thus, without asking leave, land in the country of a peace-loving king.

The news spread quickly over all the land. People from every part came hastening to the friendly shelter of the castle. The townsmen, with their goods and cattle, hurried within the walls. The sentinels on the ramparts paced uneasily to and fro, and scanned with watchful eye every stranger that came near the walls. The warders stood ready to hoist the drawbridge, and close the gate, at the first signal given by the watchman above, who was straining his eyes to their utmost in order to see the first approach of the foe.

A heavy mist hung over the meadow-lands between Santen and the sea, and nothing was visible beyond the gates of the town. The ten thousand strange warriors might be within half a league of the castle, and yet the sharpest eagle-eye could not see them.

All at once a clatter of horse's hoofs was heard; the dark mist rose up from the ground, and began to roll away, like a great cloud, into the sky; and then strange sunbeam-flashes were seen where the fog had lately rested.

"They come!" cried one of the sentinels. "I see the glitter of their shields and lances."

"Not so," said the watchman from his place on the tower above. "I see but one man, and he rides with the speed of the wind, and lightning flashes from the mane of the horse which carries him."

The drawbridge was hastily hoisted. The heavy gates were quickly shut, and fastened with bolts and bars. Every man in the castle was at his post, ready to defend the fortress with his life. In a short time the horse and his rider drew near. All who looked out upon them were dazzled with the golden brightness of the hero's armor, as well as with the lightning gleams that flashed from the horse's mane. And some whispered,—

"This is no man who thus comes in such kingly splendor. More likely it is Odin on one of his journeys, or the Shining Balder come again to earth."

As the stranger paused on the outer edge of the moat, the sentinels challenged him,—

"Who are you who come thus, uninvited and unheralded, to Santen?"

"One who has the right to come," answered the stranger. "I am Siegfried; and I have come to see my father, the good Siegmund, and my mother, the gentle Sigelind."

It was indeed Siegfried; and he had come from his kingdom in the Nibelungen Land, with his great fleet, and the noblest of his warriors, to see once more his boyhood's home, and to cheer for a time the hearts of his loving parents. For he had done many noble deeds, and had ruled wisely and well, and he felt that he was now not unworthy to be called the son of Siegmund, and to claim kinship with the heroes of the earlier days.

As soon as it was surely known that he who stood before the castle-walls was the young prince who had been gone so many years, and about whom they had heard so many wonderful stories, the drawbridge was hastily let down, and the great gates were thrown wide open. And Siegfried, whose return had been so long wished for, stood once again in his father's halls. And the fear and confusion which had prevailed gave place to gladness and gayety; and all the folk of Santen greeted the returned hero with cheers, and joyfully welcomed him home. And in the whole world there was no one more happy than Siegmund and Sigelind.

On the morrow the ten thousand Nibelungen warriors came to Santen; and Siegmund made for them a great banquet, and entertained them in a right kingly way, as the faithful liegemen of his son. And Siegfried, when he had given them rich gifts, sent them with the fleet back to Nibelungen Land; for he meant to stay for a time with his father and mother at Santen.

When the harvest had been gathered, and the fruit was turning purple and gold, and the moon rode round and full in the clear autumn sky, a gay high-tide was held for Siegfried's sake; and everybody in the Lowland country, whether high or low, rich or poor, was asked to come to the feast. For seven days, nought but unbridled gayety prevailed in Siegmund's halls. On every hand were sounds of music and laughter, and sickness and poverty and pain were for the time forgotten. A mock-battle was fought on the grassy plain not far from the town, and the young men vied with each other in feats of strength and skill. Never before had so many beautiful ladies nor so many brave men been seen in Santen. And, when the time of jollity and feasting had drawn to an end, Siegmund called together all his guests, and gave to each choice gifts,—a festal garment, and a horse with rich trappings. And Queen Sigelind scattered gold without stint among the poor, and many were the blessings she received. Then all the folk went back to their homes with light hearts and happy faces.[EN#20]

The autumn days passed quickly by, and Siegfried began to grow weary of the idle, inactive life in his father's halls; and Greyfell in his stall pined for the fresh, free air, and his mane lost all its brightness. When Siegmund saw how full of unrest his son had become, he said to him,—

"Siegfried, I have grown old and feeble, and have no longer the strength of my younger days. My kingdom would fare better were a younger ruler placed over it. Take my crown, I pray you, and let me withdraw from kingly cares."

But Siegfried would not listen to such an offer. He had his own kingdom of the Nibelungens, he said; and, besides, he would never sit on his father's throne while yet that father lived. And although he loved the pleasant companionship of his mother, and was delighted to listen to the wise counsels of his father, the craving for action, and the unrest which would not be satisfied, grew greater day by day. At last he said,—

"I will ride out into the world again. Mayhap I may find some other wrong to right, or some other kingdom to win. It was thus that my kin, in the golden age long past, went faring over the land and sea, and met their doom at last. They were not home-abiders, nor tillers of the soil; but the world was their abiding-place, and they filled the hearts of men."

And, when his father and mother heard this, they tried no longer to keep him with them; for they knew that it would be more cruel than the keeping of a caged bird away from the sunlight.

"Only go not into Burgundy," said his father. "The kings of that country are not friendly to us, and they may do you harm. Hagen, the kinsman of the kings, and the chief of their fighting-men, is old and crafty, and he cannot brook a greater hero than himself."

Siegfried laughed.

"That is all the better reason why I should go to Burgundy-land," he said.

"Then take ten thousand of my warriors," said his father, "and make yourself master of the land."

"No, no!" cried Siegfried. "One kingdom is enough for me. My own Nibelungen Land is all I want. I will take my twelve Nibelungen knights that I have with me here, and we will fare forth to see the world and its beauties, and men's work; and, when we have tired with riding, we will sail across the sea to our Nibelungen home."

Adventure IX. The Journey to Burgundy-Land.

For many days before Siegfried's departure, the queen, and all the women of the household, busily plied their needles; and many suits of rich raiment made they for the prince and his worthy comrades. At length the time for leave-taking came, and all the inmates of the castle went out to the gate to bid the heroes God-speed. Siegfried sat upon his noble horse Greyfell, and his trusty sword Balmung hung at his side. And his Nibelungen knights were mounted on lordly steeds, with gold-red saddles and silver trappings chased with gold; and their glittering helmets, and burnished shields, and war-coats of polished steel, when added to their noble bearing and manlike forms, made up a picture of beauty and strength such as no one in Santen had ever seen before, or would ever see again.

"Only go not into Burgundy-land," were the parting words of Siegmund.

And all who had come to bid them farewell wept bitterly as the young men rode out of the city, and were lost to sight in the distance.

"Only go not into Burgundy-land!" These words of his father sounded still in Siegfried's ears; and he turned his horse's head towards the west and south; and they rode through the level country, and among the fields, from which the corn had already been gathered; and at night they slept in the open air, upon the still warm ground. Thus for many days they travelled. And they left the Lowlands far behind them, and Burgundy far to the left of them; and by and by they came to a country covered with high hills, and mountains that seemed to touch the sky. The crags and peaks were covered with snow, and ice lay all summer in the dales and in the deep gorges cleft long time ago by giant hands. Here it is that the rivers take their beginning. And here it is that the purple grapes and the rare fruits of milder climes are found; for the sun shines warm in the valleys and upon the plains, and the soil is exceeding rich. It is said that these mountains are midway between the cold regions of Jotunheim and the glowing gardens of Muspelheim, and that, in ages past, they were the scene of many battles between the giants who would overwhelm the earth,—these with ice, and those with fire. Here and there were frowning caves dug out of the solid mountain-side; while higher up were great pits, half-filled with ashes, where, it is said, the dwarf-folk, when they were mighty on earth, had their forges.

Siegfried stopped not long in this land. Thoughts of the Nibelungen Land, and of his faithful liegemen who waited for his return, began to fill his mind. Then the heroes turned their horses' heads, and rode back towards the north, following the course of the River Rhine, as it wound, here and there, between hills and mountains, and through meadows where the grass was springing up anew, and by the side of woodlands, now beginning to be clothed in green again; for the winter was well over, and spring was hastening on apace. And as they rode down the valley of the Rhine they came, ere they were aware, into the Burgundian Land, and the high towers of King Gunther's castle rose up before them. Then Siegfried remembered again his father's words,—

"Only go not into Burgundy-land."

But it was now too late to go back, and they determined to stop for a few days with the Burgundian kings. They rode onwards through the meadows and the pleasant farming-lands which lay around the city; and they passed a wonderful garden of roses, said to belong to Kriemhild, the peerless princess of the Rhine country; and at last they halted before the castle-gate. So lordly was their bearing, that a company of knights came out to meet them, and offered, as the custom was, to take charge of their horses and their shields. But Siegfried asked that they be led at once to King Gunther and his brothers; and, as their stay would not be long, they said they would have no need to part with horses or with shields. Then they followed their guides, and rode through the great gateway, and into the open court, and halted beneath the palace windows.

And the three kings—Gunther, Gernot, and Giselher—and their young sister, the matchless Kriemhild, looked down upon them from above, and hazarded many guesses as to who the lordly strangers might be. And all the inmates of the castle stood at the doors and windows, or gathered in curious groups in the courtyard, and gazed with open-mouthed wonder upon the rich armor and noble bearing of the thirteen heroes. But all eyes were turned most towards Siegfried and the wondrous steed Greyfell. Some of the knights whispered that this was Odin, and some that it was Thor, the thunderer, making a tour through Rhineland. But others said that Thor was never known to ride on horseback, and that the youth who sat on the milk-white steed was little like the ancient Odin. And the ladies who looked down upon the heroes from the palace windows said that this man could be no other than the Sunbright Balder, come from his home in Breidablik, to breathe gladness and sunshine into the hearts and lives of men.

Only one among all the folk in the castle knew who the hero was who had ridden thus boldly into the heart of Burgundy-land. That one was Hagen, the uncle of the three kings, and the doughtiest warrior in all Rhineland. With a dark frown and a sullen scowl he looked out upon the little party, and already plotted in his mind how he might outwit, and bring to grief, the youth whose name and fame were known the whole world over. For his evil mind loved deeds of darkness, and hated the pure and good. By his side, at an upper window, stood Kriemhild, the peerless maiden of the Rhine; but her thoughts were as far from his thoughts as the heaven-smile on her face was unlike the sullen scowl on his grim visage. As the moon in her calm beauty is sometimes seen in the sky, riding gloriously by the side of a dark thunder-cloud,—the one more lovely, the other more dreadful, by their very nearness,—so seemed Kriemhild standing there by the side of Hagen.

"Think you not, dear uncle," she said, "that this is the Shining Balder come to earth again?"

"The gods have forgotten the earth," answered Hagen in surly tones. "But if, indeed, this should be Balder, we shall, without doubt, find another blind archer, who, with another sprig of mistletoe, will send him back again to Hela."

"What do you mean?" asked Kriemhild earnestly.

But old Hagen said not a word in answer. He quietly withdrew from the room, and left the maiden and her mother, the good dame Ute, alone.

"What does uncle Hagen mean by his strange words? and why does he look so sullen and angry?" asked Kriemhild.

"Indeed, I know not," answered the queen-mother. "His ways are dark, and he is cunning. I fear that evil will yet come to our house through him."

Meanwhile the three kings and their chiefs had gone into the courtyard to greet their unknown guests. Very kindly did Gunther welcome the strangers to his home; and then he courteously asked them whence they came, and what the favors they wished.

"I have heard," answered Siegfried, "that many knights and heroes live in this land, and that they are the bravest and the proudest in the world. I, too, am a knight; and some time, if I am worthy, I shall be a king. But first I would make good my right to rule over land and folk; and for this reason I have come hither. If, indeed, you are as brave as all the world says you are, ride now to the meadows with us, and let us fight man to man; and he who wins shall rule over the lands of both. We will wager our kingdom and our heads against yours."

King Gunther and his brothers were amazed at this unlooked-for speech.

"Such is not the way to try where true worth lies!" they cried. "We have no cause of quarrel with you, neither have you any cause of quarrel with us. Why, then, should we spill each other's blood?"

Again Siegfried urged them to fight with him; but they flatly refused. And Gernot said,—

"The Burgundian kings have never wished to rule over folk that are not their own. Much less would they gain new lands at the cost of their best heroes' blood. And they have never taken part in needless quarrels. Good men in Burgundy are worth more than the broadest lands, and we will not hazard the one for the sake of gaining the other. No, we will not fight. But we greet you most heartily as our friends and guests."

All the others joined in urging Siegfried and his comrades to dismount from their steeds, and partake of the cheer with which it was their use to entertain strangers. And at last he yielded to their kind wishes, and alighted from Greyfell, and, grasping King Gunther's hand, he made himself known. And there was great rejoicing in the castle and throughout all the land; and the most sumptuous rooms were set apart for the use of Siegfried and his Nibelungen knights; and a banquet was at once made ready; and no pains were spared in giving the strangers a right hearty welcome to the kingly halls of Burgundy. But Hagen, dark-browed and evil-eyed, stood silent and alone in his chamber and waited his time.

Adventure X. Kriemhild's Dream.

Early on the morrow morning, ere the sun had risen high, the peerless Kriemhild walked alone amid the sweet-scented bowers of her rose-garden. The dewdrops still hung thick on flower and thorn, and the wild birds carolled their songs of merry welcome to the new-born day. Every thing seemed to have put on its handsomest colors, and to be using its sweetest voice, on purpose to gladden the heart of the maiden. But Kriemhild was not happy. There was a shadow on her face and a sadness in her eye that the beauty and the music of that morning could not drive away.

"What ails thee, my child?" asked her mother, Queen Ute, who met her. "Why so sad, as if thy heart were heavy with care? Has any one spoken unkindly, or has aught grievous happened to thee?"

"Oh, no, dearest mother!" said Kriemhild. "It is nothing that saddens me,—nothing but a foolish dream. I cannot forget it."

"Tell me the dream," said her mother: "mayhap it betokens something that the Norns have written for thee."

Then Kriemhild answered, "I dreamed that I sat at my window, high up in the eastern tower; and the sun shone bright in the heavens, and the air was mild and warm, and I thought of nought but the beauty and the gladness of the hour. Then in the far north I saw a falcon flying. At first he seemed but a black speck in the sky; but swiftly he drew nearer and nearer, until at last he flew in at the open window, and I caught him in my arms. Oh, how strong and beautiful he was! His wings were purple and gold, and his eyes were as bright as the sun. Oh, a glorious prize I thought him! and I held him on my wrist, and spoke kind words to him. Then suddenly, from out of the sky above, two eagles dashed in at the window, and snatched my darling from me, and they tore him in pieces before my eyes, and laughed at my distress."

"Thy dream," said Queen Ute, "is easy to explain. A king shall come from the north-land, and a mighty king shall he be. And he shall seek thee, and love thee, and wed thee, and thy heart shall overflow with bliss. The two eagles are the foes who shall slay him; but who they may be, or whence they may come, is known only to the Norns."

"But I slept, and I dreamed again," said Kriemhild. "This time I sat in the meadow, and three women came to me. And they span, and they wove a woof more fair than any I have ever seen. And methought that another woof was woven, which crossed the first, and yet it was no whit less beautiful. Then the women who wove the woofs cried out, 'Enough!' And a fair white arm reached out and seized the rare fabrics, and tore them into shreds. And then the sky was overcast, and the thunder began to roll and the lightning to flash, and red fires gleamed, and fierce wolves howled around me, and I awoke."

"This dream," said Queen Ute, "is more than I can understand. Only this I can see and explain, that in the dim future the woof of another's fate shall cross thy own. But trouble not thyself because of that which shall be. While yet the sun shines for thee, and the birds sing, and the flowers shed their sweet perfume, it is for thee to rejoice and be light-hearted. What the Norns have woven is woven, and it cannot be undone."[EN#21]

Adventure XI. How the Spring-time Came.

Siegfried, when he came to Gunther's castle, thought of staying there but a few days only. But the king and his brothers made every thing so pleasant for their honored guest, that weeks slipped by unnoticed, and still the hero remained in Burgundy.

Spring had fairly come, and the weeping April clouds had given place to the balmy skies of May. The young men and maidens, as was their wont, made ready for the May-day games; and Siegfried and his knights were asked to take part in the sport.

On the smooth greensward, which they called Nanna's carpet, beneath the shade of ash-trees and elms, he who played Old Winter's part lingered with his few attendants. These were clad in the dull gray garb which becomes the sober season of the year, and were decked with yellow straw, and dead, brown leaves. Out of the wood came the May-king and his followers, clad in the gayest raiment, and decked with evergreens and flowers. With staves and willow-withes they fell upon Old Winter's champions, and tried to drive them from the sward. In friendly fray they fought, and many mishaps fell to both parties. But at length the May-king won; and grave Winter, battered and bruised, was made prisoner, and his followers were driven from the field. Then, in merry sport, sentence was passed on the luckless wight, for he was found guilty of killing the flowers, and of covering the earth with hoar-frost; and he was doomed to a long banishment from music and the sunlight. The laughing party then set up a wooden likeness of the worsted winter-king, and pelted it with stones and turf; and when they were tired they threw it down, and put out its eyes, and cast it into the river. And then a pole, decked with wild-flowers and fresh green leaves, was planted in the midst of the sward, and all joined in merry dance around it. And they chose the most beautiful of all the maidens to be the Queen of May, and they crowned her with a wreath of violets and yellow buttercups; and for a whole day all yielded fealty to her, and did her bidding.

It was thus that May Day came in Burgundy. And in the evening, when the party were seated in King Gunther's hall, Siegfried, at the command of the May-queen,—who was none other than Kriemhild the peerless,—amused them by telling the story of

Idun and Her Apples.

It is a story that Bragi told while at the feast in AEgir's hall. Idun is Bragi's wife. Very handsome is she; but the beauty of her face is by no means greater than the goodness of her heart. Right attentive is she to every duty, and her words and thoughts are always worthy and wise. A long time ago the good Asa-folk who dwell in heaven-towering Asgard, knowing how trustworthy Idun was, gave into her keeping a treasure which they would not have placed in the hands of any other person. This treasure was a box of apples, and Idun kept the golden key safely fastened to her girdle. You ask me why the gods should prize a box of apples so highly? I will tell you.

Old age, you know, spares none, not even Odin and his Asa-folk. They all grow old and gray; and, if there were no cure for age, they would become feeble and toothless and blind, deaf, tottering, and weak minded. The apples which Idun guarded so carefully were the priceless boon of youth. Whenever the gods felt old age coming on, they went to her, and she gave them of her fruit; and, when they had tasted, they grew young and strong and handsome again. Once, however, they came near losing the apples,—or losing rather Idun and her golden key, without which no one could ever open the box.

In those early days Odin delighted to come down now and then from his high home above the clouds, and to wander, disguised, among the woods and mountains, and by the seashore, and in wild desert places. For nothing pleases him more than to commune with Nature as she is found in the loneliness of vast solitudes, or in the boisterous uproar of the elements. Once on a time he took with him his friends Hoenir and Loki; and they rambled many days among the icy cliffs, and along the barren shores, of the great frozen sea. In that country there was no game, and no fish was found in the cold waters; and the three wanderers, as they had brought no food with them, became very hungry. Late in the afternoon of the seventh day, they reached some pasture-lands belonging to the giant Hymer, and saw a herd of the giant's cattle browsing upon the short grass which grew in the sheltered nooks among the hills.

"Ah!" cried Loki: "after fasting for a week, we shall now have food in abundance. Let us kill and eat."

So saying, he hurled a sharp stone at the fattest of Hymer's cows, and killed her; and the three quickly dressed the choicest pieces of flesh for their supper. Then Loki gathered twigs and dry grass, and kindled a blazing fire; Hoenir filled the pot with water from melted ice; and Odin threw into it the bits of tender meat. But, make the fire as hot as they would, the water would not boil, and the flesh would not cook.

All night long the supperless three sat hungry around the fire; and, every time they peeped into the kettle, the meat was as raw and gustless as before. Morning came, but no breakfast. And all day Loki kept stirring the fire, and Odin and Hoenir waited hopefully but impatiently. When the sun again went down, the flesh was still uncooked, and their supper seemed no nearer ready than it was the night before. As they were about yielding to despair, they heard a noise overhead, and, looking up, they saw a huge gray eagle sitting on the dead branch of an oak.

"Ha, ha!" cried the bird. "You are pretty fellows indeed! To sit hungry by the fire a night and a day, rather than eat raw flesh, becomes you well. Do but give me my share of it as it is, and I warrant you the rest shall boil, and you shall have a fat supper."

"Agreed," answered Loki eagerly. "Come down and get your share."

The eagle waited for no second asking. Down he swooped right over the blazing fire, and snatched not only the eagle's share, but also what the Lybians call the lion's share; that is, he grasped in his strong talons the kettle, with all the meat in it, and, flapping his huge wings, slowly rose into the air, carrying his booty with him. The three gods were astonished. Loki was filled with anger. He seized a long pole, upon the end of which a sharp hook was fixed, and struck at the treacherous bird. The hook stuck fast in the eagle's back, and Loki could not loose his hold of the other end of the pole. The great bird soared high above the tree-tops, and over the hills, and carried the astonished mischief-maker with him.

But it was no eagle. It was no bird that had thus outwitted the hungry gods: it was the giant Old Winter, clothed in his eagle-plumage. Over the lonely woods, and the snow-crowned mountains, and the frozen sea, he flew, dragging the helpless Loki through tree-tops, and over jagged rocks, scratching and bruising his body, and almost tearing his arms from his shoulders. At last he alighted on the craggy top of an iceberg, where the storm-winds shrieked, and the air was filled with driving snow. As soon as Loki could speak, he begged the giant to carry him back to his comrades,— Odin and Hoenir.

"On one condition only will I carry you back," answered Old Winter. "Swear to me that you will betray into my hands dame Idun and her golden key."

Loki asked no questions, but gladly gave the oath; and the giant flew back with him across the sea, and dropped him, torn and bleeding and lame, by the side of the fire, where Odin and Hoenir still lingered. And the three made all haste to leave that cheerless place, and returned to Odin's glad home in Asgard.

Some weeks after this, Loki, the Prince of Mischief-makers, went to Bragi's house to see Idun. He found her busied with her household cares, not thinking of a visit from any of the gods.

"I have come, good dame," said he, "to taste your apples again; for I feel old age coming on apace."

Idun was astonished.

"You are not looking old," she answered. "There is not a single gray hair upon your head, and not a wrinkle on your brow. If it were not for that scar upon your cheek, and the arm which you carry in a sling you would look as stout and as well as I have ever seen you. Besides, I remember that it was only a year ago when you last tasted of my fruit. Is it possible that a single winter should make you old?"

"A single winter has made me very lame and feeble, at least," said Loki. "I have been scarcely able to walk about since my return from the North. Another winter without a taste of your apples will be the death of me."

Then the kind-hearted Idun, when she saw that Loki was really lame, went to the box, and opened it with her golden key, and gave him one of the precious apples to taste. He took the fruit in his hand, bit it, and gave it back to the good dame. She put it in its place again, closed the lid, and locked it with her usual care.

"Your apples are not so good as they used to be," said Loki, making a very wry face. "Why don't you fill your box with fresh fruit?"

Idun was amazed. Her apples were supposed to be always fresh,— fresher by far than any that grow nowadays. None of the gods had ever before complained about them; and she told Loki so.

"Very well," said he. "I see you do not believe me, and that you mean to feed us on your sour, withered apples, when we might as well have golden fruit. If you were not so bent on having your own way, I could tell you where you might fill your box with the choicest of apples, such as Odin loves. I saw them in the forest over yonder, hanging ripe on the trees. But women will always have their own way; and you must have yours, even though you do feed the gods on withered apples."

So saying, and without waiting to hear an answer, he limped out at the door, and was soon gone from sight.

Idun thought long and anxiously upon the words which Loki had spoken; and, the more she thought, the more she felt troubled. If her husband, the wise Bragi, had been at home, what would she not have given? He would have understood the mischief-maker's cunning. But he had gone on a long journey to the South, singing in Nature's choir, and painting Nature's landscapes, and she would not see him again until the return of spring. At length she opened the box, and looked at the fruit. The apples were certainly fair and round: she could not see a wrinkle or a blemish on any of them; their color was the same golden-red,—like the sky at dawn of a summer's day; yet she thought there must be something wrong about them. She took up one of the apples, and tasted it. She fancied that it really was sour, and she hastily put it back, and locked the box again.

"He said that he had seen better apples than these growing in the woods," said she to herself. "I half believe that he told the truth, although everybody knows that he is not always trustworthy. I think I shall go to the forest and see for myself, at any rate."

So she donned her cloak and hood, and, with a basket on her arm, left the house, and walked rapidly away, along the road which led to the forest. It was much farther than she had thought, and the sun was almost down when she reached the edge of the wood. But no apple-trees were there. Tall oaks stretched their bare arms up towards the sky, as if praying for help. There were thorn-trees and brambles everywhere; but there was no fruit, neither were there any flowers, nor even green leaves. The Frost-giants had been there.

Idun was about to turn her footsteps homewards, when she heard a wild shriek in the tree-tops over her head; and, before she could look up, she felt herself seized in the eagle-talons of Old Winter. Struggle as she would, she could not free herself. High up, over wood and stream, the giant carried her; and then he flew swiftly away with her, towards his home in the chill North-land; and, when morning came, poor Idun found herself in an ice-walled castle in the cheerless country of the giants. But she was glad to know that the precious box was safely locked at home, and that the golden key was still at her girdle.

Time passed; and I fear that Idun would have been forgotten by all, save her husband Bragi, had not the gods begun to feel the need of her apples. Day after day they came to Idun's house, hoping to find the good dame and her golden key at home; and each day they went away some hours older than when they had come. Bragi was beside himself with grief, and his golden harp was unstrung and forgotten. No one had seen the missing Idun since the day when Loki had visited her, and none could guess what had become of her. The heads of all the folk grew white with age; deep furrows were ploughed in their faces; their eyes grew dim, and their hearing failed; their hands trembled; their limbs became palsied; their feet tottered; and all feared that Old Age would bring Death in his train.

Then Bragi and Thor questioned Loki very sharply; and when he felt that he, too, was growing old and feeble, he regretted the mischief he had done, and told them how he had decoyed Idun into Old Winter's clutches. The gods were very angry; and Thor threatened to crush Loki with his hammer, if he did not at once bring Idun safe home again.

So Loki borrowed the falcon-plumage of Freyja, the goddess of love, and with it flew to the country of the giants. When he reached Old Winter's castle, he found the good dame Idun shut up in the prison-tower, and bound with fetters of ice; but the giant himself was on the frozen sea, herding old Hymer's cows. And Loki quickly broke the bonds that held Idun, and led her out of her prison-house; and then he shut her up in a magic nut-shell which he held between his claws, and flew with the speed of the wind back towards the South-land and the home of the gods. But Old Winter coming home, and learning what had been done, donned his eagle-plumage and followed swiftly in pursuit.

Bragi and Thor, anxiously gazing into the sky, saw Loki, in Freyja's falcon-plumage, speeding homewards, with the nut-shell in his talons, and Old Winter, in his eagle-plumage, dashing after in sharp pursuit. Quickly they gathered chips and slender twigs, and placed them high upon the castle-wall; and, when Loki with his precious burden had flown past, they touched fire to the dry heap, and the flames blazed up to the sky, and caught Old Winter's plumage, as, close behind the falcon, he blindly pressed. And his wings were scorched in the flames; and he fell helpless to the ground, and was slain within the castle-gates. Loki slackened his speed; and, when he reached Bragi's house, he dropped the nut-shell softly before the door. As it touched the ground, it gently opened, and Idun, radiant with smiles, and clothed in gay attire, stepped forth, and greeted her husband and the waiting gods. And the heavenly music of Bragi's long-silent harp welcomed her home; and she took the golden key from her girdle, and unlocked the box, and gave of her apples to the aged company; and, when they had tasted, their youth was renewed.[EN#22]

It is thus with the seasons and their varied changes. The gifts of Spring are youth and jollity, and renewed strength; and the music of air and water and all things, living and lifeless, follow in her train. The desolating Winter plots to steal her from the earth, and the Summer-heat deserts and betrays her. Then the music of Nature is hushed, and all creatures pine in sorrow for her absence, and the world seems dying of white Old Age. But at length the Summer-heat repents, and frees her from her prison-house; and the icy fetters with which Old Winter bound her are melted in the beams of the returning sun, and the earth is young again.

Adventure XII. The War with the North-kings.

So swiftly and so pleasantly the days went by, that weeks lengthened into months, and the spring-time passed, and the summer came, and still Siegfried lingered in Burgundy with his kind friends. The time was spent in all manner of joyance,—in hunting the deer in the deep oak-woods, in riding over the daisied meadows or among the fields of corn, in manly games and sports, in music and dancing, in feasting and in pleasant talk. And of all the noble folk who had ever sat at Gunther's table, or hunted in the Burgundian woods, none were so worthy or so fair as the proud young lord of the Nibelungens.

One day in early autumn a party of strange knights rode up to the castle, and asked to speak with the Burgundian kings. They were led straightway into the great hall; and Gunther and his brothers welcomed them, as was their wont, right heartily, and asked them from what country they had come, and what was their errand.

"We come," they answered, "from the North country; and we bring word from our lords and kings, Leudiger and Leudigast."

"And what would our kingly neighbors say to us?" asked Gunther.

Then the strangers said that their lords had become very angry with the Burgundian kings, and that they meant, within twelve weeks from that day, to come with a great army, and lay the country waste, and besiege their city and castle. All this they had sworn to do unless the Burgundians would make peace with them upon such terms as Leudiger and Leudigast should please to grant.

When Gunther and his brothers heard this, they were struck with dismay. But they ordered the messengers to be well cared for and handsomely entertained within the palace until the morrow, at which time they should have the Burgundians' answer. All the noblest knights and earl-folk were called together, and the matter was laid before them.

"What answer shall we send to our rude neighbors of the North?" asked Gunther.

Gernot and the young Giselher declared at once for war. Old Hagen and other knights, whose prudence was at least equal to their bravery, said but little. It was known, that, in the armies of the North-kings, there were at least forty thousand soldiers; but in Burgundy there were not more than thirty thousand fighting-men, all told. The North-kings' forces were already equipped, and ready to march; but the Burgundians could by no means raise and arm any considerable body of men in the short space of twelve weeks. It would be the part of wisdom to delay, and to see what terms could best be made with their enemies. Such were the prudent counsels of the older knights, but Gernot and the young chief Volker would not listen to such words.

"The Burgundians are not cowards," said they. "We have never been foiled in battle; never have we been the vassals of a stranger. Why, then, shall we cringe and cower before such men as Leudiger and Leudigast?"

Then Hagen answered, "Let us ask our friend and guest Siegfried. Let us learn what he thinks about this business. Everybody knows that he is as wise in council as he is brave in the field. We will abide by what he says."

But Gunther and Gernot and the young Giselher were unwilling to do this; for it was not their custom to annoy their guests with questions which should be allowed to trouble themselves alone. And the kings and their counsellors went out of the council-chamber, each to ponder in silence upon the troublesome question.

As Gunther, with downcast head and troubled brow, walked thoughtfully through the great hall, he unexpectedly met Siegfried.

"What evil tidings have you heard?" asked the prince, surprised at the strange mien of the king. "What has gone amiss, that should cause such looks of dark perplexity?"

"That is a matter which I can tell only to friends long tried and true," answered Gunther.

Siegfried was surprised and hurt by these words; and he cried out,—

"What more would Gunther ask of me that I might prove my friendship? Surely I have tried to merit his esteem and trust. Tell me what troubles you, and I will further show myself to be your friend both tried and true."

Then Gunther was ashamed of the words he had spoken to his guest; and he took Siegfried into his own chamber, and told him all; and he asked him what answer they should send on the morrow to the overbearing North-kings.

"Tell them we will fight," answered Siegfried. "I myself will lead your warriors to the fray. Never shall it be said that my friends have suffered wrong, and I not tried to help them."

Then he and Gunther talked over the plans which they would follow. And the clouds fled at once from the brow of the king, and he was no longer troubled or doubtful; for he believed in Siegfried.

The next morning the heralds of the North-kings were brought again before Gunther and his brothers; and they were told to carry this word to their masters,—

"The Burgundians will fight. They will make no terms with their enemies, save such as they make of their own free-will."

Then the heralds were loaded with costly presents, and a company of knights and warriors went with them to the border-line of Burgundy; and, filled with wonder at what they had seen, they hastened back to their liege lords, and told all that had happened to them. And Leudiger and Leudigast were very wroth when they heard the answer which the Burgundians had sent to them; but, when they learned that the noble Siegfried was at Gunther's castle, they shook their heads, and seemed to feel more doubtful of success.

Many and busy were the preparations for war, and in a very few days all things were in readiness for the march northwards. It was settled that Siegfried with his twelve Nibelungen chiefs, and a thousand picked men, should go forth to battle against their boastful enemies. The dark-browed Hagen, as he had always done, rode at the head of the company, and by his side was Siegfried on the noble horse Greyfell. Next came Gernot and the bold chief Volker, bearing the standard, upon which a golden dragon was engraved; then followed Dankwart and Ortwin, and the twelve worthy comrades of Siegfried; and then the thousand warriors, the bravest in all Rhineland, mounted on impatient steeds, and clad in bright steel armor, with broad shields, and plumed helmets, and burnished swords, and sharp-pointed spears. And all rode proudly out through the great castle-gate. And Gunther and the young Giselher and all the fair ladies of the court bade them God-speed.

The little army passed through the forest, and went northwards, until, on the fifth day, they reached the boundaries of Saxon Land. And Siegfried gave spur to his horse Greyfell, and, leaving the little army behind him, hastened forwards to see where the enemy was encamped. As he reached the top of a high hill, he saw the armies of the North-kings resting carelessly in the valley beyond. Knights, mounted on their horses, rode hither and thither: the soldiers sauntered lazily among the trees, or slept upon the grass; arms were thrown about in great disorder, or stacked in piles near the smoking camp-fires. No one dreamed of danger; but all supposed that the Burgundians were still at home, and would never dare to attack a foe so numerous and so strong.

For it was, indeed, a mighty army which Siegfried saw before him. Full forty thousand men were there; and they not only filled the valley, but spread over the hills beyond, and far to the right and left.

While he stood at the top of the hill, and gazed upon this sight, a warrior, who had spied him from below, rode up, and paused before him. Like two black thunder-clouds, with lightning flashing between, the two knights stood facing each other, and casting wrathful glances from beneath their visors. Then each spurred his horse, and charged with fury upon the other; and the heavy lances of both were broken in shivers upon the opposing shields. Then, quick as thought, they turned and drew their swords, and hand to hand they fought. But soon Siegfried, by an unlooked-for stroke, sent his enemy's sword flying from him, broken in a dozen pieces, and by a sudden movement he threw him from his horse. The heavy shield of the fallen knight was no hinderance to the quick strokes of Siegfried's sword; and his glittering armor, soiled by the mud into which he had been thrown, held him down. He threw up his hands, and begged for mercy.

"I am Leudigast the king!" he cried. "Spare my life. I am your prisoner."

Siegfried heard the prayer of the discomfited king; and, lifting him from the ground, he helped him to remount his charger. But, while he was doing this, thirty warriors, who had seen the combat from below, came dashing up the hill to the rescue of their liege-lord. Siegfried faced about with his horse Greyfell, and quietly waited for their onset. But, as they drew near, they were so awed by the noble bearing and grand proportions of the hero, and so astonished at sight of the sunbeam mane of Greyfell, and the cold glitter of the blade Balmung, that in sudden fright they stopped, then turned, and fled in dismay down the sloping hillside, nor paused until they were safe among their friends.

In the mean while Leudiger, the other king, seeing what was going on at the top of the hill, had caused an alarm to be sounded; and all his hosts had hastily arranged themselves in battle-array. At the same time Hagen and Gernot, and their little army of heroes, hove in sight, and came quickly to Siegfried's help, and the dragon-banner was planted upon the crest of the hill. The captive king, Leudigast, was taken to the rear, and a guard was placed over him. The champions of the Rhine formed in line, and faced their foes. The great army of the North-kings moved boldly up the hill: and, when they saw how few were the Burgundians, they laughed and cheered most lustily; for they felt that the odds was in their favor—and forty to one is no small odds.

Then Siegfried and his twelve comrades, and Hagen and the thousand Burgundian knights, dashed upon them with the fury of the whirlwind. The lances flew so thick in the air, that they hid the sun from sight; swords flashed on every side; the sound of clashing steel, and horses' hoofs, and soldiers' shouts, filled earth and sky with a horrid din. And soon the boastful foes of the Burgundians were everywhere worsted, and thrown into disorder. Siegfried dashed hither and thither, from one part of the field to another, in search of King Leudiger. Thrice he cut his way through the ranks, and at last he met face to face the one for whom he sought.

King Leudiger saw the flashing sunbeams that glanced from Greyfell's mane, he saw the painted crown upon the hero's broad shield, and then he felt the fearful stroke of the sword Balmung, as it clashed against his own, and cut it clean in halves. He dropped his weapons, raised his visor, and gave himself up as a prisoner.

"Give up the fight, my brave fellows," he cried. "This is Siegfried the brave, the Prince of the Lowlands, and the Lord of Nibelungen Land. It were foolishness to fight against him. Save yourselves as best you can."

This was the signal for a frightful panic. All turned and fled. Each thought of nothing but his own safety; and knights and warriors, horsemen and foot-soldiers, in one confused mass, throwing shields and weapons here and there, rushed wildly down the hill, and through the valley and ravines, and sought, as best they could, their way homeward. The Burgundian heroes were the masters of the field, and on the morrow they turned their faces joyfully towards Rhineland. And all joined in saying that to Siegfried was due the praise for this wonderful victory which they had gained.

Heralds had been sent on the fleetest horses to carry the glad news to Burgundy; and when, one morning, they dashed into the court-yard of the castle, great was the anxiety to know what tidings they brought. And King Gunther, and the young Giselher, and the peerless Kriemhild, came out to welcome them, and eagerly to inquire what had befallen the heroes. With breathless haste the heralds told the story of all that had happened.

"And how fares our brother Gernot?" asked Kriemhild.

"There is no happier man on earth," answered the herald. "In truth, there was not a coward among them all; but the bravest of the brave was Siegfried. He it was who took the two kings prisoners; and everywhere in the thickest of the fight there was Siegfried. And now our little army is on its homeward march, with a thousand prisoners, and large numbers of the enemy's wounded. Had it not been for the brave Siegfried, no such victory could have been won."

In a few days the Rhine champions reached their home. And gayly were the castle and all the houses in the city decked in honor of them. And all those who had been left behind went out to meet them as they came down from the forest-road, and drew near to the castle. And the young girls strewed flowers in their path, and hung garlands upon their horses; and music and song followed the heroes into the city, and through the castle-gate.

When they reached the palace, the two prisoner kings, Leudiger and Leudigast, were loosed from their bonds, and handsomely entertained at Gunther's table. And the Burgundian kings assured them that they should be treated as honored guests, and have the freedom of the court and castle, if they would pledge themselves not to try to escape from Burgundy until terms of peace should be agreed upon. This pledge they gladly gave, and rich apartments in the palace were assigned for their use. Like favors were shown to all the prisoners, according to their rank; and the wounded were kindly cared for. And the Burgundians made ready for a gay high-tide,—a glad festival of rejoicing, to be held at the next full moon.

When the day drew near which had been set for this high-tide, the folk from all parts of Rhineland began to flock towards the city. They came in companies, with music and laughter, and the glad songs of the spring-time. And all the knights were mounted on gallant horses caparisoned with gold-red saddles, from which hung numbers of tinkling silver bells. As they rode up the sands towards the castle-gate, with their dazzling shields upon their saddle-bows, and their gay and many-colored banners floating in the air, King Gernot and the young Giselher, with the noblest knights of the fortress, went courteously out to meet them; and the friendly greetings which were offered by the two young kings won the hearts of all. Thirty and two princes and more than five thousand warriors came as bidden guests. The city and castle were decked in holiday attire, and all the people in the land gave themselves up to enjoyment. The sick and the wounded, who until now had thought themselves at death's door, forgot their ailments and their pains as they heard the shouts of joy and the peals of music in the streets.

In a green field outside of the city walls, arrangements had been made for the games, and galleries and high stages had been built for the lookers-on. Here jousts and tournaments were held, and the knights and warriors engaged in trials of strength and skill. When King Gunther saw with what keen enjoyment both his own people and his guests looked upon these games, and took part in the gay festivities, he asked of those around him,—

"What more can we do to heighten the pleasures of the day?"

And one of his counsellors answered,—

"My lord, the ladies of the court, and the little children, pine in silence in the sunless rooms of the palace, while we enjoy the free air and light of heaven, the music, and the gay scenes before us. There is nothing wanting to make this day's joy complete, save the presence of our dear ones to share these pleasures with us."

Gunther was delighted to hear these words; and he sent a herald to the palace, and invited all the ladies of the court and all the children to come out and view the games, and join in the general gladness.

When Dame Ute heard the message which the herald brought from her kingly son, she hastened to make ready rich dresses and costly jewels wherewith to adorn the dames and damsels of the court. And, when all were in readiness, the peerless Kriemhild, with her mother at her side, went forth from the castle; and a hundred knights, all sword in hand, went with her as a body-guard, and a great number of noble ladies dressed in rich attire followed her. As the red dawn peers forth from behind gray clouds, and drives the mists and shadows away from earth, so came the lovely one. As the bright full moon in radiant splendor moves in queen-like beauty before her train of attendant stars, and outshines them all, so was Kriemhild the most glorious among all the noble ladies there. And the thousand knights and warriors paused in their games, and greeted the peerless princess as was due to one so noble and fair. Upon the highest platform, under a rich canopy of cloth-of-gold, seats were made ready for the maiden and her mother and the fair ladies in their train; and all the most worthy princes in Rhineland sat around, and the games were begun again.

For twelve days the gay high-tide lasted, and nought was left undone whereby the joy might be increased. And of all the heroes and princes who jousted in the tournament, or took part in the games, none could equal the unassuming Siegfried; and his praises were heard on every hand, and all agreed that he was the most worthy prince that they had ever seen.

When at last the festal days came to an end, Gunther and his brothers called their guests and vassals around them, and loaded them with costly gifts, and bade them God-speed. And tears stood in the eyes of all at parting.

The captive kings, Leudiger and Leudigast, were not forgotten.

"What will ye give me for your freedom?" asked King Gunther, half in jest.

They answered,—

"If you will allow us without further hinderance to go back to our people, we pledge our lives and our honor that we will straightway send you gold, as much as half a thousand horses can carry."

Then Gunther turned to Siegfried, and said,—

"What think you, friend Siegfried, of such princely ransom?"

"Noble lord," said Siegfried, "I think you are in need of no such ransom. Friendship is worth much more than gold. If your kingly captives will promise, on their honor, never more to come towards Burgundy as enemies, let them go. We have no need of gold."

"'Tis well said," cried Gunther highly pleased.

And Leudiger and Leudigast, with tears of thankfulness, gladly made the asked-for promise, and on the morrow, with light hearts and costly gifts, they set out on their journey homewards.

When all the guests had gone, and the daily routine of idle palace-life set in again, Siegfried began to talk of going back to Nibelungen Land. But young Giselher, and the peerless Kriemhild, and King Gunther, besought him to stay yet a little longer. And he yielded to their kind wishes. And autumn passed away with its fruits and its vintage, and grim old winter came howling down from the north, and Siegfried was still in Burgundy. And then old Hoder, the king of the winter months, came blustering through the Rhine valley; and with him were the Reifriesen,—the thieves that steal the daylight from the earth and the warmth from the sun. And they nipped the flowers, and withered the grass, and stripped the trees, and sealed up the rivers, and covered the earth with a white mantle of sorrow.

But within King Gunther's wide halls there was joy and good cheer. And the season of the Yule-feast came, and still Siegfried tarried in Burgundy-land.

Adventure XIII. The Story of Balder.

There was mirth in King Gunther's dwelling, for the time of the Yule-feast had come. The broad banquet hall was gayly decked with cedar and spruce and sprigs of the mistletoe; and the fires roared in the great chimneys, throwing warmth and a ruddy glow of light into every corner of the room. The long table fairly groaned under its weight of good cheer. At its head sat the kings and the earl-folk; and before them, on a silver platter of rare workmanship, was the head of a huge wild boar,—the festal offering to the good Frey, in honor of whom the Yule-feast was held. For now the sun, which had been driven by the Frost-giants far away towards the South-land, had begun to return, and Frey was on his way once more to scatter peace and plenty over the land.

The harp and the wassail-bowl went round; and each one of the company sang a song, or told a story, or in some way did his part to add to the evening's enjoyment. And a young sea-king who sat at Siegfried's side told most bewitching tales of other lands which lie beyond Old AEgir's kingdom. Then, when the harp came to him, he sang the wondrous song of the shaping of the earth. And all who heard were charmed with the sweet sound and with the pleasant words. He sang of the sunlight and the south winds and the summer-time, of the storms and the snow and the sombre shadows of the North-land. And he sang of the dead Ymir, the giant whose flesh had made the solid earth, and whose blood the sea, and whose bones the mountains, whose teeth the cliffs and crags, and whose skull the heavens. And he sang of Odin, the earth's preserver, the Giver of life, the Father of all; and of the Asa-folk who dwell in Asgard; and of the ghostly heroes in Valhal. Then he sang of the heaven-tower of the thunder-god, and of the shimmering Asa-bridge, or rainbow, all afire; and, lastly, of the four dwarfs who hold the blue sky-dome above them, and of the elves of the mountains, and of the wood-sprites and the fairies. Then he laid aside his harp, and told the old but ever-beautiful story of the death of Balder the Good.

The Story.

Balder, as you know, was Odin's son; and he was the brightest and best of all the Asa-folk. Wherever he went, there were gladness and light-hearted mirth, and blooming flowers, and singing birds, and murmuring waterfalls. Balder, too, was a hero, but not one of the blustering kind, like Thor. He slew no giants; he never went into battle; he never tried to make for himself a name among the dwellers of the mid-world; and yet he was a hero of the noblest type. He dared to do right, and to stand up for the good, the true, and the beautiful. There are still some such heroes, but the world does not always hear of them.

Hoder, the blind king of the winter months, was Balder's brother, and as unlike him as darkness is unlike daylight. While one rejoiced, and was merry and cheerful, the other was low-spirited and sad. While one scattered sunshine and blessings everywhere, the other carried with him a sense of cheerlessness and gloom. Yet the brothers loved each other dearly.

One night Balder dreamed a strange dream, and when he awoke he could not forget it. All day long he was thoughtful and sad, and he was not his own bright, happy self. His mother, the Asa-queen, saw that something troubled him; and she asked,—

"Whence comes that cloud upon your brow? Will you suffer it to chase away all your sunshine? and will you become, like your brother Hoder, all frowns and sighs and tears?"

Then Balder told her what he had dreamed; and she, too, was sorely troubled, for it was a frightful dream, and foreboded dire disasters. Then both she and Balder went to Odin, and to him they told the cause of their uneasiness. And the All-Father also was distressed; for he knew that such dreams, dreamed by Asa-folk, were the forewarnings of evil. So he saddled his eight-footed steed Sleipner; and, without telling any one where he was going, he rode with the speed of the winds down into the Valley of Death. The dog that guards the gateway to that dark and doleful land came out to meet him. Blood was on the fierce beast's breast, and he barked loudly and angrily at the All-Father and his wondrous horse. But Odin sang sweet magic songs as he drew near; and the dog was charmed with the sound, and Sleipner and his rider went onward in safety. And they passed the dark halls of the pale-faced queen, and came to the east gate of the valley. There stood the low hut of a witch who lived in darkness, and, like the Norns, spun the thread of fate for gods and men.

Odin stood before the hut, and sang a wondrous song of witchery and enchantment; and he laid a spell upon the weird woman, and forced her to come out of her dark dwelling, and to answer his questions.

"Who is this stranger?" asked the witch. "Who is this unknown who calls me from my narrow home, and sets an irksome task for me? Long have I been left alone in my quiet house; nor recked I that the snow sometimes covered with its cold white mantle both me and my resting-place, or that the pattering rain and the gently falling dew often moistened the roof of my dwelling. Long have I rested quietly, and I do not wish now to be aroused."

"I am Valtam's son," said Odin; "and I come to learn of thee. Tell me, I pray, for whom are the soft couches prepared that I saw in the broad halls of Death? For whom are the jewels, and the rings, and the rich clothing, and the shining shield?"

"All are for Balder, Odin's son," she answered. "And the mead which has been brewed for him is hidden beneath the shining shield."

Then Odin asked who would be the slayer of Balder, and she answered that Hoder was the one who would send the shining Asa to the halls of Death.

"Who will avenge Balder, and bring distress upon his slayer?" asked Odin.

"A son of Earth but one day old shall be Balder's avenger. Go thou now home, Odin; for I know thou art not Valtam's son. Go home; and none shall again awaken me, nor disturb me at my task, until the new day shall dawn, and Balder shall rule over the young world in its purity, and there shall be no more Death."

Then Odin rode sorrowfully homeward; but he told no one of his journey to the Dark Valley, nor of what the weird witch had said to him.

Balder's mother, the Asa-queen, could not rest because of the ill-omened dream that her son had had; and in her distress she called all the Asa-folk together to consider what should be done. But they were speechless with sorrow and alarm; and none could offer advice, nor set her mind at ease. Then she sought out every living creature, and every lifeless thing, upon the earth, and asked each one to swear that it would not on any account hurt Balder, nor touch him to do him harm. And this oath was willingly made by fire and water, earth and air, by all beasts and creeping things and birds and fishes, by the rocks and by the trees and all metals; for every thing loved Balder the Good.

Then the Asa-folk thought that great honor was shown to Balder each time any thing refused to hurt him; and to show their love for him, as well as to amuse themselves, they often hewed at him with their battle-axes, or struck at him with their sharp swords, or hurled toward him their heavy lances. For every weapon turned aside from its course, and would neither mark nor bruise the shining target at which it was aimed; and Balder's princely beauty shone as bright and as pure as ever.

When Loki the Mischief-maker saw how all things loved and honored Balder, his heart was filled with jealous hate, and he sought all over the earth for some beast or bird or tree or lifeless thing, that had not taken the oath. But he could find not one. Then, disguised as a fair maiden, he went to Fensal Hall, where dwelt Balder's mother. The fair Asa-queen was busy at her distaff, with her golden spindles, spinning flax to be woven into fine linen for the gods. And her maid-servant, Fulla of the flowing hair, sat on a stool beside her. When the queen saw Loki, she asked,—

"Whence come you, fair stranger? and what favor would you ask of Odin's wife?"

"I come," answered the disguised Loki, "from the plains of Ida, where the gods meet for pleasant pastime, as well as to talk of the weightier matters of their kingdom."

"And how do they while away their time to-day?" asked the queen.

"They have a pleasant game which they call Balder's Honor," was the answer. "The shining hero stands before them as a target, and each one tries his skill at hurling some weapon toward him. First Odin throws at him the spear Gungner, which never before was known to miss its mark; but it passes harmlessly over Balder's head. Then Thor takes up a huge rock, and hurls it full at Balder's breast; but it turns in its course, and will not smite the sun-bright target. Then Tyr seizes a battle-axe, and strikes at Balder as though he would hew him down; but the keen edge refuses to touch him: and in this way the Asa-folk show honor to the best of their number."

The Asa-queen smiled in the glad pride of her mother-heart, and said, "Yes, every thing shows honor to the best of Odin's sons; for neither metal nor wood nor stone nor fire nor water will touch Balder to do him harm."

"Is it true, then," asked Loki, "that every thing has made an oath to you, and promised not to hurt your son?"

And the queen, not thinking what harm an unguarded word might do, answered, "Every thing has promised, save a little feeble sprig that men call the mistletoe. So small and weak it is, that I knew it could never harm any one; and so I passed it by, and did not ask it to take the oath."

Then Loki went out of Fensal Hall, and left the Asa-queen at her spinning. And he walked briskly away, and paused not until he came to the eastern side of Valhal, where, on the branches of an old oak, the mistletoe grew. Rudely he tore the plant from its supporting branch, and hid it under his cloak. Then he walked leisurely back to the place where the Asa-folk were wont to meet in council.

The next day the Asas went out, as usual, to engage in pleasant pastimes on the plains of Ida. When they had tired of leaping and foot-racing and tilting, they placed Balder before them as a target again; and, as each threw his weapon toward the shining mark, they laughed to see the missile turn aside from its course, and refuse to strike the honored one. But blind Hoder stood sorrowfully away from the others, and did not join in any of their sports. Loki, seeing this, went to him and said,—

"Brother of the gloomy brow, why do you not take part with us in our games?"

"I am blind," answered Hoder. "I can neither leap, nor run, nor throw the lance."

"But you can shoot arrows from your bow," said Loki.

"Alas!" said Hoder, "that I can do only as some one shall direct my aim, for I can see no target."

"Do you hear that laughter?" asked Loki. "Thor has hurled the straight trunk of a pine-tree at your brother; and, rather than touch such a glorious mark; it has turned aside, and been shivered to pieces upon the rocks over there. It is thus that the Asa-folk, and all things living and lifeless, honor Balder. Hoder is the only one who hangs his head, and fears to do his part. Come, now, let me fit this little arrow in your bow, and then, as I point it, do you shoot. When you hear the gods laugh, you will know that your arrow has shown honor to the hero by refusing to hit him."

And Hoder, thinking no harm, did as Loki wished. And the deadly arrow sped from the bow, and pierced the heart of shining Balder, and he sank lifeless upon the ground. Then the Asa-folk who saw it were struck speechless with sorrow and dismay; and, had it not been that the Ida plains where they then stood were sacred to peace, they would have seized upon Loki, and put him to death.

Forthwith the world was draped in mourning for Balder the Good; the birds stopped singing, and flew with drooping wings to the far South-land; the beasts sought to hide themselves in their lairs and in the holes of the ground; the trees shivered and sighed until their leaves fell withered to the earth; the flowers closed their eyes, and died; the rivers stopped flowing, and dark and threatening billows veiled the sea; even the sun shrouded his face, and withdrew silently towards the south.

When Balder's good mother heard the sad news, she left her golden spindle in Fensal Hall, and with her maidens hastened to the Ida-plains, where the body of her son still lay. Nanna, the faithful wife of Balder, was already there; and wild was her grief at sight of the lifeless loved one. And all the Asa-folk—save guilty Loki, who had fled for his life—stood about them in dumb amazement. But Odin was the most sorrowful of all; for he knew, that, with Balder, the world had lost its most gladsome life.

They lifted the body, and carried it down to the sea, where the great ship "Ringhorn," which Balder himself had built, lay ready to be launched. And a great company followed, and stood upon the beach, and bewailed the untimely death of the hero. First came Odin, with his grief-stricken queen, and then his troop of handmaidens, the Valkyrien, followed by his ravens Hugin and Munin. Then came Thor in his goat-drawn car, and Heimdal on his horse Goldtop; then Frey, in his wagon, behind the boar Gullinbruste of the golden bristles. Then Freyja, in her chariot drawn by cats, came weeping tears of gold. Lastly, poor blind Hoder, overcome with grief, was carried thither on the back of one of the Frost-giants. And Old AEgir, the Ocean king, raised his dripping head above the water, and gazed with dewy eyes upon the scene; and the waves, as if affrighted, left off their playing, and were still.

High on the deck they built the funeral-pile; and they placed the body upon it, and covered it with costly garments, and with woods of the finest scent; and the noble horse which had been Balder's they slew, and placed beside him, that he might not have to walk to the halls of Death. And Odin took from his finger the ring Draupner, the earth's enricher, and laid it on the pile. Then Nanna, the faithful wife, was overcome with grief, and her gentle heart was broken, and she fell lifeless at the feet of the Asa-queen. And they carried her upon the ship, and laid her by her husband's side.

When all things were in readiness to set fire to the pile, the gods tried to launch the ship; but it was so heavy that they could not move it. So they sent in haste to Jotunheim for the stout giantess Hyrroken; and she came with the speed of the whirlwind, and riding on a wolf, which she guided with a bridle of writhing snakes.

"What will you have me do?" she asked.

"We would have you launch the great ship 'Ring horn,'" answered Odin.

"That I will do!" roared the grim giantess. And, giving the vessel a single push, she sent it sliding with speed into the deep waters of the bay. Then she gave the word to her grisly steed, and she flew onwards and away, no one knew whither.

The "Ringhorn" floated nobly upon the water,—a worthy bier for the body which it bore. The fire was set to the funeral-pile, and the red flames shot upwards to the sky; but their light was but a flickering beam when matched with the sun-bright beauty of Balder, whose body they consumed.

Then the sorrowing folk turned away, and went back to their homes: a cheerless gloom rested heavily where light gladness had ruled before. And, when they reached the high halls of Asgard, the Asa-queen spoke, and said,—

"Who now, for the love of Balder and his stricken mother, will undertake an errand? Who will go down into the Valley of Death, and seek for Balder, and ransom him, and bring him back to Asgard and the mid-world?"

Then Hermod the Nimble, the brother of Balder, answered, "I will go. I will find him, and, with Hela's leave, will bring him back."

And he mounted Sleipner, the eight-footed steed, and galloped swiftly away. Nine days and nine nights he rode through strange valleys and mountain gorges, where the sun's light had never been, and through gloomy darkness and fearful silence, until he came to the black river, and the glittering, golden bridge which crosses it. Over the bridge his strong horse carried him; although it shook and swayed and threatened to throw him into the raging, inky flood below. On the other side a maiden keeps the gate, and Hermod stopped to pay the toll.

"What is thy name?" she asked.

"My name is Hermod, and I am called the Nimble," he answered.

"What is thy father's name?"

"His name is Odin. Mayhap you have heard of him."

"Why ridest thou with such thunderous speed? Five kingdoms of dead men passed over this bridge yesterday, and it shook not with their weight as it did with thee and thy strange steed. Thou art not of the pale multitude that are wont to pass this gate. What is thy errand? and why ridest thou to the domains of the dead?"

"I go to find my brother Balder," answered Hermod. "It is but a short time since he unwillingly came down into these shades."

"Three days ago," said the maiden, "Balder passed this way, and by his side rode the faithful Nanna. So bright was his presence, even here, that the whole valley was lighted up as it had never before been lighted. The black river glittered like a gem; the frowning mountains smiled for once; and Hela herself, the queen of these regions, slunk far away into her most distant halls. But Balder went on his way, and even now he sups with Nanna in the dark castle over yonder."

Then Hermod rode forward till he came to the castle walls. These were built of black marble; and the iron gate was barred and bolted, and none who went in had ever yet come out. Hermod called loudly to the porter to open the gate and let him in; but no one seemed to hear nor heed him, for the words of the living are unknown in that place. Then he drew the saddle-girths more tightly around the horse Sleipner, and urged him forward. High up, the great horse leaped; and he sprang clear over the gates, and landed at the open door of the great hall. Leaving his steed, Hermod went boldly in;

and there he found his brother Balder and the faithful Nanna seated at the festal board, and honored as the most worthy of all the guests. With Balder, Hermod staid until the night had passed; and many were the pleasant words they spoke. When morning came, Hermod went into the presence of Hela, and said,—

"O mighty queen! I come to ask a boon of thee. Balder the Good, whom both gods and men loved, has been sent to dwell with thee here in thy darksome house; and all the world weeps for him, and has donned the garb of mourning, and cannot be consoled until his bright light shall shine upon them again. And the gods have sent me, his brother, to ask thee to let Balder ride back with me to Asgard, to his noble, sorrowing mother, the Asa-queen; for then will hope live again in the hearts of men, and happiness will return to the earth."

The Death-queen was silent for a moment; and then she said in a sad voice, "Hardly can I believe that any being is so greatly loved by things living and lifeless; for surely Balder is not more the friend of earth than I am, and yet men love me not. But go thou back to Asgard; and, if every thing shall weep for Balder, then I will send him to you. But, if any thing shall refuse to weep, then I will keep him in my halls."

So Hermod made ready to return home; and Balder gave him the ring Draupner to carry to his father as a keepsake; and Nanna sent to the queen-mother a rich carpet of purest green. Then the nimble messenger mounted his horse, and rode swiftly back over the dark river, and through the frowning valleys, until he at last reached Odin's halls.

When the Asa-folk learned upon what terms they might have Balder again with them, they sent heralds all over the world to beseech every thing to mourn for him. And men and beasts, and creeping things, and birds and fishes, and trees and stones, and air and water,—all things, living and lifeless, joined in weeping for the lost Balder.

But, as the heralds were on their way back to Asgard, they met a giantess named Thok, and they asked her to join in the universal grief. And she answered, "What good thing did Balder ever do for Thok? What gladness did he ever bring her? If she should weep for him, it would be with dry tears. Let Hela keep him in her halls."[EN#23]

"And yet the day shall come," added the story-teller, "when the words of the weird woman to Odin shall prove true; and Balder shall come again to rule over a newborn world in which there shall be no wrong-doing and no more death."

Adventure XIV. How Gunther Outwitted Brunhild.

While still the festivities were at their height, an old man of noble mien, and with snow-white beard and hair, came into the great hall, and sang for the gay company. And some whispered that this must be Bragi, for surely such rare music could not be made by any other. But he sang not of spring, as Bragi does, nor yet of youth nor of beauty, nor like one whose home is with the song-birds, and who lives beside the babbling brooks and the leaping waterfalls. His song was a sorrowful one,—of dying flowers, and falling leaves, and the wailing winds of autumn, of forgotten joys, of blasted hopes, of a crushed ambition, of gray hairs, of uttering footsteps, of old age, of a lonely grave. And, as he sang, all were moved to tears by the mournful melody and the sad, sad words.

"Good friend," said Siegfried, "thy music agrees not well with this time and place; for, where nothing but mirth and joy are welcome, thou hast brought sorrowful thoughts and gloomy forebodings. Come, now, and undo the harm thou hast done, by singing a song which shall tell only of mirth and gladness."

The old man shook his head, and answered, "Were I Bragi; as some think I am, or were I even a strolling harper, I might do as you ask. But I am neither, and I know no gladsome songs. Men have called me a messenger of ill omen; and such, indeed, I have sometimes been, although through no wish of my own. I come as a herald from a far-off land, and I bear a message to all the kings and the noblest chiefs of Rhineland. If King Gunther will allow me, I will now make that message known."

"Let the herald speak on," said Gunther graciously.

"Far over the sea," said the herald, "there lies a dreamy land called Isenland; and in that land there is a glorious castle, with six and eighty towers, built of purest marble, green as grass. In that castle there lives the fairest of all Earth's daughters, Brunhild, the maiden of the spring-time. In the early days she was one of Odin's Valkyrien; and with other heavenly maidens it was her duty to follow, unseen, in the wake of armies, and when they met in battle to hover over the field, and with kisses to waken the dead heroes, and lead their souls away to Odin's glad banquet-hall. But upon a day she failed to do the All-Father's bidding, and he, in anger, sent her to live among men, and like them to be short-lived, and subject to old age and death. But the childless old king of Isenland took pity upon the friendless maiden, and called her his daughter, and made her his heir. Then Odin, still more angered, sent the thorn of sleep to wound the princess. And sleep seized upon every creature in Isenland, and silence reigned in the halls of the marble palace. For Odin said, 'Thus shall they all sleep until the hero comes, who will ride through fire, and awaken Brunhild with a kiss.'

"At last the hero so long waited for came. He passed the fiery barrier safe, and awoke the slumbering maiden; and all the castle sprang suddenly into life again. And Brunhild became known once more as the most glorious princess in this mid-world. But the sun-bright hero who freed her from her prison of sleep vanished from Isenland, and no one knew where he went; but men say that he rides through the noble world, the fairest and the best of kings. And Brunhild has sought for him in many lands; and, although all folk have heard of his deeds, none know where he dwells. And so, as a last resort, she has sent heralds into every land to challenge every king to match his skill with hers in three games of strength,—in casting the spear, in hurling the heavy stone, and in leaping. The one who can equal her in these feats shall be king of Isenland, and share with her the throne of Isenstein. And by this means she hopes to find the long-absent hero; for she believes that there is no other prince on earth whose strength and skill are equal to her own. Many men have already risked their lives in this adventure, and all have failed.

"And now, King Gunther," continued the herald, "I have come by her orders into Rhineland, and I deliver the challenge to you. If you accept, and are beaten, your life is forfeited. If you succeed, the fairest kingdom and the most beautiful queen in the world are yours; for you will have proved that you are at least the equal of the hero whom she seeks. What reply shall I carry back to Isenland?"

King Gunther answered hastily, and as one dazed and in a dream, "Say that I accept the challenge, and that when the spring-time comes again, and the waters in the river are unlocked, I shall go to Isenland, and match my skill and strength with that of the fair and mighty Brunhild."

All who stood around were greatly astonished at Gunther's reply; for, although his mind was somewhat weak, he was not given to rash and hazardous undertakings. And Siegfried, who was at his side, whispered, "Think twice, friend Gunther, ere you decide. You do not know the strength of this mighty but lovely warrior-maiden. Were your strength four times what it is, you could not hope to excel her in those feats. Give up this hasty plan, I pray you, and recall your answer to the challenge. Think no more of such an undertaking, for it surely will cost you your life."

But these warnings, and the words of others who tried to dissuade him, only made Gunther the more determined; and he vowed that nothing should hinder him from undertaking the adventure. Then the dark-browed Hagen said,—

"Our friend Siegfried seems to know much about Isenland and its maiden-queen. And indeed, if there is any truth in hearsay, he has had the best of means for learning. Now, if our good King Gunther has set his mind on going upon this dangerous enterprise, mayhap Siegfried would be willing to bear him company."

Gunther was pleased with Hagen's words; and he said to Siegfried, "My best of friends, go with me to Isenland, and help me. If we do well in our undertaking, ask of me any reward you wish, and I will give it you, so far as in my power lies."

"You know, kind Gunther," answered Siegfried, "that for myself I have no fear; and yet again I would warn you to shun the unknown dangers with which this enterprise is fraught. But if, after all, your heart is set upon it, make ready to start as soon as the warm winds shall have melted the ice from the river. I will go with you."

The king grasped Siegfried's hand, and thanked him heartily.

"We must build a fleet," said he. "A thousand fighting-men shall go with us, and we will land in Isenland with a retinue such as no other prince has had. A number of stanch vessels shall be built at once, and in the early spring they shall be launched upon the Rhine."

Siegfried was amused at Gunther's earnestness, and he answered, "Do not think of taking such a following. You would waste twelve months in building and victualling such a fleet. You would take from Burgundy its only safeguard against foes from without; and, after you should reach Isenland, you would find such a large force to be altogether useless. Take my advice: have one small vessel built and rigged and victualled for the long and dangerous voyage; and, when the time shall come, you and I, and your kinsmen Hagen and Dankwart,—we four only,—will undertake the voyage and the emprise you have decided upon."

Gunther knew that his friend's judgment in this matter was better than his own, and he agreed readily to all of Siegfried's plans.

When, at length, the winter months began to wane, many hands were busy making ready for the voyage. The peerless Kriemhild called together thirty of her maidens, the most skilful seamstresses in Burgundyland, and began the making of rich clothing for her brother and his friends.[EN#24] With her own fair hands she cut out garments from the rarest stuffs,—from the silky skins brought from the sunny lands of Lybia; from the rich cloth of Zazemang, green as clover; from the silk that traders bring from Araby, white as the drifted snow. For seven weeks the clever maidens and their gentle mistress plied their busy needles, and twelve suits of wondrous beauty they made for each of the four heroes. And the princely garments were covered with fine needle-work, and with curious devices all studded with rare and costly jewels; and all were wrought with threads of gold.

Many carpenters and ship-builders were busy with axes and hammers, and flaming forges, working day and night to make ready a vessel new and stanch, to carry the adventurers over the sea. And great stores of food, and of all things needful to their safety or comfort, were brought together and put on board.

Neither were the heroes themselves idle; for when not busy in giving directions to the workmen, or in overseeing the preparations that were elsewhere going on, they spent the time in polishing their armor (now long unused), in looking after their weapons, or in providing for the management of their business while away. And Siegfried forgot not his trusty sword Balmung, nor his cloak of darkness the priceless Tarnkappe, which he had captured from the dwarf Alberich in the Nibelungen Land.

Then the twelve suits of garments which fair fingers had wrought were brought. And when the men tried them on, so faultless was the fit, so rare and perfect was every piece in richness and beauty, that even the wearers were amazed, and all declared that such dazzling and kingly raiment had never before been seen.

At last the spring months had fairly vanquished all the forces of the cold North-land. The warm breezes had melted the snow and ice, and unlocked the river; and the time had come for Gunther and his comrades to embark. The little ship, well victualled, and made stanch and stout in every part, had been launched upon the Rhine; and she waited with flying streamers and impatient sails the coming of her crew. Down the sands at length they came, riding upon their steeds; and behind them followed a train of vassals bearing their kingly garments and their gold-red shields. And on the banks stood many of the noblest folk of Burgundy,—Gernot and the young Giselher, and Ute the queen-mother, and Kriemhild the peerless, and a number of earl-folk, and warriors, and fair dames, and blushing damsels. And the heroes bade farewell to their weeping friends, and went upon the waiting vessel, taking their steeds with them. And Siegfried seized an oar, and pushed the bark off from the shore.

"I myself will be the steersman, for I know the way," he said.

And the sails were unfurled to the brisk south wind, and the vessel sped swiftly toward the sea; and many fair eyes were filled tears as they watched it until it could be seen no more. And with sighs and gloomy forebodings the good people went back to their homes, and but few hoped ever again to see their king and his brave comrades.

Driven by favorable winds, the trusty little vessel sailed gayly down the Rhine, and, ere many days had passed, was out in the boundless sea. For a long time the heroes sailed and rowed through Old AEgir's watery kingdom. But they kept good cheer, and their hearts rose higher and higher; for each day they drew nearer the end of their voyage and the goal of their hopes. At length they came in sight of a far-reaching coast and a lovely land; and not far from the shore they saw a noble fortress, with a number of tall towers pointing toward the sky.

"What land is that?" asked the king.[EN#25]

And Siegfried answered that it was Isenland, and that the fortress which they saw was the Castle of Isenstein and the green marble hall of the Princess Brunhild. But he warned his friends to be very wary when they should arrive at the hall.

"Let all tell this story," said he: "say that Gunther is the king, and that I am his faithful vassal. The success of our undertaking depends on this." And his three comrades promised to do as he advised.

As the vessel neared the shore, the whole castle seemed to be alive. From every tower and turret-window, from every door and balcony, lords and ladies, fighting-men and serving-men, looked out to see what strangers these were who came thus unheralded to Isenland. The heroes went on shore with their steeds, leaving the vessel moored to the bank; and then they rode slowly up the beach, and across the narrow plain, and came to the drawbridge and the great gateway, where they paused.

The matchless Brunhild in her chamber had been told of the coming of the strangers; and she asked the maidens who stood around,—

"Who, think you, are the unknown warriors who thus come boldly to Isenstein without asking leave? What is their bearing? Do they seem to be worthy of our notice? or are they some straggling beggars who have lost their way?"

And one of the maidens, looking through the casement, answered, "The first is a king, I know, from his noble mien and the respect which his fellows pay to him. But the second bears himself with a prouder grace, and seems the noblest of them all. He reminds me much of the brave young Siegfried of former days. Indeed, it must be Siegfried; for he rides a steed with sunbeam mane, which can be none other than Greyfell. The third is a dark and gloomy man: he wears a sullen frown upon his brow, and his eyes seem to shoot quick glances around. How nervously he grasps his sword-hilt, as if ever guarding against surprise! I think his temper must be grim and fiery, and his heart a heart of flint. The fourth and last of the company is young and fair, and of gentle port. Little business has he with rude warriors; and many tears, methinks, would be shed for him at home should harm overtake him. Never before have I seen so noble a company of strangers in Isenland. Their garments are of dazzling lustre; their saddles are covered with gem-stones; their weapons are of unequalled brightness. Surely they are worthy of your notice."

When Brunhild heard that Siegfried was one of the company, she was highly pleased, and she hastened to make ready to meet them in the great hall. And she sent ten worthy lords to open the gate, and to welcome the heroes to Isenland.

When Siegfried and his comrades passed through the great gateway, and came into the castle-yard, their horses were led away to the stables, and the clanging armor and the broad shields and swords which they carried were taken from them, and placed in the castle armory. Little heed was paid to Hagen's surly complaint at thus having every means of defence taken away. He was told that such had always been the rule at Isenstein, and that he, like others, must submit.

After a short delay the heroes were shown into the great hall, where the matchless Brunhild already was awaiting them. Clad in richest raiment, from every fold of which rare jewels gleamed, and wearing a coronet of pearls and gold, the warrior-maiden sat on a throne of snow-white ivory. Five hundred earl-folk and warriors, the bravest in Isenland, stood around her with drawn swords, and fierce, determined looks. Surely men of mettle less heroic than that of the four knights from Rhineland would have quaked with fear in such a presence.

King Gunther and his comrades went forward to salute the queen. With a winning smile she kindly greeted them, and then said to Siegfried, "Gladly do we welcome you back to our land, friend Siegfried, We have ever remembered you as our best friend. May we ask what is your will, and who are these warriors whom you have with you?"

"Most noble queen," answered he, "right thankful am I that you have not forgotten me, and that you should deign to notice me while in the presence of this my liege lord," and he pointed towards King Gunther. "The king of all Burgundy-land, whose humble vassal I am, has heard the challenge you have sent into different lands, and he has come to match his strength with yours."

"Does he know the conditions?" asked Brunhild.

"He does," was the answer. "In case of success, the fairest of women for his queen: in case of failure, death."

"Yet scores of worthy men have made trial, and all have failed," said she. "I warn your liege lord to pause, and weigh well the chances ere he runs so great a risk."

Then Gunther stepped forward and spoke:—

"The chances, fairest queen, have all been weighed, and nothing can change our mind. Make your own terms, arrange every thing as pleases you best. We accept your challenge, and ask to make a trial of our strength."

The warrior-maiden, without more words, bade her servants help her to make ready at once for the contest. She donned a rich war-coat, brought long ago from the far-off Lybian shores,—an armor which, it was said, no sword could dint, and upon which the heaviest stroke of spear fell harmless. Her hemlet was edged with golden lace, and sparkled all over with rich gem-stones. Her lance, of wondrous length, a heavy weight for three stout men, was brought. Her shield was as broad and as bright as the sun, and three spans thick with steel and gold.

While the princess was thus arming herself, the heroes looked on with amazement and fear. But Siegfried, unnoticed, hastened quietly out of the hall, and through the open castle-gate, and sped like the wind to the seashore and to their little ship. There he arrayed himself in the Tarnkappe, and then, silent and unseen, he ran back to his friends in the great hall.

"Be of good cheer," he whispered in the ears of the trembling Gunther.

But the king could not see who it was that spoke to him, so well was the hero hidden in the cloak of darkness. Yet he knew that it must be Siegfried and he felt greatly encouraged.

Hagen's frowning face grew darker, and the uneasy glances which shot from beneath his shaggy eyebrows were not those of fear, but of anger and deep anxiety. Dankwart gave up all as lost, and loudly bewailed their folly.

"Must we, unarmed, stand still and see our liege lord slain for a woman's whim?" he cried. "Had we only our good swords, we might defy this maiden-queen and all her Isenland."

Brunhild overheard his words. Scornfully she called to her servants, "Bring to these boasters their armor, and let them have their keen-edged swords. Brunhild has no fear of such men, whether they be armed or unarmed."

When Hagen and Dankwart felt their limbs again enclosed in steel, and when they held their trusty swords in hand, their uneasiness vanished, and hope returned.

In the castle-yard a space was cleared, and Brunhild's five hundred warriors stood around as umpires. The unseen Siegfried kept close by Gunther's side.

"Fear not," he said. "Do my bidding, and you are safe. Let me take your shield. When the time comes, make you the movements, and trust me to do the work."

Then Brunhild threw her spear at Gunther's shield. The mighty weapon sped through the air with the swiftness of lightning; and, when it struck the shield, both Gunther and the unseen Siegfried fell to the ground, borne down by its weight and the force with which it was thrown. Blood gushed from the nostrils of both; and sad would have been their fate if the friendly Tarnkappe had not hidden Siegfried from sight, and given him the strength of twelve giants. Quickly they rose. And Gunther seemed to pick up the heavy shaft, but it was really Siegfried who raised it from the ground. For one moment he poised the great beam in the air, and then, turning the blunt end foremost, he sent it flying back more swiftly than it had come. It struck the huge shield which Brunhild held before her, with a sound that echoed to the farthest cliffs of Isenland. The warrior-maiden was dashed to the earth; but, rising at once, she cried,—

"That was a noble blow, Sir Gunther. I confess myself fairly outdone. But there are two chances yet, and you will do well if you equal me in those. We will now try hurling the stone, and jumping."

Twelve men came forward, carrying a huge rough stone in weight a ton or more. And Brunhild raised this mass of rock in her white arms, and held it high above her head; then she swung it backwards once, and threw it a dozen fathoms across the castle-yard. Scarcely had it reached the ground when the mighty maiden leaped after, and landed just beside it. And the thousand lookers-on shouted in admiration. But old Hagen bit his unshorn lip, and cursed the day that had brought them to Isenland.

Gunther and the unseen Siegfried, not at all disheartened, picked up the heavy stone, which was half buried in the ground, and, lifting it with seeming ease, threw it swiftly forward. Not twelve, but twenty, fathoms it flew; and Siegfried, snatching up Gunther in his arms, leaped after, and landed close to the castle-wall. And Brunhild believed that Gunther alone had done these great feats through his own strength and skill; and she at once acknowledged herself beaten in the games, and bade her vassals do homage to Gunther as their rightful liege lord.

Alas that the noblest of men-folk should gave stooped to such deed of base deception! The punishment, although long delayed, came surely at last; for not even the highest are exempt from obedience to Heaven's behests and the laws of right.

When the contest was ended, the unseen Siegfried ran quickly back to the little ship, and hastily doffed the magic Tarnkappe. Then, in his own form, he returned to the castle, and leisurely entered the castle-yard. When he met his pleased comrades and the vanquished maiden-queen, he asked in careless tones when the games would begin. All who heard his question laughed; and Brunhild said,—

"Surely, Sir Siegfried, the old sleep-thorn of Isenstein must have caught you, and held you in your ship. The games are over, and Gunther, your liege lord, is the winner."

At this news Siegfried seemed much delighted, as indeed he was. And all went together to the great banquet-hall, where a rich feast was served to our heroes and to the worthy earl-folk and warriors of Isenland.

Adventure XV. In Nibelungen Land Again.

When the folk of Isenland learned that their queen had been outwitted and won by a strange chief from a far-off and unknown land, great was their sorrow and dismay; for they loved the fair maiden-queen, and they feared to exchange her mild reign for that of an untried foreigner. Nor was the queen herself at all pleased with the issue of the late contest. She felt no wish to leave her loved people, and her pleasant home, and the fair island which was her kingdom, to take up her abode in a strange land, as the queen of one for whom she could feel no respect. And every one wondered how it was that a man like Gunther, so commonplace, and so feeble in his every look and act, could have done such deeds, and won the wary warrior-maiden.

"If it had only been Siegfried!" whispered the maidens among themselves.

"If it had only been Siegfried!" murmured the knights and the fighting-men.

"If it had only been Siegfried!" thought the queen, away down in the most secret corner of her heart. And she shut herself up in her room, and gave wild vent to her feelings of grief and disappointment.

Then heralds mounted the swiftest horses, and hurried to every village and farm, and to every high-towered castle, in the land. And they carried word to all of Brunhild's kinsmen and liegemen, bidding them to come without delay to Isenstein. And every man arose as with one accord, and hastened to obey the call of their queen. And the whole land was filled with the notes of busy preparation for war. And day by day to the castle the warriors came and went, and the sound of echoing horse-hoofs, and the rattling of ready swords, and the ringing of the war-shields, were heard on every hand.

"What means this treason?" cried Gunther in dismay. "The coy warrior-maiden would fain break her plighted word; and we, here in our weakness, shall perish from her wrath."

And even old Hagen, who had never felt a fear when meeting a host in open battle, was troubled at the thought of the mischief which was brewing.

"'Tis true, too true," he said, and the dark frown deepened on his face, "that we have done a foolish thing. For we four men have come to this cheerless land upon a hopeless errand; and, if we await the gathering of the storm, our ruin will be wrought." And he grasped his sword-hilt with such force, that his knuckles grew white as he paced fiercely up and down the hall.

Dankwart, too, bewailed the fate that had driven them into this net, from which he saw no way of escape. And both the warriors besought King Gunther to take ship at once, and to sail for Rhineland before it was too late. But Siegfried said,—

"What account will you give to the folk at home, if you thus go back beaten, outwitted, and ashamed? Brave warriors, indeed! we should be called. Wait a few days, and trust all to me. When Brunhild's warriors shall be outnumbered by our own, she will no longer hesitate, and our return to Rhineland shall be a triumphant one; for we shall carry the glorious warrior-queen home with us."

"Yes," answered Hagen, mocking, "we will wait until her warriors are outnumbered by our own. But how long shall that be? Will the lightning carry the word to Burgundy? and will the storm-clouds bring our brave men from across the sea? Had you allowed King Gunther's plans to be followed, they would have been here with us now, and we might have quelled this treason at the first."

And Dankwart said, "By this time the fields of the South-land are green with young corn, and the meadows are full of sweet-smelling flowers, and the summer comes on apace. Why should we stay longer in this chilly and fog-ridden land, waiting upon the whims of a fickle maiden,—as fickle as the winds themselves? Better face the smiles and the jeers of the folk at home than suffer shameful shipwreck in this cold Isenland."

But Siegfried would not be moved by the weak and wavering words of his once valiant comrades.

"Trust me," he said, "and all will yet be well. Wait here but a few days longer in quietness, while I go aboard ship, and fare away. Within three days I will bring to Isenstein a host of warriors such as you have never seen. And then the fickle fancies of Brunhild will flee, and she will no longer refuse to sail with us to the now sunny South-land."

Hagen frowned still more deeply; and as he strode away he muttered, "He only wants to betray us, and leave us to die in this trap which he himself has doubtless set for us."

But Gunther anxiously grasped the hand of Siegfried, and said, "Go! I trust you, and believe in you. But be sure not to linger, for no one knows what a day may bring forth in this uncertain and variable clime."

Without saying a word in reply, Siegfried turned, and hastened down to the shore. Without any loss of time he unmoored the little ship, and stepped aboard. Then he donned his Tarnkappe, spread the sails, and seized the helm; and the vessel, like a bird with woven wings, sped swiftly out of the bay, and Isenstein, with its wide halls and glass-green towers, was soon lost to the sight of the invisible helmsman. For four and twenty hours did Siegfried guide the flying vessel as it leaped from wave to wave, and sent the white foam dashing to left and right like flakes of snow. And late on the morrow he came to a rock-bound coast, where steep cliffs and white mountain-peaks rose up, as it were, straight out of the blue sea. Having found a safe and narrow inlet, he moored his little bark; and, keeping the Tarnkappe well wrapped around him, he stepped ashore. Briskly he walked along the rough shore, and through a dark mountain-pass, until he came to a place well known to him,—a place where, years before, he had seen a cavern's yawning mouth, and a great heap of shining treasures, and two princes dying of hunger. But now, upon the selfsame spot there stood a frowning fortress, dark and gloomy and strong, which Siegfried himself had built in after-years; and the iron gates were barred and bolted fast, and no living being was anywhere to be seen.

Loud and long did Siegfried, wrapped in his cloak of darkness, knock and call outside. At last a grim old giant, who sat within, and kept watch and ward of the gate, cried out,—

"Who knocks there?"

Siegfried, angrily and in threatening tones, answered,—

"Open the gate at once, lazy laggard, and ask no questions. A stranger, who has lost his way among the mountains, seeks shelter from the storm which is coming. Open the gate without delay, or I will break it down upon your dull head."

Then the giant in hot anger seized a heavy iron beam, and flung the gate wide open, and leaped quickly out to throttle the insolent stranger. Warily he glanced around on every side; but Siegfried was clad in the magic Tarnkappe, and the giant could see no one. Amazed and ashamed, he turned to shut the gate, and to go again to his place; for he began to believe that a foolish dream had awakened and deceived him. Then the unseen Siegfried seized him from behind; and though he struggled hard, and fought with furious strength, our hero threw him upon the ground, and bound him with cords of sevenfold strength.

The unwonted noise at the gate rang through the castle, and awakened the sleeping inmates. The dwarf Alberich, who kept the fortress against Siegfried's return, and who watched the Nibelungen treasure, which was stored in the hollow hill, arose, and donned his armor, and hurried to the giant's help. A right stout dwarf was Alberich; and, as we have seen in a former adventure, he was as bold as stout. Armed in a war-coat of steel, he ran out to the gate, flourishing a seven-thonged whip, on each thong of which a heavy golden ball was hung. Great was his amazement and his wrath when he saw the giant lying bound and helpless upon the ground; and with sharp, eager eyes he peered warily around to see if, perchance, he might espy his hidden foe. But, when he could find no one, his anger grew hotter than before, and he swung his golden scourge fiercely about his head. Well was it for Siegfried then, that the Tarnkappe hid him from sight; for the dwarf kept pounding about in air so sturdily and strong, that, even as it was, he split the hero's shield from the centre to the rim. Then Siegfried rushed quickly upon the doughty little fellow, and seized him by his long gray beard, and threw him so roughly upon the ground, that Alberich shrieked with pain.

"Spare me, I pray you," he cried. "I know that you are no mean knight; and, if I had not promised to serve my master Siegfried until death, I fain would acknowledge you as my lord."

But Siegfried bound the writhing dwarf, and placed him, struggling and helpless, by the side of the giant.

"Tell me, now, your name, I pray," said the dwarf; "for I must give an account of this adventure to my master when he comes."

"Who is your master?"

"His name is Siegfried; and he is king of the Nibelungens, and lord, by right, of the great Nibelungen Hoard. To me and to my fellows he long ago intrusted the keeping of this castle and of the Hoard that lies deep hidden in the hollow hill; and I have sworn to keep it safe until his return."

Then Siegfried threw off his Tarnkappe, and stood in his own proper person before the wonder-stricken dwarf.

"Noble Siegfried," cried the delighted Alberich, "right glad I am that you have come again to claim your own. Spare my life, and pardon me, I pray, and let me know what is your will. Your bidding shall be done at once."

"Hasten, then," said Siegfried, loosing him from his bonds,—"hasten, and arouse my Nibelungen hosts. Tell them that their chief has come again to Mist Land, and that he has work for them to do."

Then Alberich, when he had set the giant gatekeeper free, sent heralds to every town and castle in the land to make known the words and wishes of Siegfried. And the gallant Nibelungen warriors, when they heard that their liege lord had come again, sprang up joyously, and girded on their armor, and hastened to obey his summons. And soon the strong-built castle was full of noble men,—of earls, and the faithful liegemen who had known Siegfried of old. And joyful and happy were the words of greeting.

In the mean while, Alberich had busied himself in preparing a great feast for his master and his master's chieftains. In the long low hall that the dwarfs had hollowed out within the mountain's heart, the table was spread, and on it was placed every delicacy that could be wished. There were fruits and wines from the sunny South-land, and snow-white loaves made from the wheat of Gothland, and fish from Old AEgir's kingdom, and venison from the king's wild-wood, and the flesh of many a fowl most delicately baked, and, near the head of the board, a huge wild boar roasted whole. And the hall was lighted by a thousand tapers, each held in the hands of a swarthy elf; and the guests were served by the elf-women, who ran hither and thither, obedient to every call. But Alberich, at Siegfried's desire, sat upon the dais at his lord's right hand. Merriment ruled the hour, and happy greetings were heard on every side. And, when the feast was at its height, a troop of hill-folk came dancing into the hall; and a hundred little fiddlers, perched in the niches of the wall, made merry music, and kept time for the busy, clattering little feet. And when the guests had tired of music and laughter, and the dancers had gone away, and the tables no longer groaned under the weight of good cheer Siegfried and his earls still sat at their places, and beguiled the hours with pleasant talk and with stories of the earlier days. And Alberich, as the master of the feast, told a tale of the dwarf-folk, and how once they were visited in their hill-home by Loki the Mischief-maker.

Alberich's Story.

My story begins with the Asa-folk, and has as much to do with the gods as with my kinsmen the dwarfs. It happened long ago, when the world was young, and the elf-folk had not yet lost all their ancient glory.

Sif, as you all know, is Thor's young wife, and she is very fair. It is said, too, that she is as gentle and lovable as her husband is rude and strong; and that while he rides noisily through storm and wind, furiously fighting the foes of the mid-world, she goes quietly about, lifting up the down-trodden, and healing the broken-hearted. In the summer season, when the Thunderer has driven the Storm-giants back to their mist-hidden mountain homes, and the black clouds have been rolled away, and piled upon each other in the far east, Sif comes gleefully tripping through the meadows, raising up the bruised flowers, and with smiles calling the frightened birds from their hiding-places to frolic and sing in the fresh sunshine again. The growing fields and the grassy mountain slopes are hers; and the rustling green leaves, and the sparkling dewdrops, and the sweet odors of spring blossoms, and the glad songs of the summer-time, follow in her footsteps.

Sif, as I have said, is very fair; and, at the time of my story, there was one thing of which she was a trifle vain. That was her long silken hair, which fell in glossy waves almost to her feet. On calm, warm days, she liked to sit by the side of some still pool, and gaze at her own beauty pictured in the water below, while, like the sea-maidens of old AEgir's kingdom, she combed and braided her rich, flowing tresses. And in all the mid-world nothing has ever been seen so like the golden sunbeams as was Sif's silken hair.

At that time the cunning Mischief-maker, Loki, was still living with the Asa-folk. And, as you well know, this evil worker was never pleased save when he was plotting trouble for those who were better than himself. He liked to meddle with business which was not his own, and was always trying to mar the pleasures of others. His tricks and jokes were seldom of the harmless kind, and yet great good sometimes grew out of them.

When Loki saw how proud Sif was of her long hair, and how much time she spent in combing and arranging it, he planned a very cruel piece of mischief. He hid himself in a little rocky cavern, near the pool where Sif was wont to sit, and slily watched her all the morning as she braided and unbraided her flowing silken locks. At last, overcome by the heat of the mid-day sun, she fell asleep upon the grassy bank. Then the Mischief-maker quietly crept near, and with his sharp shears cut off all that wealth of hair, and shaved her head until it was as smooth as her snow-white hand. Then he hid himself again in the little cave, and chuckled with great glee at the wicked thing he had done.

By and by Sif awoke, and looked into the stream; but she started quickly back with horror and affright at the image which she saw. She felt of her shorn head; and, when she learned that those rich waving tresses which had been her joy and pride were no longer there, she knew not what to do. Hot, burning tears ran down her cheeks, and with sobs and shrieks she began to call aloud for Thor. Forthwith there was a terrible uproar. The lightning flashed, and the thunder rolled, and an earthquake shook the rocks and trees. Loki, looking out from his hiding-place, saw that Thor was coming, and he trembled with fear; for he knew, that, should the Thunderer catch him, he would have to pay dearly for his wicked sport. He ran quickly out of the cavern, and leaped into the river, and changed himself into a salmon, and swam as swiftly as he could away from the shore.

But Thor was not so easily fooled; for he had long known Loki, and was acquainted with all his cunning ways. So when he saw Sif bewailing her stolen hair, and beheld the frightened salmon hurrying alone towards the deep water, he was at no loss to know whose work this mischief was.

Straightway he took upon himself the form of a sea-gull, and soared high up over the water. Then, poising a moment in the air, he darted, swift as an arrow, down into the river. When he arose from the water, he held the struggling salmon tightly grasped in his strong talons.

"Vile Mischief-maker!" cried Thor, as he alighted upon the top of a neighboring crag: "I know thee who thou art; and I will make thee bitterly rue the work of this day. Limb from limb will I tear thee, and thy bones will I grind into powder."

Loki, when he saw that he could not by any means get away from the angry Thunderer, changed himself back to his own form, and humbly said to Thor,—

"What if you do your worst with me? Will that give back a single hair to Sif's shorn head? What I did was only a thoughtless joke, and I really meant no harm. Do but spare my life, and I will more than make good the mischief I have done."

"How can that be?" asked Thor.

"I will hie me straight to the secret smithies of dwarfs," answered Loki; "and those cunning little kinsmen of mine shall make golden tresses for fair Sif, which will grow upon her head like other hair, and cause her to be an hundred-fold more beautiful than before."

Thor knew that Loki was a slippery fellow, and that he did not always do what he promised, and hence he would not let him go. He called to Frey, who had just come up, and said,—

"Come, cousin Frey, help me to rid the world of this sly thief. While I hold fast to his raven hair, and his long slim arms, do you seize him by the heels, and we will give his limbs to the fishes, and his body to the birds, for food."

Loki, now thoroughly frightened, wept, and kissed Frey's feet, and humbly begged for mercy. And he promised that he would bring from the dwarf's smithy, not only the golden hair for Sif, but also a mighty hammer for Thor, and a swift steed for Frey. So earnest were his words, and so pitiful was his plea, that Thor at last set the trembling Mischief-maker free, and bade him hasten away on his errand. Quickly, then, he went in search of the smithy of the dwarfs.

He crossed the desert moorlands, and came, after three days, to the bleak hill-country, and the rugged mountain-land of the South. There the earthquake had split the mountains apart, and dug dark and bottomless gorges, and hollowed out many a low-walled cavern, where the light of day was never seen. Through deep, winding ways, and along narrow crevices,

Loki crept; and he glided under huge rocks, and downward through slanting, crooked clefts, until at last he came to a great underground hall, where his eyes were dazzled by a light which was stronger and brighter than day; for on every side were glowing fires, roaring in wonderful little forges, and blown by wonderful little bellows And the vaulted roof above was thickly set with diamonds and precious stones, that sparkled and shone like thousands of bright stars in the blue sky. And the little dwarfs, with comical brown faces, and wearing strange leathern aprons, and carrying heavy hammers, were hurrying here and there, each busy at his task. Some were smelting pure gold from the coarse rough rocks; others were making precious gems, and rich rare jewels, such as the proudest king would be glad to wear. Here, one was shaping pure, round pearls from dewdrops and maidens' tears; there, another wrought green emeralds from the first leaves of spring. So busy were they all, that they neither stopped nor looked up when Loki came into their hall, but all kept hammering and blowing and working, as if their lives depended upon their being always busy.

After Loki had curiously watched their movements for some time, he spoke to the dwarf whose forge was nearest to him, and made known his errand. But the little fellow was fashioning a flashing diamond, which he called the Mountain of Light; and he scarcely looked up as he answered,—

"I do not work in gold. Go to Ivald's sons: they will make whatever you wish."

To Ivald's sons, then, in the farthest and brightest corner of the hall, Loki went. They very readily agreed to make the golden hair for Sif, and they began the work at once. A lump of purest gold was brought, and thrown into the glowing furnace; and it was melted and drawn, and melted and drawn, seven times. Then it was given to a little brown elf with merry, twinkling eyes, who carried it with all speed to another part of the great hall, where the dwarfs' pretty wives were spinning. One of the little women took the yellow lump from the elf's hands, and laid it, like flax, upon her spinning-wheel. Then she sat down and began to spin; and, as she span, the dwarf-wives sang a strange, sweet song of the old, old days when the dwarf-folk ruled the world. And the tiny brown elves danced gleefully around the spinner, and the thousand little anvils rang out a merry chorus to the music of the singers. And the yellow gold was twisted into threads, and the threads ran into hair softer than silk, and finer than gossamer. And at last the dwarf-woman held in her hand long golden tresses ten times more beautiful than the amber locks that Loki had cut from Sif's fair head. When Ivald's sons, proud of their skill, gave the rare treasure to the Mischief-maker, Loki smiled as if he were well pleased; but in his heart he was angry because the dwarfs had made so fair a piece of workmanship. Then he said,—

"This is, indeed, very handsome, and will be very becoming to Sif. Oh, what an uproar was made about those flaxen tresses that she loved so well! And that reminds me that her husband, the gruff old Giant-killer, wants a hammer. I promised to get him one; and, if I fail, he will doubtless be rude with me. I pray you make such a hammer as will be of most use to him in fighting the Jotuns, and you may win favor both for yourselves and me."

"Not now," said the elder of Ivald's sons. "We cannot make it now; for who would dare to send a present to Thor before he has offered one to Odin, the great All-Father?"

"Make me, then, a gift for Odin," cried Loki; "and he will shelter me from the Thunderer's wrath."

So the dwarfs put iron into their furnace, and heated it to a glowing white-heat; and then they drew it out, and rolled it upon their anvils, and pounded it with heavy hammers, until they had wrought a wondrous spear, such as no man had ever seen. Then they inlaid it with priceless jewels, and plated the point with gold seven times tried.

"This is the spear Gungner," said they. "Take it to the great All-Father as the best gift of his humble earth-workers."

"Make me now a present for Frey the gentle," said Loki. "I owe my life to him; and I have promised to take him a swift steed that will bear him everywhere."

Then Ivald's sons threw gold into the furnace, and blew with their bellows until the very roof of the great cave-hall seemed to tremble, and the smoke rolled up the wide chimney, and escaped in dense fumes from the mountain-top. When they left off working, and the fire died away, a fairy ship, with masts and sails, and two banks of long oars, and a golden dragon stem, rose out of the glowing coals; and it grew in size until it filled a great part of the hall, and might have furnished room for a thousand warriors with their arms and steeds. Then, at a word from the dwarfs, it began to shrink, and it became smaller and smaller until it was no broader than an oak-leaf. And the younger of Ivald's sons folded it up like a napkin, and gave it to Loki, saying,—

"Take this to Frey the gentle. It is the ship Skidbladner. When it is wanted for a voyage, it will carry all the Asa-folk and their weapons and stores; and, no matter where they wish to go, the wind will always drive it straight to the desired port. But, when it is not needed, the good Frey may fold it up, as I have done, and carry it safely in his pocket."

Loki was much pleased; and, although he felt disappointed because he had no present for Thor, he heartily thanked the dwarfs for their kindness;

and taking the golden hair, and the spear Gungner, and the ship Skidbladner, he bade Ivald's sons good-by, and started for home. But, before he reached the narrow doorway which led out of the cave, he met two crooked-backed dwarfs, much smaller and much uglier than any he had seen before.

"What have you there?" asked one of them, whose name was Brok.

"Hair for Sif, a spear for Odin, and a ship for Frey," answered Loki.

"Let us see them," said Brok.

Loki kindly showed them the strange gifts, and told them, that, in his belief, no dwarfs in all the world had ever before wrought such wonderful things.

"Who made them?" inquired Brok.

"Ivald's sons."

"Ah! Ivald's sons sometimes do good work, but there are many other dwarfs who can do better. For instance, my brother Sindre, who stands here, can make three other treasures altogether as good as those you have."

"It cannot be!" cried Loki.

"I tell you the truth," said the dwarf. "And, to show you that I mean just what I say, I will wager against your head all the diamonds in the ceiling above us, that he will make not only as good treasures, but those which the Asas will esteem much higher."

"Agreed!" cried Loki,—"agreed! I take the wager. Let your brother try his skill at once."

The three went straightway to Sindre's forge, and the brothers began their task. When the fire was roaring hot, and the sparks flew from the chimney like showers of shooting-stars, Sindre put a pig-skin into the furnace, and bade Brok blow the bellows with all his might, and never stop until he should speak the word. The flames leaped up white and hot, and the furnace glowed with a dazzling light, while Brok plied the bellows, and Sindre, with unblinking eyes, watched the slowly changing colors that played around the melted and shapeless mass within. While the brothers were thus intent upon their work, Loki changed himself to a great horse-fly, and settled upon Brok's hand, and bit him without mercy. But the dwarf kept on blowing the bellows, and stopped not until his brother cried out,—

"Enough!"

Then Sindre drew out of the flickering blue flames a huge wild boar with long tusks of ivory, and golden bristles that glittered and shone like the beams of the sun.

"This is Golden Bristle," said the dwarf. "It is the gift of Brok and his brother to the gentle Frey. His ship Skidbladner can carry him only over the sea; but Golden Bristle shall be a trusty steed that will bear him with the speed of the wind over the land or through the air."

Next the dwarfs threw gold into the furnace, and Brok plied the bellows, and Sindre gazed into the flames, as before. And the great horse-fly buzzed in Brok's face, and darted at his eyes, and at last settled upon his neck, and stung him until the pain caused big drops of sweat to roll off of his forehead. But the dwarf stopped not nor faltered, until his brother again cried out,—

"Enough!"

This time Sindre drew out a wondrous ring of solid gold, sparkling all over with the rarest and most costly jewels.

"This is the ring Draupner," said he. "It is well worthy to be worn on Odin's finger. Every ninth day eight other rings, equal to it in every way, shall drop from it. It shall enrich the earth, and make the desert blossom as the rose; and it shall bring plentiful harvests, and fill the farmers' barns with grain, and their houses with glad good cheer. Take it to the All-Father as the best gift of the earth-folk to him and to mankind."

After this the dwarfs took iron which had been brought from the mountains of Norse Land; and, after beating it upon their bellows until it glowed white and hot, Sindre threw it into the furnace.

"This shall be the gift of gifts," said he to Brok. "Ply the bellows as before, and do not, for your life, stop or falter until the work is done."

But as Brok blew the bellows, and his brother gazed into the glowing fire, the horse-fly came again. This time he settled between the dwarf's eyes, and stung his eyelids until the blood filled his eyes, and ran down his cheeks, and blinded him so that he could not see. At last, in sore distress, and wild with pain, Brok let go of the bellows, and lifted his hand to drive the fly away. Then Sindre drew his work out of the furnace. It was a blue steel hammer, well made in every way, save that the handle was half an inch too short.

"This is the mighty Mjolner," said Sindre to Loki, who had again taken his proper shape. "The Thunderer may have the hammer that you promised him; although it is our gift, and not yours. The stoutest giant will not be able now to cope with Thor. No shield nor armor, nor mountain-wall, nor, indeed, any thing on earth, shall be proof against the lightning-strokes of Mjolner."

And Brok took the three treasures which Sindre had fashioned, and went with Loki to Asgard, the home of the Asa-folk. And they chose Odin and Thor and Frey to examine and judge which was best,—Loki's three gifts, the work of Ivald's sons; or Brok's three gifts, the work of Sindre. When the judges were seated, and all were in readiness, Loki went forward and gave to Odin the spear Gungner, that would always hit the mark; and to Frey he gave the ship Skidbladner, that would sail whithersoever he wished. Then he gave the golden hair to Thor, who placed it upon the head of fair Sif; and it grew there, and was a thousand-fold more beautiful than the silken tresses she had worn before.

After the Asas had carefully looked at these treasures, and talked of their merits, little Brok came humbly forward and offered his gifts. To Odin he gave the precious ring Draupner, already dropping richness. To Frey he gave the boar Golden Bristle, telling him that wherever he chose to go this steed would serve him well, and would carry him faster than any horse, while his shining bristles would light the way on the darkest night or in the gloomiest path. At last he gave to Thor the hammer Mjolner, and said that it, like Odin's spear, would never miss the mark, and that whatever it struck, it would crush in pieces, and whithersoever it might be hurled, it would come back to his hand again.

Then the Asas declared at once that Thor's hammer was the best of all the gifts, and that the dwarf had fairly won the wager. But, when Brok demanded Loki's head as the price of the wager, the cunning Mischief-maker said,—

"My head is, by the terms of our agreement, yours; but my neck is my own, and you shall not on any account touch or harm it."[EN#26]

So Brok went back to his brother and his smithy without the head of Loki, but he was loaded with rich and rare presents from the Asa-folk.

Adventure XVI. How Brunhild Was Welcomed Home.

When the next morning's sun arose, and its light gilded the mountain peaks, and fell in a flood of splendor down upon the rich uplands and the broad green fields of Nibelungen Land, Siegfried, with his earls and mighty men, rode through the valley, and down to the seashore. There a pleasant sight met his eyes: for the little bay was white with the sails of a hundred gold-beaked vessels which lay at anchor; and on the sandy beach there stood in order three thousand island warriors,—the bravest and the best of all the Nibelungens,—clad in armor, and ready to hear and to do their master's bidding. And Siegfried told them why he had thus hastily called them together; and he gave to each one rich gifts of gold and jewels and costly raiment. Then he chose from among them one thousand of the most trustworthy, who should follow him back to Isenland; and these went aboard the waiting vessels, amid the cheers and the farewells of their comrades who were left behind. And when every thing was in readiness, the anchors were hoisted and the sails were set, and the little fleet, wafted by pleasant winds, sailed out of the bay, and eastward across the calm blue sea. And Siegfried's vessel, with a golden dragon banner floating from the masthead, led all the rest.

On the fourth day after Siegfried's departure from Isenland, Dankwart and grim old Hagen sat in a room of the castle at Isenstein. Outside and below they heard the fair-haired warriors of Queen Brunhild pacing to and fro, and ready, at a word, to seize upon the strangers, and either to put them to death, or to drive them forever from the land. Old Hagen's brows were closely knit, and his face was dark as a thunder-cloud, and his hands played nervously with his sword-hilt, as he said,—

"Where now is Gunther, the man whom we once called king?"

"He is standing on the balcony above, talking with the queen and her maidens," answered Dankwart.

"The craven that he is!" cried Hagen hoarsely. "Once he was a king, and worthy to be obeyed; but now who is the king? That upstart Siegfried has but to say what shall be done, and our master Gunther, blindly and like a child, complies. Four days ago we might have taken ship, and sailed safely home. Now our vessel is gone, the boasted hero is gone, and nothing is left for us to do but to fight and die."

"But we are sure of Odin's favor," returned Dankwart; and a wild light gleamed from his eyes, and he brandished his sword high over his head. "A place in Valhal is promised to us; for, him who bravely dies with his blood-stained sword beside him and his heart unrent with fears, the All-Father's victory-wafters will gently carry home. Even now, methinks, I sit in the banqueting-hall of the heroes, and quaff the flowing mead."

In the mean while Gunther stood with Queen Brunhild at an upper window, and looked out upon the great sea that spread forever and away towards the setting sun. And all at once, as if by magic, the water was covered with white-sailed ships, which, driven by friendly winds and the helping hands of AEgir's daughters and the brawny arms of many a stalwart oarsman, came flying towards the bay.

"What ships are those with the snow-white sails and the dragon-stems?" asked Brunhild, wondering.

Gunther gazed for a moment towards the swift-coming fleet, and his eyes were gladdened with the sight of Siegfried's dragon-banner floating from the vessel in the van. A great load seemed lifted from his breast, for now he knew that the hoped-for help was at hand. And, smiling he answered the queen,—

"Those white-sailed ships are mine. My body-guard—a thousand of my trustiest fighting-men—are on board, and every man is ready to die for me."

And as the vessels came into the harbor, and the sailors furled the sails, and cast the anchors into the sea, Siegfried was seen standing on the golden prow of his ship, arrayed in princely raiment, with his earls and chiefs around him. And their bright armor glittered in the sunlight, and their burnished shields shone like so many golden mirrors. A fairer sight had the folk of Isenstein never seen.

Long and earnestly Queen Brunhild gazed, and then, turning away, she burst into tears; for she knew that she had been again outwitted, and that it was vain for her to struggle against the Norns' decrees. Then, crushing back the grief and the sore longing that rose in her heart, she spoke again to Gunther, and her eyes shone stern and strange.

"What now will you have me do?" she asked; "for you have fairly won me, and my wayward fancies shall no longer vex you. Shall I greet your friends with kindness, or shall we send them back again over the sea?"

"I pray you give them welcome to the broad halls of Isenstein," he answered; "for no truer, nobler men live than these my liegemen."

So the queen sent word to Siegfried and his Nibelungen warriors to leave the ships and come ashore. And she herself, as radiant now as a morning in

May, went down to meet them and welcome them. Then she had a great feast made in honor of the heroes, and the long, low-raftered feast-hall rang with the sounds of merriment, instead of with the clash of arms. The fair-haired, blue-eyed warriors of the queen sat side by side with the tall strangers from over the sea. And in the high-seat was Brunhild, her face exceeding pale, yet beauteous to behold; and by her side sat Gunther, smiling and glad, and clad in his kingly raiments. And around them were the earls and chieftains, and many a fair lady of Isenland, and Hagen, smiling through his frowns, and Dankwart, now grown fearless, and Siegfried sad and thoughtful. Mirth and gladness ruled the hour, and not until the morning star began to fade in the coming sunlight did the guests retire to rest.

Only a few days longer did the heroes tarry in Isenland; for the mild spring days were growing warmer, and all faces were southward turned, and the queen herself was anxious to haste to her South-land home. When, at last, the time for leave-taking came, the folk of Isenland gathered around to bid their queen Godspeed. Then Brunhild called to Dankwart, and gave him her golden keys, and bade him unlock her closets where her gold and jewels were stored, and to scatter with hands unstinted her treasures among the poor. And many were the tearful blessings, and many the kind words said, as the radiant queen went down to the waiting, white-winged vessel, and stepped aboard with Gunther and the heroes of the Rhine. But she was not to go alone to the land of strangers; for with her were to sail a hundred fair young damsels, and more than fourscore noble dames, and two thousand blue-eyed warriors, the bravest of her land.

When all had gone on board the waiting fleet, the anchors were hoisted, and the sails were unfurled to the breeze; and amid the tearful farewells of friends, and the joyful shouting of the sailors, the hundred heavy-laden vessels glided from the bay, and were soon far out at sea. And the sorrowing folk of Isenland turned away, and went back to their daily tasks, and to the old life of mingled pain and pleasure, of shadow and sunshine; and they never saw their loved warrior-queen again.

The gay white fleet, with its precious cargo of noble men and fair ladies, sped swiftly onwards through Old AEgir's kingdom; and it seemed as if Queen Ran had forgotten to spread her nets, so smooth and quiet was the sea; and the waves slept on the peaceful bosom of the waters: only Ripple and Sky-clear danced in the wake of the flying ships, and added to the general joy. And on shipboard music and song enlivened the dragging hours; and from morn till eve no sounds were heard, save those of merriment and sport, and glad good cheer. Yet, as day after day passed by, and no sight met their eyes but the calm blue waters beneath, and the calm blue sky above, all began to wish for a view, once more, of the solid earth, and the fields, and the wild greenwood. But the ships sailed steadily onward, and every hour brought them nearer and nearer to the wished-for haven.

At length, on the ninth day, they came in sight of a long, flat coast, stretching far away towards the Lowlands, where Old AEgir and his daughters—sometimes by wasting warfare, sometimes by stealthy strategy—ever plot and toil to widen the Sea-king's domains. When the sailors saw the green shore rising up, as it were, out of the quiet water, and the wild woodland lying dense and dark beyond, and when they knew that they were nearing the end of their long sea-voyage, they rent the air with their joyful shouts. And a brisker breeze sprang up, and filled the sails, and made the ships leap forward over the water, like glad living creatures.

It was then that the thought came to King Gunther that he ought to send fleet heralds to Burgundy-land to make known the happy issue of his bold emprise, and to tell of his glad home-coming, with Brunhild, the warrior-maiden, as his queen. So he called old Hagen to him, and told him of his thoughts, and asked him if he would be that herald.

"Nay," answered the frowning chief. "No bearer of glad tidings am I. To every man Odin has given gifts. To some he has given light hearts, and cheery faces, and glad voices; and such alone are fitted to carry good news and happy greetings. To others he has given darker souls, and less lightsome faces, and more uncouth manners; and these may bear the brunt of the battle, and rush with Odin's heroes to the slaughter: but they would be ill at ease standing in the presence of fair ladies, or telling glad tidings at court. Let me still linger, I pray, on board this narrow ship, and send your friend Siegfried as herald to Burgundy-land. He is well fitted for such a duty."

So Gunther sent at once for Siegfried, to whom, when he had come, he said,—

"My best of friends, although we are now in sight of land, our voyage still is a long one; for the river is yet far away, and, when it is reached, its course is winding, and the current will be against us, and our progress must needs be slow. The folk at home have had no tidings from us since we left them in the early spring; and no doubt their hearts grow anxious, and they long to hear of our whereabouts, and whether we prosper or no. Now, as we near the headland which juts out dark and green before us, we will set you on shore, with the noble Greyfell, and as many comrades as you wish, to haste with all speed to Burgundy, to tell the glad news of our coming to the loved ones waiting there."

Siegfried at first held back, and tried to excuse himself from undertaking this errand,—not because he felt any fear of danger, but because he scorned to be any man's thrall, to go and do at his beck and bidding. Then Gunther spoke again, and in a different tone.

"Gentle Siegfried," he said, "if you will not do this errand for my sake, I pray that you will undertake it for the sake of my sister, the fair Kriemhild, who has so long waited for our coming."

Then willingly did the prince agree to be the king's herald. And on the morrow the ship touched land; and Siegfried bade his companions a short farewell, and went ashore with four and twenty Nibelungen chiefs, who were to ride with him to Burgundy. And, when every thing was in readiness, he mounted the noble Greyfell, as did also each warrior his favorite steed, and they galloped briskly away; and their glittering armor and nodding plumes were soon lost to sight among the green trees of the wood. And the ship which bore Gunther and his kingly party weighed anchor, and moved slowly along the shore towards the distant river's mouth.

For many days, and through many strange lands, rode Siegfried and his Nibelungen chiefs. They galloped through the woodland, and over a stony waste, and came to a peopled country rich in farms and meadows, and dotted with pleasant towns. And the folk of that land wondered greatly at sight of the radiant Siegfried, and the tall warriors with him, and their noble steeds, and their sunbright armor. For they thought that it was a company of the gods riding through the mid-world, as the gods were wont to do in the golden days of old. So they greeted them with smiles, and kind, good words, and scattered flowers and blessings in their way.

They stopped for a day in Vilkina-land, where dwelt one Eigill, a famous archer, who, it is said, was a brother of Veliant, Siegfried's fellow-apprentice in the days of his boyhood. And men told them this story of Eigill. That once on a time old Nidung, the king of that land, in order to test his skill with the bow, bade him shoot an apple, or, as some say, an acorn, from the head of his own little son. And Eigill did this; but two other arrows, which he had hidden beneath his coat, dropped to the ground. And when the king asked him what these were for he answered, "To kill thee, wretch, had I slain my child."[EN#27]

After this our heroes rode through a rough hill-country, where the ground was covered with sharp stones, and the roads were steep and hard. And their horses lost their shoes, and were so lamed by the travel, that they were forced to turn aside to seek the house of one Welland, a famous smith, who re-shod their steeds, and entertained them most kindly three days and nights. And it is said by some that Welland is but another name for Veliant, and that this was the selfsame foreman whom we knew in

Siegfried's younger days. But, be this as it may, he was at this time the master of all smiths, and no one ever wrought more cunningly. And men say that his grandfather was Vilkinus, the first king of that land; and that his grandmother, Wachitu, was a fair mermaid, who lived in the deep green sea; and that his father, Wada, had carried him, when a child, upon his shoulders through water five fathoms deep, to apprentice him to the cunning dwarfs, from whom he learned his trade. And if this story is true, he could not have been Veliant. He was wedded to a beautiful lady, who sometimes took the form of a swan, and flew away to a pleasant lake near by, where, with other swan-maidens, she spent the warm summer days among the reeds and the water-lilies. And many other strange tales were told of Welland the smith: how he had once made a boat from the single trunk of a tree, and had sailed in it all around the mid-world; how, being lame in one foot, he had forged a wondrous winged garment, and flown like a falcon through the air; and how he had wrought for Beowulf, the Anglo-Saxon hero, a gorgeous war-coat that no other smith could equal.[EN#28] And so pleasantly did Welland entertain his guests that they were loath to leave him; but on the fourth day they bade him farewell, and wended again their way.

Now our heroes rode forward, with greater speed than before, across many a mile of waste land, and over steep hills, and through pleasant wooded dales. Then, again, they came to fair meadows, and broad pasture-lands, and fields green with growing corn; and every one whom they met blessed them, and bade them a hearty God-speed. Then they left the farmlands and the abodes of men far behind them; and they passed by the shore of a sparkling lake, where they heard the swan-maidens talking to each other as they swam among the rushes, or singing in silvery tones of gladness as they circled in the air above. Then they crossed a dreary moor, where nothing grew but heather; and they climbed a barren, stony mountain, where the feet of men had never been, and came at last to a wild, dark forest, where silence reigned undisturbed forever.

It was the wood in which dwells Vidar, the silent god, far from the sound of man's busy voice, in the solemn shade of century-living oaks and elms. There he sits in quiet but awful grandeur,—strong almost as Thor, but holding his mighty strength in check. Hoary and gray, he sits alone in Nature's temple, and communes with Nature's self, waiting for the day when Nature's silent but resistless forces shall be quickened into dread action. His head is crowned with sear and yellow leaves, and long white moss hangs pendent from his brows and cheeks, and his garments are rusted with age. On his feet are iron shoes, with soles made thick with the scraps of leather gathered through centuries past; and with these, it is said, he shall, in the last great twilight of the mid-world, rend the jaws of the Fenris-wolf.[EN#29]

"Who is this Fenris-wolf?" asked one of the Nibelungens as they rode through the solemn shadows of the wood.

And Siegfried thereupon related how that fierce creature had been brought up and cared for by the Asa-folk; and how, when he grew large and strong, they sought to keep him from doing harm by binding him with an iron chain called Leding. But the strength of the monster was so great, that he burst the chain asunder, and escaped. Then the Asas made another chain twice as strong, which they called Drome. And they called to the wolf, and besought him to allow them to bind him again, so that, in bursting the second chain, he might clear up all doubts in regard to his strength. Flattered by the words of the Asas, the wolf complied; and they chained him with Drome, and fastened him to a great rock. But Fenris stretched his legs, and shook himself, and the great chain was snapped in pieces. Then the Asas knew that there was no safety for them so long as a monster so huge and terrible was unbound; and they besought the swarthy elves to forge them another and a stronger chain. This the elves did. They made a most wondrous chain, smooth as silk, and soft as down, yet firmer than granite, and stronger than steel. They called it Gleipner; and it was made of the sinews of a bear, the footsteps of a cat, the beard of a woman, the breath of a fish, the sweat of a bird, and the roots of a mountain. When the Asas had obtained this chain, they lured the Fenris-wolf to the rocky Island of Lyngve, and by flattery persuaded him to be bound again. But this he would not agree to do until Tyr placed his hand in his mouth as a pledge of good faith. Then they tied him as before, and laughingly bade him break the silken cord. The huge creature stretched himself as before, and tried with all his might to burst away; but Gleipner held him fast, and the worst that he could do was to bite off the hand of unlucky Tyr. And this is why Tyr is called the one-armed god.

"But it is said," added Siegfried, "that in the last twilight the Fenris-wolf will break his chain, and that he will swallow the sun, and slay the great Odin himself, and that none can subdue him save Vidar the Silent."

It was thus that the heroes conversed with each other as they rode through the silent ways of the wood.

At length, one afternoon in early summer, the little company reached the Rhine valley; and looking down from the sloping hill-tops, green with growing corn, they saw the pleasant town of the Burgundians and the high gray towers of Gunther's dwelling. And not long afterwards they rode through the streets of the old town, and, tired and travel-stained, halted outside of the castle-gates. Very soon it became noised about that Siegfried and a company of strange knights, fair and tall, had come again to Burgundy and to the home of the Burgundian kings. But when it was certainly known that neither Gunther the king, nor Hagen of the evil eye, nor Dankwart his brother, had returned, the people felt many sad misgivings; for they greatly feared that some hard mischance had befallen their loved king. Then Gernot and the young Giselher, having heard of Siegfried's arrival, came out with glad but anxious faces to greet him.

"Welcome, worthy chief!" they cried. "But why are you alone? What are your tidings? Where is our brother? and where are our brave uncles, Hagen and Dankwart? And who are those strange, fair men who ride with you? And what about Brunhild, the warrior-maiden? Alas! if our brother has fallen by her cruel might, then woe to Burgundy! Tell us quickly all about it!"

"Have patience, friends!" answered Siegfried. "Give me time to speak, and I will gladden the hearts of all the folk of Burgundy with my news. Your brother Gunther is alive and well; and he is the happiest man in the whole mid-world, because he has won the matchless Brunhild for his bride. And he is ere now making his way up the river with a mighty fleet of a hundred vessels and more than two thousand warriors. Indeed, you may look for him any day. And he has sent me, with these my Nibelungen earls, to bid you make ready for his glad home-coming."

Then, even before he had alighted from Greyfell, he went on to tell of the things that had happened at Isenstein; but he said nothing of the part which he had taken in the strange contest. And a crowd of eager listeners stood around, and heard with unfeigned joy of the happy fortune of their king.

"And now," said Siegfried to Giselher, when he had finished his story, "carry the glad news to your mother and your sister; for they, too, must be anxious to learn what fate has befallen King Gunther."

"Nay," answered the prince, "you yourself are the king's herald, and you shall be the one to break the tidings to them. Full glad they'll be to hear the story from your own lips, for long have they feared that our brother would never be seen by us again. I will tell them of your coming, but you must be the first to tell them the news you bring."

"Very well," answered Siegfried. "It shall be as you say."

Then he dismounted from Greyfell, and, with his Nibelungen earls, was shown into the grand hall, where they were entertained in a right kingly manner.

When Kriemhild the peerless, and Ute her mother, heard that Siegfried had come again to Burgundy, and that he brought news from Gunther the king, they hastened to make ready to see him. And, when he came before them, he seemed so noble, so bright, and so glad, that they knew he bore no evil tidings.

"Most noble prince," said Kriemhild, trembling in his presence, "right welcome are you to our dwelling! But wherefore are you come? How fares my brother Gunther? Why came he not with you back to Burgundy-land? Oh! undone are we, if, through the cruel might of the warrior-queen, he has been lost to us."

"Now give me a herald's fees!" cried Siegfried, laughing. "King Gunther is alive and well. In the games of strength to which fair Brunhild challenged him, he was the winner. And now he comes up the Rhine with his bride, and a great retinue of lords and ladies and fighting-men. Indeed, the sails of his ships whiten the river for miles. And I am come by his desire to ask that every thing be made ready for his glad home-coming and the loving welcome of his peerless queen."

Great was the joy of Kriemhild and her queenly mother when they heard this gladsome news; and they thanked the prince most heartily for all that he had done.

"You have truly earned a herald's fee," said the lovely maiden, "and gladly would I pay it you in gold; for you have cheered us with pleasant tidings, and lightened our minds of a heavy load. But men of your noble rank take neither gifts nor fees, and hence we have only to offer our deepest and heartiest thanks."

"Not so," answered Siegfried gayly. "Think not I would scorn a fee. Had I a kingdom of thirty realms, I should still be proud of a gift from you."

"Then, you shall have your herald's fee!" cried Kriemhild; and she sent her maidens to fetch the gift. And with her own lily hands she gave him twenty golden bracelets, richly inwrought with every kind of rare and costly gem-stones. Happy, indeed, was Siegfried to take such priceless gift from the hand of so peerless a maiden; and his face shone radiant with sunbeams as he humbly bowed, and thanked her. But he had no need for the jewels, nor wished he to keep them long: so he gave them, with gracious wishes, to the fair young maidens at court.

From this time forward, for many days, there was great bustle in Gunther's dwelling. On every side was heard the noise of busy hands, making ready for the glad day when the king should be welcomed home. The broad halls and the tall gray towers were decked with flowers, and floating banners, and many a gay device; the houses and streets of the pleasant burgh put on their holiday attire; the shady road which led through Kriemhild's rose-garden down to the river-banks was dusted and swept with daily care; and the watchman was cautioned to keep on the lookout every moment for the coming of the expected fleet. And heralds had been sent to every burgh and castle, and to every countryside in Burgundy, announcing the happy home-coming of Gunther and his bride, and bidding every one, both high and low, to the glad merry-making.

On the morning of the eleventh day, ere the sun had dried the dew from the springing grass, the keen-eyed watchman, in his perch on the topmost tower, cried out in happy accents to the waiting folk below,—

"They come at last! I see the white-winged ships still far down the stream. But a breeze springs up from the northward, and the sailors are at the oars, and swift speed the hastening vessels, as if borne on the wings of the wind. Ride forth, O ye brave and fair, to welcome the fair and the brave!"

Then quickly the king-folk, and the warriors, and fair ladies, mounted their ready steeds, and gayly through the gates of the castle they rode out river-wards. And Ute, the noble queen-mother, went first. And the company moved in glittering array, with flying banners, and music, and the noisy flourish of drums, adown the rose-covered pathway which led to the water's side. And the peerless Kriemhild followed, with a hundred lovely maidens, all mounted on snow-white palfreys; and Siegfried, proud and happy, on Greyfell, rode beside her.

When the party reached the river-bank, a pleasant sight met their eyes; for the fleet had now drawn near, and the whole river, as far as the eye could reach, glittered with the light reflected from the shield-hung rails and the golden prows of the swift-coming ships. King Gunther's own vessel led all the rest; and the king himself stood on the deck, with the glorious Brunhild by his side. Nearer and nearer the fresh breeze of the summer morning wafted the vessel to the shore, where stood the waiting multitude. Softly the golden dragon glided in to the landing-place, and quickly was it moored to the banks; then Gunther, clad in his kingly garments, stepped ashore, and with him his lovely queen. And a mighty shout of welcome, and an answering shout of gladness, seemed to rend the sky as the waiting hosts beheld the sight. And the queen-mother Ute, and the peerless Kriemhild, and her kingly brothers, went forward to greet the pair. And Kriemhild took Brunhild by the hand, and kissed her, and said,—

"Welcome, thrice welcome, dear sister! to thy home and thy kindred and thy people, who hail thee as queen. And may thy days be full of joyance, and thy years be full of peace!"

Then all the folk cried out their goodly greetings; and the sound of their glad voices rang out sweet and clear in the morning air, and rose up from the riverside, and was echoed among the hill-slopes, and carried over the meadows and vineyards, to the farthest bounds of Burgundy-land. And the matchless Brunhild, smiling, returned the happy greeting; and her voice was soft and sweet, as she said,—

"O kin of the fair Rhineland, and folk of my new-found home! may your days be summer sunshine, and your lives lack grief and pain; and may this hour of glad rejoicing be the type of all hours to come!"

Then the lovely queen was seated in a golden wain which stood in waiting for her; and Gunther mounted his own war-steed; and the whole company made ready to ride to the castle. Never before had so pleasant a sight been seen in Rhineland, as that glorious array of king-folk and lords and ladies wending from river to fortress along the rose-strewn roadway. Foremost went the king, and by his side was Siegfried on the radiant Greyfell. Then came the queen's golden wain, drawn by two snow-white oxen, which were led with silken cords by sweet-faced maidens; and in it, on an ivory throne deep-carved with mystic runes, sat glorious Brunhild. Behind rode the queen-mother and her kingly sons, and frowning Hagen, and Dankwart, and Volker, and all the earl-folk and mighty warriors of Burgundy and of Nibelungen Land. And lastly came Kriemhild and her hundred damsels, sitting on their snow-white steeds. And they rode past the blooming gardens, and through the glad streets of the burgh, and then, like a radiant vision, they entered the castle-halls; and the lovely pageant was seen no more.

For twelve days after this, a joyful high-tide was held at the castle; and the broad halls rang with merriment and music and festive mirth. And games and tournaments were held in honor of the king's return. Brave horsemen dashed here and there at break-neck speed, or contended manfully in the lists; lances flew thick in the air; shouts and glad cries were heard on every hand; and for a time the most boisterous tumult reigned. But gladness and good-feeling ruled the hour, and no one thought of aught but merry-making and careless joy. At length, when the days of feasting were past, the guests bade Gunther and his queen farewell; and each betook himself to his own home, and to whatsoever his duty called him. And one would have thought that none but happy days were henceforth in store for the kingly folk of Burgundy. But alas! too soon the cruel frost and the cold north winds nipped the buds and blossoms of the short summer, and the days of gladness gave place to nights of gloom.

Adventure XVII.
How Siegfried Lived in Nibelungen Land.

When the twelve-days' high-tide at King Gunther's home-coming had been brought to an end, and the guests had all gone to their homes, Siegfried, too, prepared to bid farewell to the Rhineland kings, and to wend to his own country. But he was not to go alone; for Kriemhild, the peerless princess, was to go with him as his bride. They had been wedded during the merry festivities which had just closed, and that event had added greatly to the general joy; for never was there a fairer or a nobler pair than Siegfried the fearless, and Kriemhild the peerless.

"It grieves my heart to part with you," said Gunther, wringing Siegfried's hand. "It will fare but ill with us, I fear, when we no longer see your radiant face, or hear your cheery voice."

"Say not so, my brother," answered Siegfried; "for the gods have many good things in store for you. And, if ever you need the help of my arm, you have but to say the word, and I will hasten to your aid."

Then the Burgundian kings besought the hero to take the fourth part of their kingdom as his own and Kriemhild's, and to think no more of leaving them. But Siegfried would not agree to this. His heart yearned to see his father and mother once again, and then to return to his own loved Nibelungen Land. So he thanked the kings for their kind offer, and hastened to make ready for his intended journey.

Early on Midsummer Day the hero and his bride rode out of Gunther's dwelling, and turned their faces northward. And with them was a noble retinue of warriors,—five hundred brave Burgundians, with Eckewart as their chief,—who had sworn to be Queen Kriemhild's vassals in her new, far-distant home. Thirty and two fair maidens, too, went with her. And with Siegfried were his Nibelungen earls.

As the company rode down the sands, and filed gayly along the river-road, it seemed a lovely although a sad sight to their kinsmen who gazed after them from the castle-towers. Fair and young were all the folk; and the world, to most, was still untried. And they rode, in the morning sunlight, away from their native land, nor recked that never again would they return. Each warrior sat upon a charger, richly geared with gilt-red saddle, and gorgeous bridle, and trappings of every hue; and their war-coats were bright and dazzling; and their spears glanced in the sun; and their golden shields threw rays of resplendent light around them. The maidens, too, were richly dight in broidered cloaks of blue, and rare stuffs brought from far-off Araby; and each sat on a snow-white palfrey geared with silken housings, and trappings of bright blue.

For some days the company followed the course of the river, passing through many a rich meadow, and between lovely vineyards, and fields of yellow corn. Then they rode over a dreary, barren waste, and through a wild greenwood, and reached, at last, the hills which marked the beginning of King Siegmund's domains. Then Siegfried sent fleet heralds before them to carry to his father the tidings of his coming with his bride, fair Kriemhild. Glad, indeed, were old King Siegmund and Siegfried's gentle mother when they heard this news.

"Oh, happy is the day!" cried the king. "Thrice happy be the day that shall see fair Kriemhild a crowned queen, and Siegfried a king in the throne of his fathers!"

And they showered upon the heralds who had brought the happy news rich fees of gold and silver, and gave them garments of silken velvet. And on the morrow they set out, with a train of earl-folk and lovely ladies, to meet their son and his bride. For one whole day they journeyed to the old fortress of Santen, where in former days the king's dwelling had been. There they met the happy bridal-party, and fond and loving were the hearty greetings they bestowed upon Kriemhild and the radiant Siegfried. Then, without delay, they returned to Siegmund's kingly hall; and for twelve days a high tide, more happy and more splendid than that which had been held in Burgundy, was made in honor of Siegfried's marriage-day. And, in the midst of those days of sport and joyance, the old king gave his crown and sceptre to his son; and all the people hailed Siegfried, king of the broad Lowlands, and Kriemhild his lovely queen.

Old stories tell how Siegfried reigned in peace and glad contentment in his fatherland; and how the joyous sunshine shone wherever he went, and poured a flood of light and warmth and happiness into every nook and corner of his kingdom; and how, at length, after the gentle Sigelind had died, he moved his court to that other country of his,—the far-off Nibelungen Land. And it is in that strange, dream-haunted land, in a strong-built mountain fortress, that we shall next find him.

Glad were the Nibelungen folk when their own king and his lovely wife came to dwell among them; and the mists once more were lifted, and the skies grew bright and clear, and men said that the night had departed, and the better days were near. Golden, indeed, and most glorious, was that summer-time; and long to be remembered was Siegfried's too brief reign in Nibelungen Land. And, ages afterward, folk loved to sing of his care for his people's welfare, of his wisdom and boundless lore, of his deeds in the time of warring, and the victories gained in peace. And strong and brave were the men-folk, and wise and fair were the women, and broad and rich were the acres, in Siegfried's well-ruled land. The farm-lands were yellow with the abundant harvests, fruitful orchards grew in the pleasant dales, and fair vineyards crowned the hills. Fine cities sprang up along the seacoast, and strong fortresses were built on every height. Great ships were made, which sailed to every land, and brought home rich goods from every clime,— coffee and spices from India, rich silks from Zazemang, fine fruits from the Iberian shore, and soft furs, and ivory tusks of the sea-beast, from the frozen coasts of the north. Never before was country so richly blessed; for Siegfried taught his people how to till the soil best, and how to delve far down into the earth for hidden treasures, and how to work skilfully in iron and bronze and all other metals, and how to make the winds and the waters, and even the thunderbolt, their thralls and helpful servants. And he was as great in war as in peace; for no other people dared harm, or in any way impose upon, the Nibelungen folk, or any of his faithful liegemen.

It is told how, once on a time, he warred against the Hundings, who had done his people an injury, and how he sailed against them in a long dragon-ship of a hundred oars. When he was far out in the mid-sea, and no land was anywhere in sight, a dreadful storm arose. The lightnings flashed, and the winds roared, and threatened to carry the ship to destruction. Quickly the fearful sailors began to reef the sails, but Siegfried bade them stop.

"Why be afraid?" he cried. "The Norns have woven the woof of every man's life, and no man can escape his destiny. If the gods will that we should drown, it is folly for us to strive against fate. We are bound to the shore of the Hundings' land, and thither must our good ship carry us. Hoist the sails high on the masts, even though the wind should tear them into shreds, and split the masts into splinters!"

The sailors did as they were bidden; and the hurricane caught the ship in its mighty arms, and hurried it over the rolling waves with the speed of lightning. And Siegfried stood calmly at the helm, and guided the flying vessel. Presently they saw a rocky point rising up out of the waters before them; and on it stood an old man, his gray cloak streaming in the wind, and his blue hood tied tightly down over his head.

"Whose ship is that which comes riding on the storm?" cried the man.

"King Siegfried's ship," answered the man at the prow. "There lives no braver man on earth than he."

"Thou sayest truly," came back from the rock. "Lay by your oars, reef the sails, and take me on board!"

"What is your name?" asked the sailor, as the ship swept past him.

"When the raven croaks gladly over his battle-feast, men call me Hnikar. But call me now Karl from the mountain, Fengr, or Fjolner. Reef, quick, your sails, and take me in!"

The men, at Siegfried's command, obeyed. And at once the wind ceased blowing, and the sea was calm, and the warm sun shone through the rifted clouds, and the coast of Hundings Land lay close before them. But when they looked for Fjolner, as he called himself, they could not find him.

One day Siegfried sat in his sun-lit hall in Nibelungen Land; and Kriemhild, lovely as a morning in June, sat beside him. And they talked of the early days when alone he fared through the mid-world, and alone did deeds of wondrous daring. And Siegfried bethought him then of the glittering Hoard of Andvari, and the cave and the mountain fortress, where the faithful dwarf Alberich still guarded the measureless treasure.

"How I should like to see that mountain fastness and that glittering hoard!" cried Kriemhild.

"You shall see," answered the king.

And at once horses were saddled, and preparations were made for a morning's jaunt into the mountains. And, ere an hour had passed, Siegfried and his queen, and a small number of knights and ladies, were riding through the passes. About noon they came to Alberich's dwelling,—a frowning fortress of granite built in the mountain-side. The gate was opened by the sleepy giant who always sat within, and the party rode into the narrow court-yard. There they were met by Alberich, seeming smaller and grayer, and more pinched and wan, than ever before.

"Hail, noble master!" cried he, bowing low before Siegfried. "How can Alberich serve you to-day?"

"Lead us to the treasure-vaults," answered the king. "My queen would fain feast her eyes upon the yellow, sparkling hoard."

The dwarf obeyed. Through a narrow door they were ushered into a long, low cavern, so frowning and gloomy, that the queen started back in affright. But, re-assured by Siegfried's smiling face, she went forward again. The entrance-way was lighted by little torches held in the hands of tiny elves, who bowed in humble politeness to the kingly party. But, when once beyond the entrance-hall, no torches were needed to show the way; for the huge pile of glittering gold and sparkling jewels, which lay heaped up to the cavern's roof, lighted all the space around with a glory brighter than day.

"There is the dwarf's treasure!" cried Siegfried. "Behold the Hoard of Andvari, the gathered wealth of the ages! Henceforth, fair Kriemhild, it is yours—all yours, save this serpent-ring."

"And why not that too?" asked the queen; for she admired its glittering golden scales, and its staring ruby eyes.

"Alas!" answered he, "a curse rests upon it,—the curse which Andvari the ancient laid upon it when Loki tore it from his hand. A miser's heart—selfish, cold, snaky—is bred in its owner's being; and he thenceforth lives a very serpent's life. Or, should he resist its influence, then death through the guile of pretended friends is sure to be his fate."

"Then why," asked the queen,—"why do you keep it yourself? Why do you risk its bane? Why not give it to your sworn foe, or cast it into the sea, or melt it in the fire, and thus escape the curse?"

Siegfried answered by telling how, when in the heyday of his youth, he had slain Fafnir, the keeper of this hoard, upon the Glittering Heath; and how, while still in the narrow trench which he had dug, the blood of the horrid beast had flown in upon him, and covered him up.

"And this I have been told by Odin's birds," he went on to say, "that every part of my body that was touched by the slimy flood was made forever proof against sword and spear, and sharp weapons of every kind. Hence I have no cause to fear the stroke, either of open foes or of traitorous false friends."

"But was all of your body covered with the dragon's blood? Was there no small spot untouched?" asked the queen, more anxious now than she had ever seemed to be before she had known aught of her husband's strange security from wounds.

"Only one very little spot between the shoulders was left untouched," answered Siegfried. "I afterwards found a lime-leaf sticking there, and I know that the slimy blood touched not that spot. But then who fears a thrust in the back? None save cowards are wounded there."

"Ah!" said the queen, toying tremulously with the fatal ring, "that little lime-leaf may yet bring us unutterable woe."

But Siegfried laughed at her fears; and he took the serpent-ring, and slipped it upon his forefinger, and said that he would wear it there, bane or no bane, so long as Odin would let him live.

Then, after another long look at the heaps of glittering gold and priceless gem-stones, the company turned, and followed Alberich back, through the gloomy entranceway and the narrow door, to the open air again. And mounting their steeds, which stood ready, they started homewards. But, at the outer gate, Siegfried paused, and said to the dwarf at parting,—

"Hearken, Alberich! The Hoard of Andvari is no longer mine. I have made a present of it to my queen. Hold it and guard it, therefore, as hers and hers alone; and, whatever her bidding may be regarding it, that do."

"Your word is law, and shall be obeyed," said the dwarf, bowing low.

Then the drowsy gate-keeper swung the heavy gate to its place, and the kingly party rode gayly away.

On their way home the company went, by another route, through the narrow mountain pass which led towards the sea, and thence through a rocky gorge between two smoking mountains. And on one side of this road a great cavern yawned, so dark and deep that no man had ever dared to step inside of it. And as they paused before it, and listened, they heard, away down in its dismal depths, horrid groans, sad moanings, and faint wild shrieks, so far away that it seemed as if they had come from the very centre of the earth. And, while they still listened, the ground around them trembled and shook, and the smoking mountain on the other side of the gorge smoked blacker than before.

"Loki is uneasy to-day," said Siegfried, as they all put spurs to their horses, and galloped swiftly home.

It was the Cavern of the Mischief-maker which the party had visited; and that evening, as they again sat in Siegfried's pleasant hall, they amused themselves by telling many strange old tales of the mid-world's childhood, when the gods, and the giants, and the dwarf-folk, had their dwelling on the earth. But they talked most of Loki, the flame, the restless, the evil-doer. And this, my children, is the story that was told of the Doom of the Mischief-maker.[EN#30]

The Story.

You have heard of the feast that old AEgir once made for the Asa-folk in his gold-lit dwelling in the deep sea; and how the feast was hindered, through the loss of his great brewing-kettle, until Thor had obtained a still larger vessel from Hymer the giant. It is very likely that the thief who stole King AEgir's kettle was none other than Loki the Mischief-maker; but, if this was so, he was not long unpunished for his meanness.

There was great joy in the Ocean-king's hall, when at last the banquet was ready, and the foaming ale began to pass itself around to the guests. But Thor, who had done so much to help matters along, could not stay to the merry-making: for he had heard that the Storm-giants were marshalling their forces for a raid upon some unguarded corner of the mid-world; and so, grasping his hammer Mjolner, he bade his kind host good-by, and leaped into his iron car.

"Business always before pleasure!" he cried, as he gave the word to his swift, strong goats, and rattled away at a wonderful rate through the air.

In old AEgir's hall glad music resounded on every side; and the gleeful Waves danced merrily as the Asa-folk sat around the festal-board, and partook of the Ocean-king's good fare. AEgir's two thralls, the faithful Funfeng and the trusty Elder, waited upon the guests, and carefully supplied their wants. Never in all the world had two more thoughtful servants been seen; and every one spoke in praise of their quickness, and their skill, and their ready obedience.

Then Loki, unable to keep his hands from mischief, waxed very angry, because every one seemed happy and free from trouble, and no one noticed or cared for him. So, while good Funfeng was serving him to meat, he struck the faithful thrall with a carving-knife, and killed him. Then arose a great uproar in the Ocean-king's feast-hall. The Asa-folk rose up from the table, and drove the Mischief-maker out from among them; and in their wrath they chased him across the waters, and forced him to hide in the thick greenwood. After this they went back to AEgir's hall, and sat down again to the feast. But they had scarcely begun to eat, when Loki came quietly out of his hiding-place, and stole slyly around to AEgir's kitchen, where he found Elder, the other thrall, grieving sadly because of his brother's death.

"I hear a great chattering and clattering over there in the feast-hall," said Loki. "The greedy, silly Asa-folk seem to be very busy indeed, both with their teeth and their tongues. Tell me, now, good Elder, what they talk about while they sit over their meat and ale."

"They talk of noble deeds," answered Elder. "They speak of gallant heroes, and brave men, and fair women, and strong hearts, and willing hands, and gentle manners, and kind friends. And for all these they have words of praise, and songs of beauty; but none of them speak well of Loki, the thief and the vile traitor."

"Ah!" said Loki wrathfully, twisting himself into a dozen different shapes, "no one could ask so great a kindness from such folk. I must go into the feast-hall, and take a look at this fine company, and listen to their noisy merry-making. I have a fine scolding laid up for those good fellows; and, unless they are careful with their tongues, they will find many hard words mixed with their ale."

Then he went boldly into the great hall, and stood up before the wonder-stricken guests at the table. When the Asa-folk saw who it was that had darkened the doorway, and was now in their midst, a painful silence fell upon them, and all their merriment was at an end. And Loki stretched himself up to his full height, and said to them,—

"Hungry and thirsty come I to AEgir's gold lit hall. Long and rough was the road I trod, and wearisome was the way. Will no one bid me welcome? Will none give me a seat at the feast? Will none offer me a drink of the precious mead? Why are you all so dumb? Why so sulky and stiff-necked, when your best friend stands before you? Give me a seat among you,—yes, one of the high-seats,—or else drive me from your hall! In either case, the world will never forget me. I am Loki."

Then one among the Asa-folk spoke up, and said, "Let him sit with us. He is mad; and when he slew Funfeng, he was not in his right mind. He is not answerable for his rash act."

But Bragi the Wise, who sat on the innermost seat, arose, and said, "Nay, we will not give him a seat among us. Nevermore shall he feast or sup with us, or share our good-fellowship. Thieves and murderers we know, and will shun."

This speech enraged Loki all the more; and he spared not vile words, but heaped abuse without stint upon all the folk before him. And by main force he seized hold of the silent Vidar, who had come from the forest solitudes to be present at the feast, and dragged him away from the table, and seated himself in his place. Then, as he quaffed the foaming ale, he flung out taunts and jeers and hard words to all who sat around, but chiefly to Bragi the Wise. Then he turned to Sif, the beautiful wife of Thor, and began to twit her about her golden hair.

"Oh, how handsome you were, when you looked at your bald head in the mirror that day! Oh, what music you made when your hands touched your smooth pate! And now whose hair do you wear?"

And the wretch laughed wickedly, as he saw the tears welling up in poor Sif's eyes.

Then suddenly a great tumult was heard outside. The mountains shook and trembled; and the bottom of the sea seemed moved; and the waves, affrighted and angry, rushed hither and thither in confusion. All the guests looked up in eager expectation, and some of them fled in alarm from the hall. Then the mighty Thor strode through the door, and up to the table, swinging his hammer, and casting wrathful glances at the Mischief-maker. Loki trembled, and dropped his goblet, and sank down upon his knees before the terrible Asa.

"I yield me!" he cried. "Spare my life, I pray you, and I will be your thrall forever!"

"I want no such thrall," answered Thor. "And I spare your life on one condition only,—that you go at once from hence, and nevermore presume to come into the company of Asa-folk."

"I promise all that you ask," said Loki, trembling more than ever. "Let me go."

Thor stepped aside; and the frightened culprit fled from the hall, and was soon out of sight. The feast was broken up. The folk bade AEgir a kind farewell, and all embarked on Frey's good ship Skidbladner; and fair winds wafted them swiftly home to Asgard.

Loki fled to the dark mountain gorges of Mist Land, and sought for a while to hide himself from the sight of both gods and men. In a deep ravine by the side of a roaring torrent, he built himself a house of iron and stone, and placed a door on each of its four sides, so that he could see whatever passed around him. There, for many winters, he lived in lonely solitude, planning with himself how he might baffle the gods, and regain his old place in Asgard. And now and then he slipped slyly away from his hiding-place, and wrought much mischief for a time among the abodes of men. But when Thor heard of his evil-doings, and sought to catch him, and punish him for his evil deeds, he was nowhere to be found. And at last the Asa-folk determined, that, if he could ever be captured, the safety of the world required that he should be bound hand and foot, and kept forever in prison.

Loki often amused himself in his mountain home by taking upon him his favorite form of a salmon, and lying listlessly, beneath the waters of the great Fanander Cataract, which fell from the shelving rocks a thousand feet above him. One day while thus lying, he bethought himself of former days, when he walked the glad young earth in company with the All-Father. And among other things he remembered how he had once borrowed the magic net of Ran, the Ocean-queen, and had caught with it the dwarf Andvari, disguised, as he himself now was, in the form of a slippery salmon.

"I will make me such a net!" he cried. "I will make it strong and good; and I, too, will fish for men."

So he took again his proper shape, and went back to his cheerless home in the ravine. And he gathered flax and wool and long hemp, and spun yarn and strong cords, and wove them into meshes, after the pattern of Queen Ran's magic net; for men had not, at that time, learned how to make or use nets for fishing. And the first fisherman who caught fish in that way is said to have taken Loki's net as a model.

Odin sat, on the morrow, in his high hall of Hlidskialf, and looked out over all the world, and saw, even to the uttermost corners, what men-folk were everywhere doing. When his eye rested upon the dark line which marked the mountain-land of the Mist Country, he started up in quick surprise, and cried out,

"Who is that who sits by the Fanander Force, and ties strong cords together?"

But none of those who stood around could tell, for their eyes were not strong enough and clear enough to see so far.

"Bring Heimdal!" then cried Odin.

Now, Heimdal the White dwells among the blue mountains of sunny Himminbjorg, where the rainbow, the shimmering Asa-bridge, spans the space betwixt heaven and earth. He is the son of Odin, golden-toothed, pure-faced, and clean-hearted; and he ever keeps watch and ward over the mid-world and the homes of frail men-folk, lest the giants shall break in, and destroy and slay. He rides upon a shining steed named Goldtop; and he holds in his hand a horn called Gjallar-horn, with which, in the last great twilight, he shall summon the world to battle with the Fenris-wolf and the sons of Loki. This watchful guardian of the mid-world is as wakeful as the birds. And his hearing is so keen, that no sound on earth escapes him,—not even that of the rippling waves upon the seashore, nor of the quiet sprouting of the grass in the meadows, nor even of the growth of the soft wool on the backs of sheep. And his eyesight, too, is wondrous clear and sharp; for he can see by night as well as by day, and the smallest thing, although a hundred leagues away, cannot be hidden from him.

To Heimdal, then, the heralds hastened, bearing the words which Odin had spoken. And the watchful warder of the mid-world came at once to the call of the All-Father.

"Turn your eyes to the sombre mountains that guard the shadowy Mist-land from the sea," said Odin, "Now look far down into the rocky gorge in which the Fanander Cataract pours, and tell me what you see."

Heimdal did as he was bidden.

"I see a shape," said he, "sitting by the torrent's side. It is Loki's shape, and he seems strangely busy with strong strings and cords."

"Call all our folk together!" commanded Odin. "The wily Mischief-maker plots our hurt. He must be driven from his hiding-place, and put where he can do no further harm."

Great stir was there then in Asgard. Every one hastened to answer Odin's call, and to join in the quest for the Mischief-maker. Thor came on foot, with his hammer tightly grasped in his hands, and lightning flashing from beneath his red brows. Tyr, the one-handed, came with his sword. Then followed Bragi the Wise, with his harp and his sage counsels; then Hermod the Nimble, with his quick wit and ready hands; and, lastly, a great company of elves and wood-sprites and trolls. Then a whirlwind caught them up in its swirling arms, and carried them through the air, over the hill-tops and the country-side, and the meadows and the mountains, and set them down in the gorge of the Fanander Force.

But Loki was not caught napping. His wakeful ears had heard the tumult in the air, and he guessed who it was that was coming. He threw the net, which he had just finished, into the fire, and jumped quickly into the swift torrent, where, changing himself into a salmon, he lay hidden beneath the foaming waters.

When the eager Asa-folk reached Loki's dwelling, they found that he whom they sought had fled; and although they searched high and low, among the rocks and the caves and the snowy crags, they could see no signs of the cunning fugitive. Then they went back to his house again to consult what next to do. And, while standing by the hearth, Kwaser, a sharp-sighted elf, whose eyes were quicker than the sunbeam, saw the white ashes of the burned net lying undisturbed in the still hot embers, the woven meshes unbroken and whole.

"See what the cunning fellow has been making!" cried the elf. "It must have been a trap for catching fish."

"Or rather for catching men," said Bragi; "for it is strangely like the Sea-queen's net."

"In that case," said Hermod the Nimble, "he has made a trap for himself; for, no doubt, he has changed himself, as is his wont, to a slippery salmon, and lies at this moment hidden beneath the Fanander torrent. Here are plenty of cords of flax and hemp and wool, with which he intended to make other nets. Let us take them, and weave one like the pattern which lies there in the embers; and then, if I mistake not, we shall catch the too cunning fellow."

All saw the wisdom of these words, and all set quickly to work. In a short time they had made a net strong and large, and full of fine meshes, like the model among the coals. Then they threw it into the roaring stream, Thor holding to one end, and all the other folk pulling at the other. With great toil, they dragged it forwards, against the current, even to the foot of the waterfall. But the cunning Loki crept close down between two sharp stones, and lay there quietly while the net passed harmlessly over him.

"Let us try again!" cried Thor. "I am sure that something besides dead rocks lies at the bottom of the stream."

So they hung heavy weights to the net, and began to drag it a second time, this time going down stream. Loki looked out from his hiding-place, and saw that he would not be able to escape again by lying between the rocks, and that his only chance for safety was either to leap over the net, and hide himself behind the rushing cataract itself, or to swim with the current out to the sea. But the way to the sea was long, and there were many shallow places; and Loki had doubts as to how old AEgir would receive him in his kingdom. He feared greatly to undertake so dangerous and uncertain a course. So, turning upon his foes, and calling up all his strength, he made a tremendous leap high into the air, and clean over the net. But Thor was too quick for him. As he fell towards the water, the Thunderer quickly threw out his hand, and caught the slippery salmon, holding him firmly by the tail.

When Loki found that he was surely caught, and could not by any means escape, he took again his proper shape. Fiercely did he struggle with mighty Thor, and bitter were the curses which he poured down upon his enemies. But he could not get free. Into the deep, dark cavern, beneath the smoking mountain, where daylight never comes, nor the warmth of the sun, nor the sound of Nature's music, the fallen Mischief-maker was carried. And they bound him firmly to the sharp rocks, with his face turned upwards toward the dripping roof; for they said that nevermore, until the last dread twilight, should he be free to vex the world with his wickedness. And Skade, the giant wife of Niord and the daughter of grim Old Winter, took a hideous poison snake, and hung it up above Loki, so that its venom would drop into his upturned face. But Sigyn, the loving wife of the suffering wretch, left her home in the pleasant halls of Asgard, and came to his horrible prison-house to soothe and comfort him; and evermore she holds a basin above his head, and catches in it the poisonous drops as they fall. When the basin is filled, and she turns to empty it in the tar-black river that flows through that home of horrors, the terrible venom falls upon his unprotected face, and Loki writhes and shrieks in fearful agony, until the earth around him shakes and trembles, and the mountains spit forth fire, and fumes of sulphur-smoke.

And there the Mischief-maker, the spirit of evil, shall lie in torment until the last great day and the dread twilight of all mid-world things. How strange and how sad, that, while Loki lies thus bound and harmless, evil still walks the earth, and that so much mischief and such dire disasters were prepared for Siegfried and the folk of Nibelungen Land!

Adventure XVIII. How the Mischief Began to Brew.

One day a party of strangers came to Siegfried's Nibelungen dwelling, and asked to speak with the king.

"Who are you? and what is your errand?" asked the porter at the gate.

"Our errand is to the king, and he will know who we are when he sees us," was the answer.

When Siegfried was told of the strange men who waited below, and of the strange way in which they had answered the porter's question, he asked,—

"From what country seem they to have come? For surely their dress and manners will betray something of that matter to you. Are they South-land folk, or East-land folk? Are they from the mountains, or from the sea?"

"They belong to none of the neighbor-lands," answered the earl who had brought the word to the king. "No such men live upon our borders. They seem to have come from a far-off land; for they are travel-worn, and their sea-stained clothing betokens a people from the south. They are tall and dark, and their hair is black, and they look much like those Rhineland warriors who came hither with our lady the queen. And they carry a blood-red banner with a golden dragon painted upon it."

"Oh, they must be from Burgundy!" cried the queen, who had overheard these words. And she went at once to the window to see the strangers, who were waiting in the courtyard below.

There, indeed, she saw thirty tall Burgundians, clad in the gay costume of Rhineland, now faded and worn with long travel. But all save one were young, and strangers to Kriemhild. That one was their leader,—an old man with a kind face, and a right noble bearing.

"See!" said the queen to Siegfried: "there is our brave captain Gere, who, ever since my childhood, has been the trustiest man in my brother Gunther's household. Those men are from the fatherland, and they bring tidings from the dear old Burgundian home."

"Welcome are they to our Nibelungen Land!" cried the delighted king.

And he ordered that the strangers should be brought into the castle, and that the most sumptuous rooms should be allotted to them, and a plenteous meal prepared, and every thing done to entertain them in a style befitting messengers from Kriemhild's fatherland. Then Gere, the trusty captain, was led into the presence of the king and queen. Right gladly did they welcome him, and many were the questions they asked about their kin-folk, and the old Rhineland home.

"Tell us, good Gere," said Siegfried, "what is thy message from our friends; for we are anxious to know whether they are well and happy, or whether some ill luck has overtaken them. If any harm threatens them, they have but to speak, and I, with my sword and my treasures, will hasten to their help."

"They are all well," answered the captain. "No ill has befallen them, and no harm threatens them. Peace rules all the land; and fair weather and sunshine have filled the people's barns, and made their hearts glad. And thus it has been ever since Gunther brought to his dwelling the warrior-maiden Brunhild to be his queen. And this is my errand and the message that I bring: King Gunther, blessed with happiness, intends to hold a grand high-tide of joy and thanksgiving at the time of the harvest-moon. And nothing is wanting to complete the gladness of that time, but the sight of you and the peerless Kriemhild in your old places at the feast. And it is to invite you to this festival of rejoicing that I have come, at the king's command, to Nibelungen Land."

Siegfried sat a moment in silence, and then thoughtfully answered,—

"It is a long, long journey from this land to Burgundy, and many dangers beset the road; and my own people would sadly miss me while away, and I know not what mishaps might befall."

Then Gere spoke of the queen-mother Ute, now grown old and feeble, who wished once more, ere death called her hence, to see her daughter Kriemhild. And he told how all the people, both high and low, yearned for another sight of the radiant hero who in former days had blessed their land with his presence and his noble deeds. And his persuasive words had much weight with Siegfried, who said at length,—

"Tarry a few days yet for my answer. I will talk with my friends and the Nibelungen earls; and what they think best, that will I do."

For nine days, then, waited Gere at Siegfried's hall; but still the king put off his answer.

"Wait until to-morrow," he said each day, for his heart whispered dim forebodings.

At length, as midsummer was fast drawing near, the impatient captain could stay no longer; and he bade his followers make ready to go back forthwith to Burgundy. When the queen saw that they were ready to take their leave, and that Gere could wait no longer upon the king's pleasure, she urged her husband to say to Gunther that they would come to his harvest festival. And the lords and noble earl-folk added their persuasions to hers.

"Send word back to the Burgundian king," said they, "that you will go, as he desires. We will see to it that no harm comes to your kingdom while you are away."

So Siegfried called Gere and his comrades into the hall, and loaded them with costly gifts such as they had never before seen, and bade them say to their master that he gladly accepted the kind invitation he had sent, and that, ere the harvest high-tide began, he and Kriemhild would be with him in Burgundy.

And the messengers went back with all speed, and told what wondrous things they had seen in Nibelungen Land, and in what great splendor Siegfried lived. And, when they showed the rare presents which had been given them, all joined in praising the goodness and greatness of the hero-king. But old chief Hagen frowned darkly as he said,—

"It is little wonder that he can do such things, for the Shining Hoard of Andvari is his. If we had such a treasure, we, too, might live in more than kingly grandeur."

Early in the month of roses, Siegfried and his peerless queen, with a retinue of more than a thousand warriors and many fair ladies, started on their long and toilsome journey to the South-land. And the folk who went with them to the city gates bade them mane tearful farewells, and returned to their homes, feeling that the sunshine had gone forever from the Nibelungen Land. But the sky was blue and cloudless, and the breezes warm and mild, and glad was the song of the reapers as adown the seaward highway the kingly company rode. Two days they rode through Mist Land, to the shore of the peaceful sea. Ten days they sailed on the waters. And the winds were soft and gentle; and the waves slept in the sunlight, or merrily danced in their wake. But each day, far behind them, there followed a storm-cloud, dark as night, and the pleasant shores of Mist Land were hidden forever behind it. Five days they rode through the Lowlands, and glad were the Lowland folk with sight of their hero-king. Two days through the silent greenwood, and one o'er the barren moor, and three amid vineyards and fields, and between orchards fruitful and fair, they rode. And on the four and twentieth day they came in sight of the quiet town, and the tall gray towers, where dwelt the Burgundian kings. And a great company on horseback, with flashing shields and fine-wrought garments and nodding plumes, came out to meet them. It was King Gernot and a thousand of the best men and fairest women in Burgundy; and they welcomed Siegfried and Kriemhild and their Nibelungen-folk to the fair land of the Rhine. And then they turned, and rode back with them to the castle. And, as the company passed through the pleasant streets of the town, the people stood by the wayside, anxious to catch sight of the radiant Siegfried on his sunbright steed, and of the peerless Kriemhild, riding on a palfrey by his side. And young girls strewed roses in their pathway, and hung garlands upon their horses; and every one shouted, "Hail to the conquering hero! Hail to the matchless queen!"

When they reached the castle, King Gunther and Giselher met them, and ushered them into the old familiar halls, where a right hearty welcome greeted them from all the kingly household. And none seemed more glad in this happy hour than Brunhild the warrior-queen, now more gloriously beautiful than even in the days of yore.

When the harvest-moon began to shine full and bright, lighting up the whole world from evening till morn with its soft radiance, the gay festival so long looked forward to began. And care and anxiety, and the fatigues of the long journey, were forgotten amid the endless round of pleasure which for twelve days enlivened the whole of Burgundy. And the chiefest honors were everywhere paid to Siegfried the hero-king, and to Kriemhild the peerless queen of beauty.

Then Queen Brunhild called to mind, how, on a time, it had been told her in Isenland that Siegfried was but the liegeman and vassal of King Gunther; and she wondered why such honor should be paid to an underling, and why the king himself should treat him with so much respect. And as she thought of this, and of the high praises with which every one spoke of Kriemhild, her mind became filled with jealous broodings. And soon her bitter jealousy was turned to deadly hate; for she remembered then, how, in the days long past, a noble youth, more beautiful and more glorious than the world would ever see again, had awakened her from the deep sleep that Odin's thorn had given; and she remembered how Gunther had won her by deeds of strength and skill which he never afterwards could even imitate; and she thought how grand indeed was Kriemhild's husband compared with her own weak and wavering and commonplace lord. And her soul was filled with sorrow and bitterness and deepest misery, when, putting these thoughts together, she believed that she had in some way been duped and cheated into becoming Gunther's wife.

When at last the gay feast was ended, and most of the guests had gone to their homes, she sought her husband, and thus broached the matter to him.

"Often have I asked you," said she, "why your sister Kriemhild was given in marriage to a vassal, and as often have you put me off with vague excuses. Often, too, have I wondered why your vassal, Siegfried, has never paid you tribute for the lands which he holds from you, and why he has never come to render you homage. Now he is here in your castle; but he sets himself up, not as your vassal, but as your peer. I pray you, tell me what such strange things mean. Was an underling and a vassal ever known before to put himself upon a level with his liege lord?"

Gunther was greatly troubled, and he knew not what to say; for he feared to tell the queen how they had deceived her when he had won the games at Isenstein, and how the truth had ever since been kept hidden from her.

"Ask me not to explain this matter further than I have already done," he answered. "It is enough that Siegfried is the greatest of all my vassals, and that his lands are broader even than my own. He has helped me out of many straits, and has added much to the greatness and strength of my kingdom: for this reason he has never been asked to pay us tribute, and for this reason we grant him highest honors."

But this answer failed to satisfy the queen.

"Is it not the first duty of a vassal," she asked, "to help his liege lord in every undertaking? If so, Siegfried has but done his duty, and you owe him nothing. But you have not told me all. You have deceived me, and you would fain deceive me again. You have a secret, and I will find it out."

The king made no answer, but walked silently and thoughtfully away.

It happened one evening, not long thereafter, that the two queens sat together at an upper window, and looked down upon a company of men in the courtyard below. Among them were the noblest earl-folk of Burgundy, and Gunther the king, and Siegfried. But Siegfried towered above all the rest; and he moved like a god among men.

"See my noble Siegfried!" cried Kriemhild in her pride. "How grandly he stands there! What a type of manly beauty and strength! No one cares to look at other men when he is near."

"He maybe handsome," answered Brunhild sadly; "and, for aught I know, he may be noble. But what is all that by the side of kingly power? Were he but the peer of your brother Gunther, then you might well boast."

"He is the peer of Gunther," returned Kriemhild. "And not only his peer, but more; for he stands as high above him in kingly power and worth as in bodily stature."

"How can that be?" asked Brunhild, growing angry. "For, when Gunther so gallantly won me at Isenstein, he told me that Siegfried was his vassal; and often since that time I have heard the same. And even your husband told me that Gunther was his liege lord."

Queen Kriemhild laughed at these words, and answered, "I tell you again that Siegfried is a king far nobler and richer and higher than any other king on earth. Think you that my brothers would have given me to a mere vassal to be his wife?"

Then Brunhild, full of wrath, replied, "Your husband is Gunther's vassal and my own, and he shall do homage to us as the humblest and meanest of our underlings. He shall not go from this place until he has paid all the tribute that has so long been due from him. Then we shall see who is the vassal, and who is the lord."

"Nay," answered Kriemhild. "It shall not be. No tribute was ever due; and, if homage is to be paid, it is rather Gunther who must pay it."

"It shall be settled once for all!" cried Brunhild, now boiling over with rage. "I will know the truth. If Siegfried is not our vassal, then I have been duped; and I will have revenge."

"It is well," was the mild answer. "Let it be settled, once for all; and then, mayhap, we shall know who it was who really won the games at Isenstein, and you for Gunther's wife."

And the two queens parted in wrath.[EN#31]

Kriemhild's anger was as fleeting as an April cloud, which does but threaten, and then passes away in tears and sunshine. But Brunhild's was like the dread winter storm that sweeps down from Niflheim, and brings ruin and death in its wake. She felt that she had been cruelly wronged in some way, and that her life had been wrecked, and she rested not until she had learned the truth.

It was Hagen who at last told her the story of the cruel deceit that had made her Gunther's wife; and then her wrath and her shame knew no bounds.

"Woe betide the day!" she cried,—"woe betide the day that brought me to Rhineland, and made me the wife of a weakling and coward, and the jest of him who might have done nobler things!"

Hagen smiled. He had long waited for this day.

"It was Siegfried, and Siegfried alone, who plotted to deceive you," he said. "Had it not been for him, you might still have been the happy maiden-queen of Isenland. And now he laughs at you, and urges his queen, Kriemhild, to scorn you as she would an underling."

"I know it, I know it," returned the queen in distress. "And yet how grandly noble is the man! How he rushed through the flames to awaken me, when no one else could save! How brave, how handsome,—and yet he has been my bane. I can have no peace while he lives."

Hagen smiled again, and a strange light gleamed from his dark eye. Then he said, "Truly handsome and brave is he, but a viler traitor was never born. He even now plots to seize this kingdom, and to add it to his domain. Why else should he bring so great a retinue of Nibelungen warriors to Burgundy? I will see King Gunther at once, and we will put an end to his wicked projects."

"Do even so, good Hagen," said Brunhild. "Take him from my path, and bring low the haughty pride of his wife, and I shall be content."

"That I will do!" cried Hagen. "That I will do! Gunther is and shall be the king without a peer; and no one shall dare dispute the worth and the queenly beauty of his wife."

Then the wily chief sought Gunther, and with cunning words poisoned his weak mind. The feeble old king was easily made to believe that Siegfried was plotting against his life, and seeking to wrest the kingdom from him. And he forgot the many kind favors he had received at the hero's hand. He no longer remembered how Siegfried had slain the terror of the Glittering Heath, and freed the Burgundians from many a fear; and how he had routed the warlike hosts of the North-land, and made prisoners of their kings; and how he had brought his voyage to Isenland to a happy and successful ending. He forgot, also, that Siegfried was his sister's husband. He had ears and mind only for Hagen's wily words.

"While this man lives," said the dark-browed chief, "none of us are safe. See how the people follow him! Hear how they shout at his coming! They look upon him as a god, and upon Gunther as a nobody. If we are wise, we shall rid ourselves of so dangerous a man."

"It is but a week until he takes his leave of us, and goes back to his own home in Nibelungen Land. Watch him carefully until that time, but do him no harm. When he is once gone, he shall never come back again," said the king. But he spoke thus, not because of any kind feelings towards Siegfried, but rather because he feared the Nibelungen hero.

"He has no thought of going at that time," answered Hagen. "He speaks of it, only to hide his wicked and traitorous plots. Instead of going home, his plans will then be ready for action, and it will be too late for us to save ourselves. Still, if you will not believe me, take your own course. You have been warned."

The cunning chief arose to leave the room; but Gunther, now thoroughly frightened, stopped him.

"Hagen," he said, "you have always been my friend, and the words which you say are wise. Save us and our kingdom now, in whatsoever way you may deem best. I know not what to do."

Then the weak king and the warrior-chief talked long together in low, hoarse whispers. And, when they parted, shame and guilt were stamped in plain lines on Gunther's face, from which they were nevermore erased; and he dared not lift his gaze from the floor, fearing that his eyes would betray him, if seen by any more pure-hearted than he. But a smile of triumph played under the lurking gleams of Hagen's eye; and he walked erect and bold, as if he had done a praiseworthy deed.

That night a storm came sweeping down from the North, and the cold rain fell in torrents; and great hailstones pattered on the roofs and towers of the castle, and cruelly pelted the cattle in the fields, and the birds in the friendly shelter of the trees. And old Thor fought bravely with the Storm-giants; and all night long the rattle of his chariot-wheels, and the heavy strokes of his dread hammer, were heard resounding through the heavens. In his lonely chamber Hagen sat and rubbed his hands together, and grimly smiled.

"The time so long waited for has come at last," he said.

But the guilty king, unable to sleep, walked restlessly to and fro, and trembled with fear at every sound of the storm-gust without.

When day dawned at last, a sad scene met the eyes of all beholders. The earth was covered with the broken branches of leafy trees; the flowers and shrubs were beaten pitilessly to the ground; and here and there lay the dead bodies of little feathered songsters, who, the day before, had made the woods glad with their music.

The sun had scarcely risen above this sorrowful scene, gilding the gray towers and turrets and the drooping trees with the promise of better things, than a strange confusion was noticed outside of the castle-gates. Thirty and two horsemen wearing the livery of the North-lands stood there, and asked to be led to the Burgundian kings.

"Who are you? and what is your errand?" asked the gate-keeper.

"We come as heralds and messengers from Leudiger and Leudigast, the mighty kings of the North," they answered. "But our errand we can tell to no man save to Gunther your king, or to his brothers Gernot and Giselher."

Then they were led by the king's command into the council-hall, where sat Gunther, Gernot, and the noble Giselher; and behind them stood their uncle and chief, brave old Hagen.

"What message bring you from our old friends Leudiger and Leudigast?" asked Gunther of the strangers.

"Call them not your friends," answered the chief of the company. "We bring you this message from our liege lords, whom you may well count as enemies. Many years ago they were sorely beaten in battle, and suffered much hurt at your hands. And they vowed then to avenge the injury, and to wipe out the disgrace you had caused them, just so soon as they were strong enough to do so. Now they are ready, with fifty thousand men, to march into your country. And they swear to lay waste your lands, and to burn your towns and villages and all your castles, unless you at once acknowledge yourselves their vassals, and agree to pay them tribute. This is the kings' message. And we were further ordered not to wait for an answer, but to carry back to them without delay your reply, whether you will agree to their terms or no."

King Gunther, as was his wont, turned to Hagen for advice.

"Send for Siegfried," whispered the chief.

It was done. And soon the hero came into the hall. His kingly grace and warlike bearing were such that Gunther dared not raise his guilty eyes from the ground; and Hagen's furtive glances were, for the moment, freighted with fear and shame. The message of the heralds was repeated to Siegfried; and Gunther said,—

"Most noble friend, you hear what word these traitorous kings dare send us. Now, we remember, that, long years ago, you led us against them, and gave us a glorious victory. We remember, too, how, by your counsel, their lives were spared, and they were sent home with costly gifts. It is thus they repay our kindness. What answer shall we send them?"

"Say that we will fight," answered Siegfried at once. "I will lead my brave Nibelungens against them, and they shall learn how serious a thing it is to break an oath, or to return treason for kindness."

The news soon spread through all the town and through the country-side, that Leudiger and Leudigast, with fifty thousand men, were marching into Burgundy, and destroying every thing in their way. And great flight and confusion prevailed. Men and women hurried hither and thither in dismay. Soldiers busily sharpened their weapons, and burnished their armor, ready for the fray. Little children were seen cowering at every sound, and anxious faces were found everywhere.

When Queen Kriemhild saw the busy tumult, and heard the shouts and cries in the street and the courtyard, and learned the cause of it all, she was greatly troubled, and went at once to seek Siegfried. When she found him, she drew him aside, and besought him not to take part in the war which threatened, but to hasten with all speed back to their own loved Nibelungen Land.

"And why would my noble queen wish me thus to play the part of a coward, and to leave my friends when they most need my help?" asked Siegfried in surprise.

"I would not have you play the coward," answered Kriemhild, and hot tears stood in her eyes. "But some unseen danger overhangs. There are other traitors than Leudiger and Leudigast, and men to be more feared than they. Last night I dreamed a fearful dream, and it follows me still. I dreamed that you hunted in the forest, and that two wild boars attacked you. The grass and the flowers were stained with your gore, and the cruel tusks of the beasts tore you in pieces, and no one came to your help. And I cried out in my distress, and awoke; and the storm-clouds roared and threatened, and the hail pattered on the roof, and the wind and rain beat against the windowpanes. Then I slept again, and another dream, as fearful as the first, came to me. I dreamed that you rode in the forest, and that music sprang up in your footsteps, and all things living called you blessed, but that suddenly two mountains rose up from the ground, and their high granite crags toppled over, and fell upon you, and buried you from my sight forever. Then I awoke again, and my heart has ever since been heavy with fearful forebodings. I know that some dread evil threatens us; yet, what it is, I cannot tell. But go not out against the North-kings. Our Nibelungen-folk wait too long for your coming."

Siegfried gayly laughed at his queen's fears, and said, "The woof of every man's fate has been woven by the Norns, and neither he nor his foes can change it. When his hour comes, then he must go to meet his destiny."

Then he led her gently back to her room in the castle, and bade her a loving farewell, saying, "When the foes of our Burgundian hosts are put to flight, and there is no longer need for us here, then will we hasten back to Nibelungen Land. Have patience and hope for a few days only, and all will yet be well. Forget your foolish dreams, and think only of my glad return."

It was arranged, that, in the march against the North-kings, Siegfried with his Nibelungens should take the lead; while Hagen, with a picked company of fighting-men, should bring up the rear. Every one was eager to join in the undertaking; and no one, save King Gunther and his cunning counsellor, and Ortwin and Dankwart, knew that the pretended heralds from the North-kings were not heralds at all, but merely the false tools of wicked Hagen. For the whole was but a well-planned plot, as we shall see, to entrap unwary, trusting Siegfried.

Soon all things were in readiness for the march; but, as the day was now well spent, it was agreed, that, at early dawn of the morrow, the little army should set out. And every one went home to put his affairs in order, and to rest for the night.

Late that evening old Hagen went to bid Siegfried's queen good-by. Kriemhild had tried hard to drown her gloomy fears, and to forget her sad, foreboding dreams; but it was all in vain, for deep anxiety still rested heavily upon her mind. Yet she welcomed her dark-browed uncle with the kindest words.

"How glad I am," she said, "that my husband is here to help my kinsfolk in this their time of need! I know right well, that, with him to lead, you shall win. But, dear uncle, remember, when you are in the battle, that we have always loved you, and that Siegfried has done many kindnesses to the Burgundians; and, if any danger threaten him, turn it aside, I pray you, for Kriemhild's sake. I know that I merit Queen Brunhild's anger, because of the sharp words I lately spoke to her; but let not my husband suffer blame for that which is my fault alone."

"Kriemhild," answered Hagen, "no one shall suffer blame,—neither Siegfried nor yourself. We are all forgetful, and sometimes speak hasty words; but that which we say in angry thoughtlessness should not be cherished up against us. There is no one who thinks more highly of Siegfried than I, and there is nothing I would not do to serve him."

"I should not fear for him," said she, "if he were not so bold and reckless. When he is in the battle, he never thinks of his own safety. And I tremble lest at some time he may dare too much, and meet his death. If you knew every thing, as I do, you would fear for him too."

"What is it?" asked Hagen, trying to hide his eagerness,—"what is it that gives you cause for fear? Tell me all about it, and then I will know the better how to shield him from danger. I will lay down my life for his sake."

Then Kriemhild, trusting in her uncle's word, and forgetful of every caution, told him the secret of the dragon's blood, and of Siegfried's strange bath, and of the mischief-working lime-leaf.

"And now," she added, "since I know that there is one spot which a deadly weapon might reach, I am in constant fear that the spear of an enemy may, perchance, strike him there. Is there not some way of shielding that spot?"

"There is," answered Hagen. "Make some mark, or put some sign, upon his coat, that I may know where that spot is. And, when the battle rages, I will ride close behind him, and ward off every threatened stroke."

And Kriemhild joyfully promised that she would at once embroider a silken lime-leaf on the hero's coat, just over the fatal spot. And Hagen, well pleased, bade her farewell, and went away.

Without delay the chief sought the weak-minded Gunther, and to him he related all that the trustful Kriemhild had told him. And, until the midnight hour, the two plotters sat in the king's bed-chamber, and laid their cunning plans. Both thought it best, now they had learned the fatal secret, to give up the sham march against the North-kings, and to seek by other and easier means to lure Siegfried to his death.

"The chiefs will be much displeased," said Gunther. "For all will come, ready to march at the rising of the sun. What shall we do to please them, and make them more ready to change their plans?"

Hagen thought a moment, and then the grim smile that was wont to break the dark lines of his face when he was pleased spread over his features.

"We will have a grand hunt in the Odenwald to-morrow," he hoarsely whispered.

Adventure XIX. How They Hunted in the Odenwald.

Next morning, at earliest daybreak, while yet the stars were bright, and the trees hung heavy with dew-drops, and the clouds were light and high, King Siegfried stood with his warriors before the castle-gate. They waited but for the sunrise, and a word from Gunther the king, to ride forth over dale and woodland, and through forest and brake and field, to meet, as they believed, the hosts of the North-land kings. And Siegfried moved among them, calm-faced and bright as a war-god, upon the radiant Greyfell. And men said, long years afterward, that never had the shining hero seemed so glorious to their sight. Within the spacious courtyard a thousand Burgundian braves stood waiting, too, for the signal, and the king's word of command. And at their head stood Hagen, dark as a cloud in summer, guilefully hiding his vile plots, and giving out orders for the marching. There, too, were honest Gernot, fearless and upright, and Giselher, true as gold; and neither of them dreamed of evil, or of the dark deed that day was doomed to see. Close by the gate was Ortwin, bearing aloft the blood-red dragon-banner, which the Burgundians were wont to carry in honor of Siegfried's famous fight with Fafnir. And there was Dankwart, also, ever ready to boast when no danger threatened, and ever willing to do chief Hagen's bidding. And next came Volker the Fiddler good, with the famed sword Fiddle-bow by him, on which, it is said, he could make the sweetest music while fighting his foes in battle.

At length the sun began to peep over the eastern hills, and his beams fell upon the castle-walls, and shot away through the trees, and over the meadows, and made the dewdrops glisten like myriads of diamonds among the dripping leaves and blossoms. And a glad shout went up from the throats of the waiting heroes; for they thought that the looked-for moment had come, and the march would soon begin. And the shout was echoed from walls to turrets, and from turrets to trees, and from trees to hills, and from the hills to the vaulted sky above. And nothing was wanting now but King Gunther's word of command.

Suddenly, far down the street, the sound of a bugle was heard, and then of the swift clattering of horses' hoofs coming up the hill towards the castle.

"Who are they who come thus to join us at the last moment?" asked Hagen of the watchman above the gate.

"They are strangers," answered the watchman; "and they carry a peace-flag."

In a few moments the strange horsemen dashed up, and halted some distance from the castle-gate, where Siegfried and his heroes stood.

"Who are you? and what is your errand?" cried Hagen, in the king's name.

They answered that they were heralds from the North-land kings, sent quickly to correct the message of the day before; for their liege lords, Leudiger and Leudigast, they said, had given up warring against Burgundy, and had gone back to their homes. And they had sent humbly to ask the Rhineland kings to forget the rash threats which they had made, and to allow them to swear fealty to Gunther, and henceforth to be his humble vassals, if only they might be forgiven.

"Right cheerfully do we forgive them!" cried Gunther, not waiting to consult with his wise men. "And our forgiveness shall be so full, that we shall ask neither fealty nor tribute from them."

Then he turned to Siegfried, and said, "You hear, friend Siegfried, how this troublesome matter has been happily ended. Accept our thanks, we pray you, for your proffered help; for, without it, it might have gone but roughly with us in a second war with the Northland kings. But now you are free to do what pleases you. If, as you said yesterday, you would fain return to Nibelungen Land, you may send your warriors on the way to-day, for they are already equipped for the journey. But abide you with us another day, and to-morrow we will bid you God-speed, and you may easily overtake your Nibelungen friends ere they have reached our own boundaries."

Siegfried was not well pleased to give up an undertaking scarce begun, and still less could he understand why the king should be so ready to forgive the affront which the North-land kings had offered him. And he was not slow in reading the look of shame and guilt that lurked in Gunther's face, or the smile of jealous hate that Hagen could no longer hide. Yet no word of displeasure spoke he, nor seemed he to understand that any mischief was brewing; for he feared neither force nor guile. So he bade his Nibelungens to begin their homeward march, saying that he and Kriemhild, and the ladies of her train, would follow swiftly on the morrow.

"Since it is your last day with us," said Gunther, grown cunning through Hagen's teaching, "what say you, dear Siegfried, to a hunt in Odin's Wood?"

"Right glad will I be to join you in such sport," answered Siegfried. "I will change my war-coat for a hunting-suit, and be ready within an hour."

Then Siegfried went to his apartments, and doffed his steel-clad armor, and searched in vain through his wardrobe for his favorite hunting-suit. But it was nowhere to be found; and he was fain to put on the rich embroidered coat which he sometimes wore in battle, instead of a coat-of-mail. And he did not see the white lime-leaf that Kriemhild with anxious care had worked in silk upon it. Then he sought the queen, and told her of the unlooked-for change of plans, and how, on the morrow, they would ride towards Nibelungen Land; but to-day he said he had promised Gunther to hunt with him in the Odenwald.

But Kriemhild, to his great surprise, begged him not to leave her, even to hunt in the Odenwald. For she had begun to fear that she had made a great mistake in telling Hagen the story of the lime-leaf; and yet she could not explain to Siegfried the true cause of her uneasiness.

"Oh, do not join in the hunt!" she cried. "Something tells me that danger lurks hidden in the wood. Stay in the castle with me, and help me put things in readiness for our journey homewards to-morrow. Last night I had another dream. I thought that Odin's birds, Hugin and Munin, sat on a tree before me. And Hugin flapped his wings, and said, 'What more vile than a false friend? What more to be feared than a secret foe? Harder than stone is his unfeeling heart; sharper than the adder's poison-fangs are his words; a snake in the grass is he!' Then Munin flapped his wings too, but said nothing. And I awoke, and thought at once of the sunbright Balder, slain through Loki's vile deceit. And, as I thought upon his sad death, a withered leaf came fluttering through the casement, and fell upon my couch. Sad signs and tokens are these, my husband; and much grief, I fear, they foretell."

But Siegfried was deaf to her words of warning, and he laughed at the foolish dream. Then he bade her farewell till even-tide, and hastened to join the party of huntsmen who waited for him impatiently at the gate.

When the party reached the Odenwald, they separated; each man taking his own course, and following his own game. Siegfried, with but one trusty huntsman and his own fleet-footed hound, sought at once the wildest and thickest part of the wood. And great was the slaughter he made among the fierce beasts of the forest; for nothing that was worthy of notice could hide from his sight, or escape him. From his lair in a thorny thicket, a huge wild boar sprang up; and with glaring red eyes, and mouth foaming, and tusks gnashing with rage, he charged fiercely upon the hero. But, with one skilful stroke from his great spear, Siegfried laid the beast dead on the heather. Next he met a tawny lion, couched ready to spring upon him; but, drawing quickly his heavy bow, he sent a quivering arrow through the animal's heart.

Then, one after another, he slew a buffalo, four bisons, a mighty elk with branching horns, and many deers and stags and savage beasts.

At one time the hound drove from its hiding-place another wild boar, much greater than the first, and far more fierce. Quickly Siegfried dismounted from his horse, and met the grizzly creature as it rushed with raving fury towards him. The sword of the hero cleft the beast in twain, and its bloody parts lay lifeless on the ground. Then Siegfried's huntsman, in gay mood, said, "My lord, would it not be better to rest a while! If you keep on slaughtering at this rate, there will soon be no game left in Odenwald."

Siegfried laughed heartily at the merry words, and at once called in his hound, saying, "You are right! We will hunt no more until our good friends have joined us."

Soon afterward the call of a bugle was heard; and Gunther and Hagen and Dankwart and Ortwin, with their huntsmen and hounds, came riding up.

"What luck have you had, my friends?" asked Siegfried.

Then Hagen told what game they had taken,—a deer, a young bear, and two small wild boars. But, when they learned what Siegfried had done, the old chief's face grew dark, and he knit his eyebrows, and bit his lips in jealous hate: for four knights, ten huntsmen, and four and twenty hounds, had beaten every bush, and followed every trail; and yet the Nibelungen king, with but one follower and one hound, had slain ten times as much game as they.

While they stood talking over the successes of the day, the sound of a horn was heard, calling the sportsmen together for the mid-day meal; and knights and huntsmen turned their steeds, and rode slowly towards the trysting-place. Suddenly a huge bear, roused by the noise of baying hounds and tramping feet, crossed their pathway.

"Ah!" cried Siegfried, "there goes our friend Bruin, just in time to give us a bit of fun, and some needed sport at dinner. He shall go with us, and be our guest!"

With these words he loosed his hound, and dashed swiftly forwards after the beast. Through thick underbrush and tangled briers, and over fallen trees, the frightened creature ran, until at last it reached a steep hillside. There, in a rocky cleft, it stood at bay, and fought fiercely for its life. When Siegfried came up, and saw that his hound dared not take hold of the furious beast, he sprang from his horse, and seized the bear in his own strong arms, and bound him safely with a stout cord. Then he fastened an end of the cord to his saddle-bows, and remounted his steed. And thus he rode through the forest to the place where the dinner waited, dragging the unwilling bear behind him, while the dog bounded gayly along by his side.

No nobler sight had ever been seen in that forest than that which Gunther's people saw that day. The Nibelungen king was dressed as well became so great a hero. His suit was of the speckled lynx's hide and rich black silk, upon which were embroidered many strange devices, with threads of gold. (But, alas! between the shoulders was the silken lime-leaf that Queen Kriemhild's busy fingers had wrought.) His cap was of the blackest fur, brought from the frozen Siberian land. Over his shoulder was thrown his well-filled quiver, made of lion's skin; and in his hands he carried his bow of mulberry,—a very beam in size, and so strong that no man save himself could bend it. A golden hunting-horn was at his side, and his sunbright shield lay on his saddle-bow; while his mighty sword, the fire-edged Balmung, in its sheath glittering with gemstones, hung from his jewelled belt.

The men who stood around chief Hagen, and who saw the hero coming thus god-like through the greenwood, admired and trembled; and Dankwart whispered a word of caution to his dark-browed brother. But the old chief's face grew gloomier than before; and he scowled fiercely upon the faint-hearted Dankwart, as he hoarsely whispered in return,—

"What though he be Odin himself, still will I dare! It is not I: it is the Norns, who shape every man's fate."

When Siegfried reached the camp with his prize, the huntsmen shouted with delight; and the hounds howled loudly, and shook their chains, and tried hard to get at the shaggy beast. The king leaped to the ground, and unloosed the cords which bound him; and at the same time the hounds were unleashed, and set upon the angry, frightened creature. Hemmed in on every side, the bear rushed blindly forwards, and leaped over the fires, where the cooks were busy with the dinner. Pots and kettles were knocked about in great confusion, and the scared cooks thrown sprawling upon the ground; and many a dainty dish and savory mess was spoiled. The bear fled fast down the forest road, followed by the baying hounds and the fleet-footed warriors. But none dared shoot an arrow at him for fear of killing the dogs; and it seemed as if he would surely escape, so fast he ran away. Then Siegfried bounded forwards, swifter than a deer, overtook the bear, and with one stroke of the sword gave him his death-blow. And all who saw this feat of strength and quickness wondered greatly, and felt that such a hero must indeed be without a peer.

When Gunther's cooks had made the dinner ready, the company sat down on the grass, and all partook of a merry meal; for the bracing air and the morning's sport had made sharp appetites. But, when they had eaten, they were surprised to find that there was nothing to drink. Indeed, there was neither wine nor water in the camp.

"How glad I am," said Siegfried gayly, "that I am not a huntsman by trade, if it is a huntsman's way to go thus dry! Oh for a glass of wine, or even a cup of cold spring-water, to quench my thirst!"

"We will make up for this oversight when we go back home," said Gunther; and his heart was black with falsehood. "The blame in this matter should rest on Hagen, for it was he who was to look after the drinkables."

"My lord," said Hagen, "I fell into a mistake by thinking that we would dine, not here, but at the Spessart Springs; and thither I sent the wine."

"And is there no water near?" asked Siegfried.

"Yes," answered Hagen. "There is a cool, shady spring not far from here, where the water gushes in a clear, cold stream from beneath a linden-tree. Do but forgive me for the lack of wine, and I will lead you to it. It is a rare spring, and the water is almost as good as wine."

"Better than wine for me!" cried Siegfried. And he asked to be shown to the spring at once.

Hagen arose, and pointed to a tree not far away, beneath whose spreading branches Siegfried could see the water sparkling in the sunlight.

"Men have told me," said the chief, "that the Nibelungen king is very fleet of foot, and that no one has ever outstripped him in the race. Time was, when King Gunther and myself were spoken of as very swift runners; and, though we are now growing old, I fancy that many young men would, even now, fail to keep pace with us. Suppose we try a race to the spring, and see which of the three can win."

"Agreed!" cried Siegfried. "We will run; and, if I am beaten, I will kneel down in the grass to him who wins. I will give the odds in your favor too; for I will carry with me my spear, and my shield, and my helmet and sword, and all the trappings of the chase, while you may doff from your shoulders whatever might hinder your speed."

So Gunther and Hagen laid aside all their arms, and put off their heavy clothing; but Siegfried took up his bow and quiver, and his heavy shield, and his beamlike spear. Then the word was given, and all three ran with wondrous speed. Gunther and his chief flew over the grass as light-footed as two wild panthers: but Siegfried sped swift as an arrow shot from the hand of a skilful bowman. He reached the spring when yet the others were not half way to it. He laid his spear and sword, and bow and quiver of arrows, upon the ground, and leaned his heavy shield against the linden-tree; and then he waited courteously for King Gunther to come up, for his knightly honor would not allow him to drink until his host had quenched his thirst.

Gunther, when he reached the spring, stooped over, and drank heartily of the cool, refreshing water; and, after he had risen, Siegfried knelt upon the grass at the edge of the pool to quaff from the same gushing fountain. Stealthily then, and with quickness, did chief Hagen hide his huge bow and his quiver, and his good sword Balmung, and, seizing the hero's spear, he lifted it in air, and with too steady aim struck the silken lime-leaf that the loving Kriemhild had embroidered. Never in all the wide mid-world was known a deed more cowardly, never a baser act. The hero was pierced with his own weapon by one he had deemed his friend. His blood gushed forth in torrents, and dyed the green grass red, and discolored the sparkling water, and even filled the face and eyes of vile Hagen.

Yet, in the hour of death, King Siegfried showed how noble was his soul, how great his strength of will. Up he rose from his bended knees, and fiercely glanced around. Then, had not the evil-eyed chief, who never before had shunned a foe, fled with fleet-footed fear, quick vengeance would have overtaken him. In vain did the dying king look for his bow and his trusty sword: too safely had they been hidden. Then, though death was fast dimming his eyes, he seized his heavy shield, and sprang after the flying Hagen. Swift as the wind he followed him, quickly he overtook him. With his last strength he felled the vile wretch to the ground, and beat him with the shield, until the heavy plates of brass and steel were broken, and the jewels which adorned it were scattered among the grass. The sound of the heavy blows was heard far through the forest; and, had the hero's strength held out, Hagen would have had his reward.[EN#32] But Siegfried, weak and pale from the loss of blood, now staggered, and fell among the trampled flowers of the wood.

Then with his last breath he thus upbraided his false friends:—

"Cowards and traitors, ye! A curse shall fall upon you. My every care has been to serve and please you, and thus I am requited. Bitterly shall you rue this deed. The brand of traitor is set upon your foreheads, and it shall be a mark of loathing and shame to you forever."

Then the weak old Gunther began to wring his hands, and to bewail the death of Siegfried. But the hero bade him hush, and asked him of what use it was to regret an act which could have been done only by his leave and sanction.

"Better to have thought of tears and groans before," said he. "I have always known that you were a man of weak mind, but never did I dream that you could lend yourself to so base a deed. And now, if there is left aught of manliness in your bosom, I charge you to have a care for Kriemhild your sister. Long shall my loved Nibelungen-folk await my coming home."

The glorious hero struggled in the last agony. The grass and flowers were covered with his blood; the trees shivered, as if in sympathy with him, and dropped their leaves upon the ground; the birds stopped singing, and sorrowfully flew away; and a solemn silence fell upon the earth, as if the very heart of Nature had been crushed.

And the men who stood around—all save the four guilty ones—bowed their heads upon their hands, and gave way to one wild burst of grief. Then tenderly they took up Siegfried, and laid him upon a shield, with his mighty weapons by him. And, when the sorrowing Night had spread her black mantle over the mid-world, they carried him silently out of the forest, and across the river, and brought him, by Gunther's orders, to the old castle, which now nevermore would resound with mirth and gladness. And they laid him at Kriemhild's door, and stole sadly away to their own places, and each one thought bitterly of the morrow.[EN#33]

Adventure XX.
How the Hoard Was Brought to Burgundy.

And what was done on the morrow?

Too sad is the tale of Kriemhild's woe and her grief for the mighty dead. Let us pass it by in tearful, pitying silence, nor wish to awaken the echoes of that morning of hopeless anguish which dawned on the cold and cheerless dwelling of the kings. For peace had fled from Burgundy, nevermore to return.

Siegfried was dead. Faded, now, was the glory of the Nibelungen Land, and gone was the mid-world's hope.

It is told in ancient story, how men built a funeral-pile far out on the grassy meadows, where the quiet river flows; and how, in busy silence, they laid the sun-dried beams of ash and elm together, and made ready the hero's couch; and how the pile was dight with many a sun-bright shield, with war-coats and glittering helms, and silks and rich dyed cloths from the South-land, and furs, and fine-wrought ivory, and gem-stones priceless and rare; and how, over all, they scattered sweet spices from Araby, and the pleasantest of all perfumes. Then they brought the golden Siegfried, and laid him on his couch; and beside him were his battered shield, and Balmung with its fire-edge bare. And, as the sun rose high in heaven, the noblest earl-folk who had loved Siegfried best touched fire to the funeral-pile. And a pleasant breeze from the Southland fanned the fire to a flame, and the white blaze leaped on high, and all the folk cried out in mighty agony to the gods.

Such was the story that men told to each other when the world was still young, and the heroes were unforgotten.[EN#34] And some said, too, that Brunhild, the fair and hapless queen, died then of a broken heart and of a hopeless, yearning sorrow, and that she was burned with Siegfried on that high-built funeral-pile.

"They are gone,—the lovely, the mighty, the hope of the ancient earth: It shall labor and bear the burden as before the day of their birth:... It shall yearn, and be oft-times holpen, and forget their deeds no more, Till the new sun beams on Balder and the happy sealess shore."[EN#35]

Another and much later story is sometimes told of these last sad days,— how the hero's body was laid in a coffin, and buried in the quiet earth, amid the sorrowful lamentations of all the Rhineland folk; and how, at Kriemhild's earnest wish, it was afterwards removed to the place where now stands the little minster of Lorsch. As to which of these stories is the true one, it is not for me to say. Enough it is to know that Siegfried was dead, and that the spring-time had fled, and the summer-season with all its golden glories had faded away from Rhineland, and that the powers of darkness and of cold and of evil had prevailed.

To this day the city where was the dwelling of the Burgundian kings is called Worms, in remembrance of the dragon, or worm, which Siegfried slew; and a figure of that monster was for many years painted upon the city arms, and borne on the banner of the Burgundians. And, until recently, travellers were shown the Reisen-haus,—a stronghold, which, men say, Siegfried built; and in it were many strange and mighty weapons, which, they claim, were wielded by the hero. The lance which was shown there was a great beam nearly eighty feet in length; and the war-coat, wrought with steel and gold, and bespangled with gem-stones, was a wonder to behold. And now, in the Church of St. Cecilia, you may see what purports to be the hero's grave. And a pleasant meadow, not far from the town, is still called Kriemhild's Rose-garden; while farther away is the place called Drachenfels, or the dragon's field, where, they say, Siegfried met Fafnir. But whether it is the same as the Glittering Heath of the ancient legend, I know not.

And what became of the Hoard of Andvari?

The story is briefly told.[EN#36] When the days of mourning were past, and the people had gone back sadly to their homes, Queen Kriemhild began to speak of returning to the land of the Nibelungens. But Ute, her aged mother, could not bear to part with her, and besought her to stay, for a while at least, in the now desolate Burgundian castle. And Gernot and Giselher, her true and loving brothers, added their words of entreaty also. And so, though heart-sick, and with many misgivings, she agreed to abide for a season in this cheerless and comfortless place. Many days, even months, dragged by, and still she remained; for she found it still harder and harder to tear herself away from her mother, and all that her heart held dear. Yet never, for three years and more, did she even speak to Gunther, or by any sign show that she remembered him. And, as for Hagen, no words could utter the deep and settled hate she felt towards him. But the dark-browed chief cared nought either for love or hate; and he walked erect, as in the days of yore, and he smiled and frowned alike for both evil and good. And he said, "It was not I: it was the Norns, who wove the woof of his life and mine."

The years went by on leaden wings, and brought no sunlight to Gunther's dwelling; for his days were full of sadness, and his nights of fearful dreams. At length he said to chief Hagen, "If there is aught in the mid-world that can drive away this gloom, I pray thee to help me find it; for madness steals upon me."

"There is one thing," answered Hagen, "which might brighten our land again, and lift up your drooping spirits, and bring gladness to your halls."

"What is that?" asked the king.

"It is the Nibelungen Hoard," said the chief. "It is the wondrous treasure of Andvari, which Siegfried gave as a gift to Kriemhild. If it were ours, we might become the masters of the world."

"But how can we obtain it?"

"It is Kriemhild's," was the answer. "But she does not care for it; neither could she use it if she wished. If you could only gain her favor and forgiveness, I feel sure that she would let you do with it as you wish."

Then Gunther besought his younger brothers to intercede for him with Kriemhild, that she would so far forgive him as to look upon his face, and speak with him once more. And this the queen at last consented to do. And, when Gunther came into her presence, she was so touched at sight of his haggard face and whitened locks, and his earnest words of sorrow, that she forgave him the great wrong that he had done, and welcomed him again as her brother. And he swore that never would he again wrong her or hers, nor do aught to grieve her. But it was not until a long time after this, that he proposed to her that they should bring the Hoard of Andvari away from the Nibelungen Land.

"For, if it were here, dear sister," he said, "it might be of great use to you."

"Do whatever seems best to you," answered Kriemhild. "Only remember the oath that you have given me."

Then Gunther, because he was anxious to see the wondrous Hoard, but more because he was urged on by Hagen, made ready to send to the Nibelungen Land to bring away the treasure by Kriemhild's command. Eight thousand men, with Gernot and Giselher as their leaders, sailed over the sea in stanch vessels, and landed on the Nibelungen shore. And when they told who they were, and whence they came, and showed the queen's signet-ring, they were welcomed heartily by the fair-haired folk of Mist Land, who gladly acknowledged themselves the faithful liegemen of the loved Kriemhild.

When the Burgundians made known their errand to Alberich the dwarf, who still held watch and ward over the mountain stronghold, he was much amazed, and he grieved to part with his cherished treasure.

"But," said he to his little followers, who stood around him by thousands, each anxious to fight the intruders,—"but there is Queen Kriemhild's order and her signet-ring, and we must, perforce, obey. Yet had we again the good Tarnkappe which Siegfried took from us, the Hoard should never leave us."

Then sadly he gave up the keys, and the Burgundians began to remove the treasure. For four whole days and nights they toiled, carrying the Hoard in huge wagons down to the sea. And on the fifth day they set sail, and without mishap arrived in good time at Worms. And many of Alberich's people, the swarthy elves of the cave, came with Gernot to Rhineland; for they could not live away from the Hoard. And it is said, that hidden among the gold and the gem-stones was the far-famed Wishing-rod, which would give to its owner the power of becoming the lord of the wide mid-world.

And the vast treasure was stored in the towers and vaults of the castle. And Queen Kriemhild alone held the keys, and lavishly she scattered the gold wherever it was needed most. The hungry were fed, the naked were clothed, the sick were cared for; and everybody near and far blessed the peerless Queen of Nibelungen Land.

Then Hagen, always plotting evil, whispered to King Gunther, and said, "It is dangerous to suffer your sister to hold so vast a treasure. All the people are even now ready to leave you, and follow her. She will yet plot to seize the kingdom, and destroy us."

And he urged the king to take the keys and to make the Nibelungen Hoard his own.

But Gunther answered, "I have already done too great a wrong. And I have sworn to my sister never to harm her again, or to do aught that will grieve her."

"Let the guilt, then, rest on me," said Hagen. And he strode away, and took the keys from Kriemhild by force.

When Gernot and Giselher heard of this last vile act of the evil-eyed chief, they waxed very angry, and vowed that they would help their sister regain that which was her own. But the wary Hagen was not to be foiled; for, while the brothers were away from the burgh, he caused the great Hoard to be carried to the river, at a place called Lochheim, and sunk, fathoms deep, beneath the water. And then, for fear of the vengeance which might be wreaked upon him, he fled from Rhineland, and hid himself for a while among the mountains and the barren hill-country of the South.

And this was the end of the fated Hoard of Andvari.

The After Word.

Such is the story of Siegfried (or Sigurd), as we gather it from various German and Scandinavian legends. In this recital I have made no attempt to follow any one of the numerous originals, but have selected here and there such incidents as best suited my purpose in constructing one connected story which would convey to your minds some notion of the beauty and richness of our ancient myths. In doing this, I have drawn, now from the Volsunga Saga, now from the Nibelungen Lied, now from one of the Eddas, and now from some of the minor legends relating to the great hero of the North. These ancient stories, although differing widely in particulars, have a certain general relationship and agreement which proves beyond doubt a common origin. "The primeval myth," says Thomas Carlyle, "whether it were at first philosophical truth, or historical incident, floats too vaguely on the breath of men: each has the privilege of inventing, and the far wider privilege of borrowing and new modelling from all that preceded him. Thus, though tradition may have but one root, it grows, like a banian, into a whole overarching labyrinth of trees."

If you would follow the tradition of Siegfried to the end; if you would learn how, after the great Hoard had been buried in the Rhine, the curse of the dwarf Andvari still followed those who had possessed it, and how Kriemhild wreaked a terrible vengeance upon Siegfried's murderers,—you must read the original story as related in the Volsung Myth or in the Nibelungen Song. Our story ends with Siegfried.

The episodes which I have inserted here and there—the stories of AEgir, and of Balder, and of Idun, and of Thor—do not, as you may know, belong properly to the legend of Siegfried; but I have thrown them in, in order to acquaint you with some of the most beautiful mythical conceptions of our ancestors.

A grand old people were those early kinsmen of ours,—not at all so savage and inhuman as our histories would sometimes make us believe. For however mistaken their notions may have been, and however ignorant they were, according to our ideas of things, they were strong-hearted, brave workers; and, so far as opportunity was afforded them, they acted well their parts. What their notions were of true manhood,—a strong mind in a strong body, good, brave, and handsome,—may be learned from the story of Siegfried.

End of The Story of Siegfried.

The Story of Siegfried Endnotes.

[EN#1] Siegfried's Boyhood.

"All men agree that Siegfried was a king's son. He was born, as we here have good reason to know, 'at Santen in Netherland,' of Siegmund and the fair Siegelinde; yet by some family misfortune or discord, of which the accounts are very various, he came into singular straits during boyhood, having passed that happy period of life, not under the canopies of costly state, but by the sooty stithy, in one Mimer, a blacksmith's shop."— Thomas Carlyle, The Nibelungen Lied.

The older versions of this story represent Siegfried, under the name of Sigurd, as being brought up at the court of the Danish King Hialprek; his own father Sigmund having been slain in battle, as related in this chapter. He was early placed under the tuition of Regin, or Regino, an elf, who instructed his pupil in draughts, runes, languages, and various other accomplishments.—See Preface to Vollmer's Nibelunge Not, also the Song of Sigurd Fafnisbane, in the Elder Edda, and the Icelandic Volsunga Saga.

[EN#2]—Mimer.

"The Vilkinasaga brings before us yet another smith, Mimer, by whom not only is Velint instructed in his art, but Sigfrit (Siegfried) is brought up,—another smith's apprentice. He is occasionally mentioned in the later poem of Biterolf, as Mime the Old. The old name of Munster in Westphalia was Mimigardiford; the Westphalian Minden was originally Mimidun; and Memleben on the Unstrut, Mimileba.. .. The elder Norse tradition names him just as often, and in several different connections. In one place, a Mimingus, a wood-satyr, and possessor of a sword and jewels, is interwoven into the myth of Balder and Hoder. The Edda gives a higher position to its Mimer. He has a fountain, in which wisdom and understanding lie hidden: drinking of it every morning, he is the wisest, most intelligent, of men. To Mimer's fountain came Odin, and desired a drink, but did not receive it till he had given one of his eyes in pledge, and hidden it in the fountain: this accounts for Odin being one-eyed.... Mimer is no Asa, but an exalted being with whom the Asas hold converse, of whom they make use,—the sum total of wisdom, possibly an older Nature-god. Later fables degraded him into a wood-sprite, or clever smith."—Grimm's Deutsche Mythologie, I. p. 379.

Concerning the Mimer of the Eddas, Professor Anderson says, "The name Mimer means the knowing. The Giants, being older than the Asas, looked deeper than the latter into the darkness of the past. They had witnessed the birth of the gods and the beginning of the world, and they foresaw their downfall. Concerning both these events, the gods had to go to them for knowledge. It is this wisdom that Mimer keeps in his fountain."—Norse Mythology, p 209.

In the older versions of the legend, the smith who cared for Siegfried (Sigurd) is called, as we have before noticed, Regin. He is thus described by Morris:—

> "The lore of all men he knew,
>
> And was deft in every cunning, save the dealings of the
>
> sword.
>
> So sweet was his tongue-speech fashioned, that men
>
> trowed his every word.
>
> His hand with the harp-strings blended was the mingler
>
> of delight
>
> With the latter days of sorrow: all tales he told
>
> aright.
>
> The Master of the Masters in the smithying craft was
>
> he;
>
> And he dealt with the wind and the weather and the
>
> stilling of the sea;
>
> Nor might any learn him leech-craft, for before that
>
> race was made,
>
> And that man-folk's generation, all their life-days had
>
> he weighed."
>
> Sigurd the Volsung, Bk. II.

[EN#3]—The Sword.

"By this sword Balmung also hangs a tale. Doubtless it was one of those invaluable weapons sometimes fabricated by the old Northern smiths, compared with which our modern Foxes and Ferraras and Toledos are mere leaden tools. Von der Hagen seems to think it simply the sword Mimung under another name; in which case, Siegfried's old master, Mimer, had been the maker of it, and called it after himself, as if it had been his son."—Carlyle, on the Nibelungen Lied, note.

In Scandinavian legends, the story of Mimer and Amilias is given, differing but slightly from the rendering in this chapter.—See Weber and Jamieson's Illustrations of Northern Antiquities.

In the older versions of the myth, the sword is called Gram, or the Wrath. It was wrought from the shards, or broken pieces, of Sigmund's sword, the gift of Odin. It was made by Regin for Sigurd's (Siegfried's) use, and its temper was tested as here described.

[EN#4]—Sigmund The Volsung.

Sigmund the Volsung, in the Volsunga Saga, is represented as the father of Sigurd (Siegfried); but there is such a marked contrast between him, and the wise, home-abiding King Siegmund of the later stories, that I have thought proper to speak of them here as two different individuals. The word "Sigmund," or "Siegmund," means literally the mouth of victory. The story of the Volsungs, as here supposed to be related by Mimer, is derived mainly from the Volsunga Saga.

[EN#5]—Siegfried's Journey Into The Forest.

"In the shop of Mimer, Siegfried was nowise in his proper element, ever quarrelling with his fellow-apprentices, nay, as some say, breaking the hardest anvils into shivers by his too stout hammering; so that Mimer, otherwise a first-rate smith, could by no means do with him there. He sends him, accordingly, to the neighboring forest to fetch charcoal, well aware that a monstrous dragon, one Regin, the smith's own brother, would meet him, and devour him. But far otherwise it proved."—Carlyle, on The Nibelungen Lied.

[EN#6]—The Norns.

The Norns are the Fates, which watch over man through life. They are Urd the Past, Verdande the Present, and Skuld the Future. They approach every new-born child, and utter his doom. They are represented as spinning the thread of fate, one end of which is hidden by Urd in the far east, the other by Verdande in the far west. Skuld stands ready to rend it in pieces.—See Grimm's Teutonic Mythology, p. 405, also Anderson's Norse Mythology, p. 209.

The three weird women in Shakespeare's Tragedy of Macbeth represent a later conception of the three Norns, now degraded to mere witches.

Compare the Norns with the Fates of the Greek Mythology. These, also, are three in number. They sit clothed in white, and garlanded, singing of destiny. Clotho, the Past, spins; Lachesis, the Present, divides; and Atropos, the Future, stands ready with her shears to cut the thread.

[EN#7]—The Idea of Fatality.

Throughout the story of the Nibelungs and Volsungs, of Sigurd and of Siegfried,—whether we follow the older versions or the mote recent renderings,—there is, as it were, an ever-present but indefinable shadow of coming fate, "a low, inarticulate voice of Doom," foretelling the inevitable. This is but in consonance with the general ideas of our Northern ancestors regarding the fatality which shapes and controls every man's life. These ideas are embodied in more than one ancient legend. We find them in the old Anglo-Saxon poem of Beowulf. "To us," cries Beowulf in his last fight, "to us it shall be as our Weird betides,—that Weird that is every man's lord!" "Each man of us shall abide the end of his life-work; let him that may work, work his doomed deeds ere death comes!" Similar ideas prevailed among the Greeks. Read, for example, that passage in the Iliad describing the parting of Hector and Andromache, and notice the deeper meaning of Hector's words.

[EN#8]—Regin.

As we have already observed (EN#1), the older versions of this myth called Siegfried's master and teacher Regin, while the more recent versions call him Mimer. We have here endeavored to harmonize the two versions by representing Mimer as being merely Regin in disguise.

[EN#9]—Gripir.

"A man of few words was Gripir; but he knew of all deeds that had been; And times there came upon him, when the deeds to be were seen: No sword had he held in his hand since his father fell to field, And against the life of the slayer he bore undinted shield: Yet no fear in his heart abided, nor desired he aught at all: But he noted the deeds that had been, and looked for what should befall." Morris's Sigurd the Volsung, Bk. II.

[EN#10]—The Hoard.

This story is found in both the Elder and the Younger Eddas, and is really the basis upon which the entire plot of the legend of Sigurd, or Siegfried, is constructed. See also EN#18.

[EN#11]—The Dragon.

The oldest form of this story is the Song of Sigurd Fafnisbane, in the Elder Edda. The English legend of St. George and the Dragon was probably derived from the same original sources. A similar myth may be found among all Aryan peoples. Sometimes it is a treasure, sometimes a beautiful maiden, that the monster guards, or attempts to destroy. Its first meaning was probably this: The maiden, or the treasure, is the earth in its beauty and fertility. "The monster is the storm-cloud. The hero who fights it is the sun, with his glorious sword, the lightning-flash. By his victory the earth is relieved from her peril. The fable has been varied to suit the atmospheric peculiarities of different climes in which the Aryans found themselves.... In Northern mythology the serpent is probably the winter cloud, which broods over and keeps from mortals the gold of the sun's light and heat, till in the spring the bright orb overcomes the powers of darkness and tempest, and scatters his gold over the face of the earth." This myth appears in a great variety of forms among the Scandinavian and German nations. In the Eddas, Sigurd (Siegfried) is represented as roasting the heart of Fafnir, and touching it to his lips. We have ventured to present a less revolting version.—See Baring-Gould's Curious Myths of the Middle Ages.

"The slaying of the dragon Fafnir reminds us of Python, whom Apollo overcame; and, as Python guarded the Delphic Oracle, the dying Fafnir prophesies."—Jacob Grimm.

[EN#12.]

In order to harmonize subsequent passages in the story as related in different versions, we here represent Siegfried as turning his back upon the Glittering Heath, and leaving the Hoard to some other hero or discoverer. In the Younger Edda, Siegfried (Sigur) rides onward until he comes to Fafnir's bed, from which "he took out all the gold, packed it in two bags, and laid it on Grane's (Greyfell's) back, then got on himself and rode away."

[EN#13]—BRAGI. This episode of Bragi and his vessel is no part of the original story of Siegfried, but is here introduced in order to acquaint you with some of the older myths of our ancestors. Bragi was the impersonation of music and eloquence, and here represents the music of Nature,—the glad songs and sounds of the spring-time. "Above any other god," says Grimm, "one would like to see a more general veneration of Bragi revived, in whom was vested the gift of poetry and eloquence.... He appears to have stood in pretty close relation to AEgir."

[EN#14]—AEgir.

"AEgir was the god presiding over the stormy sea. He entertains the gods every harvest, and brews ale for them. The name still survives in provincial English for the sea-wave on rivers."—Anderson's Norse Mythology. See Carlyle's Heroes and Hero-Worship.

[EN#15]—The Valkyries.

See Grimm's Teutonic Mythology, p. 417, and Anderson's Norse Mythology, p. 265.

[EN#16]—Brunhild.

In the Elder Edda, Brunhild's inaccessible hall stands on a mountain, where she was doomed to sleep under her shield until Sigurd should release her. In the Nibelungen Lied, she is represented as ruling in Isenland, an island far over the sea. The well-known story of the Sleeping Beauty is derived from this myth.

[EN#17]—Nibelungen Land.

"Vain were it to inquire where that Nibelungen Land specially is. Its very name is Nebel-land, or Nifl-land, the land of Darkness, of Invisibility.... Far beyond the firm horizon, that wonder-bearing region swims on the infinite waters, unseen by bodily eye, or, at most, discerned as a faint streak hanging in the blue depths, uncertain whether island or cloud."—Carlyle, on The Nibelungen Lied.

[EN#18]—Schilbung and Nibelung.

"Old King Nibelung, the former lord of the land, had left, when he died, a mighty hoard concealed within a mountain-cavern. As Siegfried rode past the mountain-side alone, he found Schilbung and Nibelung, the king's sons, seated at the mouth of the cavern surrounded by more gold and precious stones than a hundred wagons could bear away. Espying Siegfried, they called upon him to settle their dispute, offering him as reward their father's mighty sword Balmung."—Auber Forestier's Translation of the Nibelungen Lied.

We have here made some slight variations from the original versions. (See also EN#12.)

An ancient legend relates how King Schilbung had obtained the Hoard in the upper Rhine valley, and how he was afterwards slain by his brother Niblung. This Niblung possessed a magic ring in the shape of a coiled serpent with ruby eyes. It had been presented to him by a prince named Gunthwurm, who had come to him in the guise of a serpent, desiring the hand of his daughter in marriage. This ring, according to the Eddas, was the one taken by Loki from the dwarf Andvari, and was given by Sigurd (Siegfried) to Brunhild in token of betrothal. It was the cause of all the disasters that afterwards occurred.—See W. Jordan's Sigfridssaga. See also EN#10.

[EN#19]

> "... *Siegfried the hero good*

> *Failed the long task to finish: this stirred their angry mood.*
> *The treasure undivided he needs must let remain,*
> *When the two kings indignant set on him with their train;*
> *But Siegfried gripped sharp Balmung (so hight their father's sword),*
> *And took from them their country, and the beaming, precious hoard."*
>
> The Nibelungenlied, Lettsom, 96, 97

[EN#20]—Siegfried's Welcome Home.

In the Nibelungen Lied this is our first introduction to the hero. The "High-tide" held in honor of Siegfried's coming to manhood, and which we suppose to have occurred at this time, forms the subject of the Second Adventure in that poem.

[EN#21]—Kriemhild's Dream.

This forms the subject of the first chapter of the Nibelungen Lied. "The eagles of Kriemhild's dream," says Auber Forestier, "are winter-giants, whose wont it was to transform themselves into eagles; while the pure gods were in the habit of assuming the falcon's form."

[EN#22]—Idun.

The story of Idun and her Apples is related in the Younger Edda. It is there represented as having been told by Bragi himself to his friend AEgir. This myth means, that the ever-renovating spring (Idun) being taken captive by the desolating winter (Thjasse), all Nature (all the Asa-folk) languishes until she regains her freedom through the intervention of the summer's heat (Loki). —See Anderson's Norse Mythology.

[EN#23]—Balder.

The story of Balder is, in reality, the most ancient form of the Siegfried myth. Both Balder and Siegfried are impersonations of the beneficent light of the summer's sun, and both are represented as being treacherously slain by the powers of winter. The errand of Hermod to the Halls of Death (Hela) reminds us of the errand of Hermes to Hades to bring back Persephone to her mother Demetre. We perceive also a resemblance in this story to the myth of Orpheus, in which that hero is described as descending into the lower regions to bring away his wife Eurydice.

[EN#24]

The making of rich clothing for the heroes is frequently referred to in the Nibelungen Lied. Carlyle says, "This is a never-failing preparative for all expeditions, and is always specified and insisted on with a simple, loving, almost female impressiveness."

[EN#25]—The Winning of Brunhild.

The story of the outwitting of Brunhild, as related in the pages which follow, is essentially the same as that given in the Nibelungen Lied. It is quite different from the older versions.

[EN#26]—Sif.

Sif corresponds to the Ceres of the Southern mythology. (See Grimm, p. 309.) The story of Loki and the Dwarfs is derived from the Younger Edda. It has been beautifully rendered by the German poet Oelenschlager, a translation of whose poem on this subject may be found in Longfellow's Poets and Poetry of Europe.

[EN#27]—Eigill.

Eigill is the original William Tell. The story is related in the Saga of Thidrik. For a full history of the Tell myth, see Grimm's Teutonic Mythology, p. 380, and Baring-Gould's Curious Myths of the Middle Ages, p. 110.

[EN#28]—Welland the Smith.

The name of this smith is variously given as Weland, Wieland, Welland, Volundr, Velint etc. The story is found in the Vilkina Saga, and was one of the most popular of middle age myths. (See Grimm's Mythology.) Sir Walter Scott, in his novel of Kenilworth, has made use of this legend in introducing the episode of Wayland Smith.

[EN#29]—Vidar[FN#1] the Silent.

"Vidar is the name of the silent Asa. He has a very thick shoe, and he is the strongest next to Thor. From him the gods have much help in all hard tasks."—The Younger Edda (Anderson's translation).

[FN#1] The word Vidar means forest.

[EN#30]—Loki.

"Loki, in nature, is the corrupting element in air, fire, and water. In the bowels of the earth he is the volcanic flame, in the sea he appears as a fierce serpent, and in the lower world we recognize him as pale death. Like Odin, he pervades all nature. He symbolizes sin, shrewdness, deceitfulness, treachery, malice etc."—Anderson's Mythology, p. 372.

He corresponds to the Ahriman of the Persians, to the Satan of the Christians, and remotely to the Prometheus of the Greeks.

[EN#31]—The Quarrel of the Queens.

In the ancient versions, the culmination of this quarrel occurred while the queens were bathing in the river: in the Nibelungen Lied it happened on the steps leading up to the door of the church.

[EN#32]—Hagen.

Hagen corresponds to the Hoder of the more ancient myth of Balder. In the Sigurd Sagas he is called Hogni, and is a brother instead of an uncle, of Gunther (Gunnar).

[EN#33]—The Death of Siegfried.

This story is related here essentially as found in the Nibelungen Lied. It is quite differently told in the older versions. Siegfried's invulnerability save in one spot reminds us of Achilles, who also was made invulnerable by a bath, and who could be wounded only in the heel.

[EN#34]—The Burial of Siegfried.

The story of the burning of Siegfried's body upon a funeral-pile, as related of Sigurd in the older myths, reminds us of the burning of Balder upon the ship "Ringhorn." (See p. 162.) The Nibelungen Lied represents him as being buried in accordance with the rites of the Roman-Catholic Church. This version of the story must, of course, have been made after the conversion of the Germans to Christianity. "When the Emperor Frederick III. (1440-93) visited Worms after his Netherlands campaign," says Forestier, "he undertook to have the mighty hero's bones disinterred, probably in view of proving the truth of the marvellous story then sung throughout Germany; but, although he had the ground dug into until water streamed forth, no traces of these became manifest."

[EN#35]—Morris: Sigurd the Volsung, Bk. III.

[EN#36]—The Hoard.

The story of bringing the Hoard from Nibelungen Land belongs to the later versions of the myth, and fitly closes the First Part of the Nibelungen Lied. Lochheim, the place where the Hoard was sunk, was not far from Bingen on the Rhine.

[EN#37]—a Short Vocabulary of the Principal Proper Names Mentioned in this Story.

AEGIR. *The god of the sea.*

ALBERICH and ANDVARI. *Dwarfs who guard the great Hoard.*

ASA. *A name applied to the gods of the Norse mythology.*

ASGARD. *The home of the gods.*

BALDER. *The god of the summer sunlight.*

BRAGI. *The god of eloquence and of poetry.*

DRAUPNER. *Odin's ring, which gives fertility to the earth.*

FAFNIR. *The dragon whom Siegfried slays.*

FENRIS-WOLF. *The monster who in the last twilight slays Odin.*

FREYJA. *The goddess of love.*

REY. *The god of peace and plenty.*

GRIPIR. *The giant who gives wise counsel to Siegfried (Sigurd).*

GUNTHER. *In the older myths called Gunnar.*

HEIMDAL. *The heavenly watchman.*

HELA. *The goddess of death.*

HERMOD. *The quick messenger who is sent to Hela for Balder.*

HODER. *The winter-god. He slays Balder.*

HOENIR. *One of the three most ancient gods.*

HUGIN. *Odin's raven, Thought.*

IDUN. *The goddess of spring.*

IVALD. *A skilful dwarf.*

JOTUNHEIM. *The home of the giants.*

KRIEMHILD. *In the older myths called Gudrun.*

LOKI. *The mischief-maker. The god of evil.*

MIMER. *In the later German mythology a skilful smith. In the older mythology a wise giant.*

NORNS. *The three Fates,—Urd, Verdande, and Skuld.*

ODIN. *The chief of the gods.*

REGIN. *The teacher of Sigurd, by whom he is slain.*

SIEGFRIED. *In the older myths called Sigurd.*

SIF. *Thor's wife.*

SLEIPNER. *Odin's eight-footed horse.*

TYR. *The god of war.*

THOR. *The god of thunder. The foe of the giants.*

VALHAL. *The hall of the slain.*

VALKYRIES. *The choosers of the slain. Odin's handmaidens.*

VIDAR. *The silent god.*

YMIR. *The huge giant out of whose body the world was made.*

Milton Keynes UK
Ingram Content Group UK Ltd.
UKHW030906151124
451262UK00006B/958